Life and Thought in the Ancient Near East

Life and Thought in the

ANCIENT NEAR EAST

Louis L. Orlin

THE UNIVERSITY OF MICHIGAN PRESS   ANN ARBOR

Copyright © by the University of Michigan 2007
All rights reserved
Published in the United States of America by
The University of Michigan Press
Manufactured in the United States of America
⊗ Printed on acid-free paper

2010   2009   2008   2007   4   3   2   1

A CIP catalog record for this book is available from the British Library.

Library of Congress Cataloging-in-Publication Data

Orlin, Louis L. (Louis Lawrence)
    Life and thought in the ancient Near East / Louis L. Orlin.
       p.   cm.
    Includes bibliographical references and index.
    ISBN-13: 978-0-472-09992-4 (cloth : alk. paper)
    ISBN-10: 0-472-09992-2 (cloth : alk. paper)
    ISBN-13: 978-0-472-06992-7 (pbk. : alk. paper)
    ISBN-10: 0-472-06992-6 (pbk. : alk. paper)
    1. Middle East—Civilization—To 622.   I. Title.

DS57.O75   2008
939'.4—dc22   2007001728

To Jenny, my loving and wonderful wife, my children, grand-children, and great-grandchildren, and to all the students I have been privileged to teach and learn from—undergraduates, graduate students, and senior citizens—at the University of Michigan and other colleges and universities in this country and abroad during the last half century.

L. L. O.

Contents

Maps

Illustrations

Abbreviations

ANET   *Ancient Near Eastern Texts Relating to the Old Testament.* Ed. J. B. Pritchard. Princeton: Princeton University Press, 1969.

CANE   *Civilizations of the Ancient Near East.* Ed. J. M. Sasson. New York: Charles Scribner's Sons, 1995.

HANE   *A History of the Ancient Near East, ca. 3000–323 B.C.,* by Marc Van De Mieroop. Oxford: Blackwell, 2004.

Preface

This book takes a different approach to writing about the ancient Near East than is usually found in works intended for general readers or students. It does not concentrate on a single culture and does not limit its chronological scope. Instead it uses sources from the archives of most of the peoples who inhabited the area for millennia before the conquests of Alexander the Great in the late fourth century. It aims to offer an anthology of human activities, concerns, and thoughts as reflected both in official political and religious documents and in the records of everyday life. In doing so, it seeks to establish a link between ourselves and our ancestors of five thousand years ago, who lived in Egypt, the Palestinian corridor, central Anatolia (in present-day Turkey), and Mesopotamia (today the region of Iraq).

Western religious heritage is the living reminder of our connection to the ancient Near East. Biblical texts bring us intimately into the world of our religious origins. But no living tradition links us to the rest of the peoples who inhabited the territories of the Near East. Although we have collectively hundreds of thousands of records from numbers of ancient Near Eastern civilizations, the too usual academic view is that since these civilizations are "dead"—and therefore off the main paths of human development—the people who daily struggled with their lives in antiquity have little in common with us. But where there are records there *is* life. And it is selected samples of this life that I present here as short essays, scenes, and sketches.

Readers may be confused that the terms *Near East* and *Middle East* refer to the same general area. *Near East* is preferred by historians and other scholars of antiquity in that it alludes to civilizations that occupied the Arabian Peninsula and its immediately bordering areas—Egypt, Anatolia, and western Iran. *Middle East* today includes North African states and areas as far east as central Asia. It is a term normally used by contemporary political and social analysts and media representatives. The archaeologist tends to work in the Near East. The news commentator reports from the Middle East. They may both, however, meet for lunch in the same restaurant in Cairo or Beirut.

Acknowledgments

Grateful acknowledgment is given to the following individuals at the University of Michigan who aided the author in producing this book:

Professor Alexander Knysh, recent chair of the Department of Near Eastern Studies, who granted me a stipend to partially cover typing costs.

Lisa Michelin (key administrator) and Margaret Casazza (academic services secretary) of the Department of Near Eastern Studies, who always cheerfully assisted me while the book was being composed.

Robin Meador-Woodruff, associate curator of Slides/Photographs, Kelsey Museum of Archaeology, who gave generously of her interest and time to photograph clay tablets for the book.

Kari Neely, an outstanding graduate teaching fellow in the Department of Near Eastern Studies, who typed the manuscript meticulously and prepared it for publication.

Ann Tai, director of the Learning in Retirement program, and her associates and staff for their assistance in providing teaching facilities and office and classroom support.

Further acknowledgment is given to the owners of copyrighted materials used in this book:

George Braziller, Inc., New York, for permission to use maps 4, 5, 6, and 7 (The Ancient Near East, Mesopotamia, Egypt, and Palestine), from Paul Lampl, *Cities and Planning in the Ancient Near East* (New York:

George Braziller, 1968), and fig. 33, "Irrigation ditches of the Euphrates."

The Minnesota Council for Geographic Education and Professor John Adams, chair of the Department of Geography at the University of Minnesota, for permission to use maps 2 and 3 (Physical Regions of the Near East and Land Use and Vegetation of the Modern Near East), designed as teaching materials.

The Greenwood Publishing Group, Westport, Connecticut, for permission to reprint parts of my article "Ancient Near Eastern Literature," which appeared in *The Reader's Adviser: A Layman's Guide to Literature,* ed. E. J. Sypher (New York and London: R. R. Bowker Co., 1977), 2:601–2 (text, without booklist).

Karl Longstreth, Map Librarian, Head, Map Library, the University of Michigan Library, for the satellite color image of the Near East.

Fate Magazine, for permission to use my essay "Lost Writings of Lost Cities," 36, no. 2, issue 395 (February 1983): 38–45, under its new title, "The Decipherment of Cuneiform Writing" in the present volume.

The Kelsey Museum of Archaeology at the University of Michigan for permission to use the photographs of cuneiform tablets (KM89147, KM89177, KM89257, and KM89277) from the museum's collection.

Figures 30 and 31 originally appeared in Robert Koldewey, *Excavations at Babylon* (London: Macmillan and Co., 1914).

All other photographs in the book (except for figs. 30 an 31) were taken by the author in Near Eastern and Mediterranean regions during various expeditions, surveys, and lecturing and teaching projects and remain under copyright to the University of Michigan and the author.

The director of the University of Michigan Press, Philip M. Pochoda, who saw a future for this book; my former editor, Christopher Collins, and his assistants Sarah Mann and Amy Anderson; my current editor, Christopher Hebert, and his assistants Julia Goldstein and Christy Byks for their advice and assistance in the writing and production of the work, and to Mary Hashman, my copyediting coordinator, who greatly assisted in the preparation of the text for publication.

A Yardstick of Time

Ancient history has always been a source of fascination for young and old alike, yet it has never been a popular field of study. All those languages to learn, all those dates and funny names to remember. And it's so *old!* Yet, in fact, the civilizations of the ancient world are close contemporaries of ours if you look at them from the standpoint of the age of the earth itself.

Scientific research concludes that the earth formed about four billion six hundred million years ago. This number is impossible to comprehend in itself. So let's use a one-thousand-page book to represent the time span. Each page would then represent four million six hundred thousand years. Let's assume that each page also contains one hundred lines of print. Each line in our book would represent forty-six thousand years. Suppose that each line contained ten words. Each word would then represent four thousand six hundred years. Now, if we propose that each word had four syllables, each syllable would represent one thousand one hundred fifty years.

Using this analogy for calculation, writing was invented about a word ago, and the birth of Christ occurred less than two syllables ago. To bring things closer to home, our American Revolution is just a letter away, and current events are hardly noticeable at the very bottom of the last page of our book.

Looked at from this perspective, ancient Near Eastern civilizations are very much closer to us than we think. What better reason for us to see the life of these civilizations as practically contemporaneous to ours in the greater scheme of things?

Introduction

The idea for this book originated in the classes I taught for senior
citizens in the University of Michigan's Learning in Retirement
program. The subject matter was selected from ancient Near Eastern and classical history and literature, and the interest my students
showed in these materials stimulated me to suggest a possible book to the
University of Michigan Press. It was not to be the ordinary type of academic book—a straight history, the proposal or defense of a specific
theme, or yet the introduction of new information. Rather, it would be
a collection of vignettes taken from source materials of the ancient
peoples themselves. The idea of a vignette includes such forms as short
essays, sketches, glimpses, and other abbreviated perceptions about a
variety of subjects. If there is a unifying principle of the material it is simply geographical and chronological—the area covered by Anatolia, Iran,
the civilizations that occupied Mesopotamia (Sumeria, Babylonia, and
Assyria), and neighboring societies as well. What I conceived of was
essence, not formal structure. By this I mean the question, "What does
the institution or behavior described tell the reader about human
thought and behavior?" This does not mean that the essentials of historical reporting are dispensed with in this work. There are plenty of dates,
descriptions of places, and physical facts, as required in the narration. I
did not want the reader, however, to be inundated by the often confusing and contradictory problems with which the professional scholar
must contend. Readers are left with the option of further reading to
develop their interests, for which introductory bibliographies are provided at the ends of some of the vignettes.

While the life circumstances of ancient Near Easterners were vastly different from ours, people of the early civilizations possessed the same physical and mental potential as we do. They were born; were married; created families; found their niches in their contemporary societies; struggled against pestilence, war, and all the trials that humans have always faced; and left records of what they achieved and clues as to what they did not, even as we create records of our accomplishments and failures. At base it is the human being of any period who furthers the ongoing saga of our continual struggle to understand the meaning of existence and to exploit the strategies of survival. Whether it is the ancient Egyptian or Mesopotamian or the contemporary American whom we survey, at base it will always be the human being who creates the story that is worthy of recounting.

I came to the study of the ancient Near East after intensive training in European and American history, intellectual history, political theory, comparative literature, and philosophy. My formal university training began at Princeton following my enlistment in the Army Specialized Training Program in 1943. It was interrupted by combat service in World War II and was later completed at the University of Michigan, where I received my Ph.D. in 1960. Unlike the majority of my colleagues here and abroad, I did not enter the study of the ancient Near East through the path of philology, theology, or archaeology, but rather through an intellectual journey whose natural end, for me, was to encounter the origins of human thought and activity as recorded in the earliest available records. These sources numbered in the hundreds of thousands. This thought is worth recounting not only because it shaped my teaching and research career but also because the impetus for the type of book now in your hands has always been latent in my own notions of arousing interest in Near Eastern antiquity. It took the faith in me exhibited by the first chair of the newly founded Department of Near Eastern Studies in 1948, George G. Cameron, when I had already been teaching history and English at the University of Michigan, to launch me into the study of Hittite and Assyro-Babylonian.

I would never have met George Cameron had I not, on a whim, decided to attend his inaugural lecture at the University of Michigan. Its subject was his work in Iran on the great trilingual inscription incised on the cliff walls at Bisitun. This inscription—a royal proclamation of the Old Persian Dynasty—was written in three languages and had been a vital key to unlocking the mysteries of the Babylonian language. The face of the inscription had weathered severely at one edge, and Professor Cameron, at great personal risk while working high up on the cliff face, undertook to coat the damaged parts with latex rubber so as to remove a cast of the original writing. The lecture was enthralling. At its end he added the sentence that was to change my academic objectives and my academic career: He had as yet no colleagues and no students, and if anyone was interested in the subject, would they see him in his office the following week? I decided to take up his offer. With two other brave souls I embarked on the study of cuneiform and the histories of ancient Near Eastern societies while at the same time teaching in the humanities curriculum of the College of Literature, Science and the Arts at the university. Eventually I finished my doctoral studies and was ultimately invited to join the faculty of the Department of Near Eastern Studies, from which I retired in 1989. My career allowed me to lecture and teach in many parts of the world, to do archaeological investigations and explorations in all parts of the Near East, and finally to teach in the University of Michigan's Learning in Retirement program for senior citizens.

My interests and competencies have never been narrowly defined as solely linguistic or historical or literary. I have always seen the parts of the universe of knowledge as being interconnected. I have always felt, as a scholar, that the aim of scholarly life is, of course, primarily to work in a field of expertise, but the aim also is to try to understand how the chosen field of endeavor helps to illuminate other areas of human understanding. This belief lies behind my interest in writing this book. There have been objections from Assyriologists within the field that it is far too early to attempt to generalize about Mesopotamian life because there are many thousands of cuneiform tablets yet to be discovered and read and so very few scholars to read them at the best of times. Agreed. But that is no reason, in my view, why summaries and pro tem appraisals should not be written.

Like ancient Gaul under the Romans, this book is divided into three parts, each fulfilling a different but, one hopes, desirable function for its readers.

The first part consists of vignettes.

The second part consists of background material in the form of a more highly concentrated scope and treatment than that given to the vignettes. This provides a geographical and historical framework setting of ancient Near Eastern life—a summation of more general background information than could be offered in the first part.

The third part, entitled "Especially for Students," contains items that I have found particularly helpful for students during my teaching career and that often have been overlooked by instructors because of the particular time demands imposed by their curricular syllabi.

Accordingly the book presents invitations to readers with different interests and purposes—pick and choose the subjects of interest to you, whether for casual browsing, the larger screen, or special in-depth study of particular issues.

There is a general bibliography in the back of the book, but some of the vignettes offer their own lists of a small group of texts that will carry the reader's interests forward. I have tried to offer older—in my view deeply insightful—books along with more recent, up-to-date publications so as to marry, so to speak, the insights of earlier outstanding scholars in the various fields with new data and information that may have been but recently discovered.

I invite the reader of this book to enter the world of the ancient Near East knowing that there is still too much that we do not know about the subject but certainly enough to stimulate our serious interest in what is, after all, the earliest written records of life on this planet.

Bibliographical Note

Nothing can be more discouraging to readers new to the civilizations of the ancient Near East and the classical worlds than long lists of detailed bibliographical references, a majority of which are in foreign languages because of the worldwide scope of scholarship on the area. I have decided to limit detailed bibliographical lists in favor of short notations of books of an introductory nature. However, I have not followed this rule in every case. There is a brief "Further Reading" addition to some of the vignettes, as previously mentioned, mostly materials written in English. I trust that sufficient copies of the latter are still available in bookstores or on-line. Otherwise, the reader will have to depend on accessibility to academic libraries or public libraries in larger municipalities. The single most comprehensive collection of translations of ancient Near Eastern source materials in English is found in James B. Pritchard, ed., *Ancient Near Eastern Texts Relating to the Old Testament* (Princeton: Princeton University Press, 1950, 1955, 1969). Materials from the hardbound editions have also been issued, some in abridged form, in paperback: vol. 1, *The Ancient Near East: An Anthology of Texts and Pictures,* and vol. 2, *A New Anthology of Texts and Pictures.* In this book the abbreviation *ANET* (1969) refers to the hardbound edition of that year.

Since the vast majority of dates in this book refer to the pre-Christian era, the usual designation, BC, will be omitted throughout.

∽ *Vignettes* ∽

MESOPOTAMIA

In the Tablet Houses of Mesopotamia

The title of this vignette will doubtless suggest to readers an archaeological tour through abandoned buildings complete with elaborate columns, porticos, plazas, and terraced gardens, the sort of tour one imagines taking place in the cool of the evening in a pleasant classical setting. Unfortunately, we shall not be dealing with freestanding buildings but rather with remains of rooms in various types of structures that have been crushed under literally tons of earth accumulated over thousands of years on the sites of ancient towns and cities in the Tigris-Euphrates river plain of Iraq. These structures, having been constructed not of stone or marble but of mud brick, have crumbled into rubble and have formed earth mounds that encase the clay tablets they once protected.

The setting in which the first archives and libraries were produced was the ancient Mesopotamian city. The appearance of villages, towns, and cities, which historians label "the urban revolution," was the single most significant step taken by early peoples in their development out of the late Stone Age in Iraq. With permanent settlement came the collateral appearance of formal political and religious institutions, as well as organizations that directed the economic, judicial, and social lives of the new urbanites. The growth of population, coupled with an ever-increasing need to keep track of economic transactions contracted by individuals who often bore the same names, was an important stimulus for the invention of writing. Contrary to popular belief, the desire to record and preserve the great thoughts of great thinkers was a later development. Early on, the need for accurate record keeping by traders, tax officials, and other administrators took precedence. Though writing is often overlooked for primacy in lists of humankind's greatest inventions, the ability that writing affords humans to capture speech in permanent form allows us to study our record as a species in all areas of thought and experience.

Once the principles of writing were understood, the medium for its use was, in Mesopotamia, instantly available. Clay, when moistened and shaped into a small, pillow-shaped mass in the palm of the hand, and the stylus, with which the clay was incised, rapidly served as the "pen and paper" of the scribe. Depending upon need, clay tablets of various shapes, from miniature to large blocks, could be developed. When these were baked in the sun they became hard as rock and could then be stored in containers—large vases, baskets, boxes of clay—or individually on shelves in public buildings, such as palaces and temples, or in workrooms of private houses.

Most writing in ancient Mesopotamia was directed toward specific and practical ends. Only a relatively small number of clay tablets were devoted to what we would think of as aesthetic productions—myths, epics, speculations about the meaning of life, and the like. By far the greatest number were administrative texts, letters, texts of commercial or legal import, and those dealing with priestly concerns or those of omen takers, stargazers, and a host of temple administrators. This led to a practice among Assyriologists of dividing clay tablets into two general types: the "Stream of Tradition" texts and the "day-to-day" texts.

A survey of a major collection of "Stream of Tradition" cuneiform texts originated from the library gathered together about 650 by the Assyrian king Assurbanipal in Nineveh, the Assyrian capital at that time, suggests that the collection was a diviner's reference source—traditional texts to be consulted for advising and guiding the king in his many royal obligations and activities. The obsessions of the Mesopotamians in preserving such materials almost unaltered as they copied and recopied them throughout the centuries testify to the collection's "frozen tradition." The aim and need to look backward to beginnings amply testify to Mesopotamian religious conservatism. To learn to be a scribe meant long hours learning the originals and reduplicating them. Graduates of scribal schools might then be employed in positions requiring their specialized training.

Archives

The earliest archives seem to have developed in connection with storage rooms. These rooms also appear to have served as schools. Linguistic and archaeological evidence supports the notion of such an interrelated use. Two archive buildings were uncovered during excavations at Tello dating to about 2000 and situated in southern Mesopotamia. Seventy thousand tablets were found in these buildings, in connecting rooms, but no external doors led into the buildings. Entry seems to have been from above. Similar structures have been found at other sites. An archival site could be attached to a temple, though separated from it by a wall and a private entry. Along the walls of the Lagash complex stood benches, 1.5 feet high by 1.5 feet wide, on which tablets had been stacked.[1]

Archive Technique

At Ur, also in southern Mesopotamia, collections of tablets were found in a container to which a small clay label hung by a reed strand for identification purposes. Usually such labels gave information about the contents of the tablets, for example, legal verdicts, financial accounts, expenses, and receipts. At the end was an indication of the period covered, which in most cases was a year. In some instances the beginning period and the ending period, in years or months, were noted, as well as the finishing year or month. On some labels, the years and months were summed up.

An interesting and significant shift in the development of archives came with the use of containers to store longer-term collection of tablets, those comprising multiple years' worth of business or administrative records. Palace records, especially letters and other types of communications between previously reigning kings and their functionaries or between those functionaries themselves, could then become the basis of historical inquiry.[2]

Libraries

The production of literary and didactic texts required different preparation. A tale or ceremonial tablet would routinely require far more space than that needed for the single debt or receipt tablet, so the need arose to store a series of large tablets in a useful way. What the scribes and archive keepers devised was a method of indicating how many large tablets were part of the composition, where in the series a particular tablet belonged, how many tablets made up the series, and sometimes the name of the scribe who had created or copied the text. Although archives and libraries each employed similar techniques, early libraries had to provide space and protection for the larger tablets; the solution, found as a result of excavation at Korsabad of a late eighth-century palace belonging to Sargon II of Assyria, showed rows of niches set into the walls, like modern bookcases, which could accommodate oversized tablets.

To store clay tablets and find ways to protect them was one thing; to retrieve them was another. No one was permanently seated at a desk to deal with requests from passersby. Since libraries were attached to temples and palaces, there were chains of communications and procedures that had to authorize the removal of tablets. These originated at the very top, with the king or chief priest or other designated officials. To gain entrance to the relevant storage area, a doorkeeper had to be summoned, who would then have to find the requested tablet(s) and hand them over to the requesters (sometimes a whole delegation) and record the removal.

The modern librarian will be pleased to know that ancient patrons of libraries in Mesopotamia could suffer severely if they damaged a borrowed tablet. If you broke a tablet or immersed it in water so as to make it illegible, you would be cursed with the curses of troops of deities, including the highest of the land; merciless curses for as long as you lived; and curses including your family. If you feared the gods, you were enjoined to return the tablet on the same or following day. Nor should the borrower refuse to let officials consult the tablet(s). Those who complain today about the rising cost of fines for overdue or damaged books might ponder how lucky they are.

Of all the occupations both in Mesopotamia and in Egypt, that of scribe was clearly the most desirable. Scribal training was long, involved, and arduous. The students first underwent elementary training in how to form clay tablets of various sizes; how to hold the styluses, which were usually made from reeds though sometimes of wood; how to moisten a tablet's surface so that it could be incised; and generally how to preserve it once it was finished. The real task was learning the lists of Sumerian signs, approximately six hundred in number, which represented both an idea and the sound that expressed it. When Semites adapted the Sumerian writing system to express their own language in southern Mesopotamia, they retained the Sumerian logograms but used them normally as individual syllables with which their own Semitic vocabulary could be written phonetically. Since Semitic religious, political, and literary documents were heavily indebted to Sumerian models, the scribe had to learn to use basic elements of two writing systems. Beyond this, the most proficient scribes had also to be translators of messages in foreign languages if such came from royal courts.

The methods of teaching began with the copying of simple exercises. On one side of a round tablet the teacher, known as "father," would inscribe an exercise. The student learned by reproducing the text on the other. As a student's proficiency increased, the exercises doubtless became more complicated, and if such were completed satisfactorily, the student proceeded to copying actual texts from the standard materials of archives and libraries—that is, economic, legal, and political texts and texts used by temples and priests in religious, magical, and omenistic functions. Because the curriculum allowed it, the teaching technique was to progress from one text type to another as soon as a class had mastered the opening tablets of a multitablet series. We often find the beginnings of such series as epics and myths, without middles and ends, in the course of excavations.

Since Mesopotamian cities and towns were widely engaged in economic activities, scribes had to be trained to reckon accounts for palaces and temples, as well as for private entrepreneurs. Mathematics was therefore an important course for the would-be scribe. Some scribes chose (or were chosen for) a career in temple or palace bookkeeping; others rode with trading caravans. For still others, there were specialties in lexical, magical, ecclesiastical, or diplomatic pursuits. The best students were recruited by the major centers of activity such as the palaces, just as the average graduate, so to speak, could find street work by writing letters for illiterate passersby or by explaining intricacies of legal procedure to the ignorant. This allowed a decent life compared to what a person had to do by working in fields or storehouses or in "factories" of potters, weavers, or metalsmiths, and the like. The "inside scribe" led a protected and well-rewarded life within a temple or a palace and could count himself among the social elite of his community. A military scribe carried waxed tablets to record events in the field as notes for eventual inclusion in tablets relating to the glorification of campaigns and individual battles honoring the reigning king.[3]

New Year's Day in Babylon

In the Babylonian New Year's Festival, a twelve-day event that took place at the spring equinox (March–April of our calendar), we recognize two major themes of Mesopotamian religious and political life, which have been artfully blended together: from earliest times, on the one hand, the theme of renewal of life, the onset, once again, of agricultural growth and abundance; on the other, an assertion that political and social stability will continue during the new year—therefore, an affirmation, though infused with apprehension, that nature itself and the state and human society would continue to function in a benignly harmonious way.[1]

We have come to Babylon to observe this most pivotal event in its ritual history. The sight of its great outer walls as we approach down the Euphrates River from the north reveals how great and powerful this ancient city had become. From a much smaller town in the time of Hammurabi, almost two thousand years earlier, Babylon had endured to become a fabled capital city known far and wide in the ancient Near East. Our boat docks at one of the city's quays, and now we will walk the city's streets to identify a few of the chief buildings and monuments. As we begin, we see a bridge across the river that connects the older civic and religious center on the east bank with a newer residential district on the west.

Eight gates are set in the walls, but we shall enter the city through the beautiful Ishtar Gate, named after the Babylonian goddess of love and war. Its entry arch is set in a massive structure whose piers and walls are covered with colored glazed bricks. Gracefully executed figures of bulls and dragons are set in the walls, a wonderfully impressive entrance to the city (a reduced-sized reconstruction of this gate exists in the Vorderasiatischen Museum of Berlin). Once through this ceremonial gate we encounter huge citadels with massive defensive walls and palace and temple precincts, which define the skyline of the city. As we walk southward along the broad processional thoroughfare we soon see two magnificent temple complexes. The first is called Etemenanki, which means, in the oldest, Sumerian, language of Mesopotamia, "The House [Temple] at the boundary of the heaven and earth." The second is called Esagila, or "The House [Temple] which raises up its head." This was the abode of Marduk/Bel, head of the Babylonian pantheon and patron deity of Babylon itself. Within the precinct of Etemenanki stands a ziggurat, which was an edifice in the shape of a stepped pyramid. Not far away, beautifying the city's landscape, we can see the fabled Hanging Gardens of Babylon.

Unlike the kinds of houses of worship we are familiar with, where people join together in prayer and participate in the divine service, Mesopotamian temples were structures wherein the gods and their households were physically in residence. The statues and other images of these gods were not merely representations or symbols but rather were considered to be the deities themselves. The ancient Babylonian temple was not a public building. At best, people could congregate in its outermost courts. Since the statues were treated as though they were alive, they had to be awakened in the morning, dressed, fed, carried about, and tended to in innumerable ways by the temple staffs, which consisted of large numbers of priests of various grades and functions and many specialists in performance of rites and rituals. These could be exorcists, slaughterers of sacrificial animals, artisans who created sacerdotal objects in precious metals and woods, musicians, and singers. Women were included in the temple staffs, notably to function in fertility rites. Because a temple in a Mesopotamian city or town was a large landholder, dating from most ancient times, it had economic functions and had to maintain facilities such as accounting offices, stables or other enclosures for sacrificial animals, archives, and facilities for the training of acolytes and scribes. All in all, the temple was a complicated and very busy divine household that would rival the structure and functions of a modern, multifunctional corporation.

Returning now to the precinct of the temple Etemenanki, we look briefly at the ziggurat, whose origins as a religious edifice go back to earliest Sumerian civilization in lower Mesopotamia (about 3000). On top of this structure was placed some sort of chapel, whether early made of reeds or later of wood, brick, or stone. Some scholars think that this chapel represented a special link between heaven and earth. Traditionally in Mesopotamia, it appears to have been used in fertility ceremonies involving a city ruler and a high priestess. So well known was Babylon's ziggurat in the ancient Near East that the Hebrews, dwelling far to the west in Palestine, satirized it in the Bible, when they called the "Tower of Babylon" (from *bab ili,* Gate of the Gods) by the title "Tower of Confusion" (Hebrew, *balal*).

Continuing down the Processional Way, we next come to Esagila, the huge temple of Marduk/Bel with its fifty-five chapels to this god. This was the chief temple of Babylon and of Babylonia, the center of the realm's religious life, and home of the head of the Babylonian pantheon. Marduk, whose more customary appellation was Bel, was not one of the most ancient gods of Mesopotamia. Before him, in earliest mythic memory reigned Anu, the sky god; Enlil, the god of storm; Ea, the god of waters; and other nature gods whom Marduk supplanted after a great cosmic war. This epic conflict will be recited on the fourth day of the New Year's Festival. To understand what the reciter will be saying, you need a very short summary of the long poem called *Enuma Elish,* which we call the "Creation Epic." It culminates in the elevation of Marduk/Bel to supreme god in the universe.[2]

According to the story, from their abode in the ocean the primeval gods find themselves greatly disturbed by the uproarious doings of younger gods, who also inhabit the watery depths (perhaps "sweet water"?), and resolve to destroy them. They choose Tiamat to lead them against the revelers. Supported by a host of demons in her retinue, Tiamat marshals her forces and thoroughly intimidates the younger gods until the latter seek a champion. The young Marduk is given great magical powers. He engages Tiamat's forces and in a fierce battle defeats her. Thereupon he puts the universe in order and creates humankind. The members of Marduk's divine forces, grateful for his victory, establish Babylon as his home and build for him the temple Esagila, within whose precincts we will watch the ceremonies of the New Year's Festival unfold.

Although the temple rites and rituals to be followed exclude the general public, we have been given dispensation to observe the events of this most sacred celebration. We've arrived in time for the first day's schedule. The high priest has arisen before dawn and now stands before Marduk/Bel's statue. He has already washed himself with waters from both the Tigris and the Euphrates Rivers. He offers a prayer to the god that stresses the god's glory, his omnipotence, and omniscience and then petitions him to grant mercy to Babylon and to reconfirm the liberty of its citizens, his subjects (to be discussed later in conjunction with the ceremonies for the fifth day). Following this personal prayer, other priests and singers are allowed to enter the temple's inner precincts to perform their traditional rites before the statues of Bel and his consort, Beltiya.

The second day mirrors the first day, but the third day brings some new developments. After the familiar predawn rising, washing, and praying by the high priest and the entrance of auxiliary priests and singers have taken place, the high priest summons a group of artisans to craft two small images. These artisans include a metalworker (perhaps a goldsmith), a wood-carver, and a weaver. The images, one of cedarwood and one of tamarisk wood, are to be decorated with precious stones mounted in gold. The images are then to be dressed in red garments, which are tied by palm branches around their waists. After three days, during which the images are presented with food from a special tray, a slaughterer comes to strike off their heads. They then are burned in the presence of the statue of Nabu, Marduk/Bel's son. Although the meaning of the ritual is not self-evident, it suggests some sort of exorcism or rite of purification.

The main events of the fourth day begin to move toward an important climax. It is a day in which the temple itself is purified and the high priest will recite the entire "Creation Epic." The exorcist priest sprinkles water from the Tigris and the Euphrates within the edifice and then beats a kettledrum inside the temple. This drum was part of the equipment of Mesopotamian temples. There are ritual instructions for the replacement of the drumhead, which suggests the drum may have possessed magical properties. The exorcist priest has also smeared all the sanctuary doors with cedar resin or oil to purify them. Most significant on this day is the slaughtering of a ram; two priests proceed outside the city to the Euphrates, face west, and throw the body into the river. The priests must not return to the city until after the New Year's Festival is over.

The meaning of this act, with its accompanying prohibition, appears to be connected to a rite familiar in other ancient Near Eastern cultures—the expulsion of the "scapegoat." The animal assumes the burden of evil and impurity in a society and is ritually killed or expelled so as to cleanse the group and regain its favor in the eyes of the gods.

Now that the major purification of Esagila has been performed, we prepare for the arrival of the god Nabu from his temple, Ezida, in Borsippa, which is located slightly southwest of Babylon. Nabu will travel upriver in a splendidly caparisoned boat named *Iddahedu*. In Nabu's earliest manifestation in Mesopotamia, he was considered to be the god of wisdom. In the course of time he became closely associated with Marduk/Bel and ultimately was considered to be the latter's son. On Nabu's journey northward, he is ministered to by his own retinue of priests and other attendants. When he arrives at Babylon, he will be greeted by a host of artisans carrying a ceremonial tray of food in his honor.

At this point, on the fifth day of the festival, the ceremonial emphasis shifts to the role of the Babylonian king. We see him washing his hands in waters taken from the Tigris and Euphrates and then being escorted from his palace into the temple, Esagila. When the king reaches the approach to the sanctuary of Marduk/Bel, the high priest, who appears to have been within the sanctuary, emerges and strips the king of his royal insignia and puts them on a stool in Bel's sanctuary. After this he comes back and strikes the king on his cheek. Quite violently, he drags the king by his ears and then forces him to bow down to the ground.

At this point, the king recites a negative confession. He has not been neglectful of the god. He has not sinned. He has not destroyed Babylon, nor has he incited civic violence. He has not overlooked the rites of Esagila. He has not assaulted any important subordinate or humiliated them. He affirms that he was diligent in protecting his citizens. Next, the high priest assures the king that Marduk will listen to his confession and will bless him and protect his kingdom. After these assurances, the cleric restores the king's regalia to the now doubtless much relieved king. But a final action is required. The high priest strikes the king's cheek again. If tears flow as a result, all is well; Marduk will be friendly. If, on the other hand, no tears flow, Marduk will be angry and enemies will cut short the king's reign. (We can wonder how pleased the high priest might have been to be able to land a solid blow on the royal face without being in danger of losing his life!)

The practice of humiliating the king of Babylon is rooted in an age-old Mesopotamian idea, that of the *kidinnutu,* or status of freedom, granted to cities by earlier rulers. Some notable cities, Babylon being one, were designated as "free cities"; their inhabitants were absolved from taxation and work on royal projects and were granted freedom from other civic obligations to the king and state. Babylon had a long and proud tradition of civic independence and even asserted its rights to conquerors. Its citizens enjoyed the kidinnutu, and before one of its gates, or inside the city, stood the kidinnu, the symbol of the city's free status. Recall that in the king's negative confession, he denies ever striking a subordinate. This would have been anathema, given the city's traditions.

The high point of the New Year's Festival has now been reached. What happens subsequent to the reaffirmation of the king's reign must be gathered from hints incorporated in texts other than the incomplete texts devoted to the festival. A great ingathering of divine statues from other important Babylonian cities suggests the homage given to Bel by lesser gods of the pantheon. The king will also "take the hands of Bel," who thereby further affirms the king's legitimacy for the new year by pronouncing his destiny.

The public phase of the celebration includes a parade of fulsomely clothed and decorated divine statues along Babylon's Processional Way, as well as a display of the king's treasures for the excited citizens. Following this, the king embarks upstream to a structure called the *akitu* house, where the sacred marriage most likely took place.

This house, or chapel, whose origins go back to earliest Mesopotamian times, was the place where early priest-kings "married" the priestesses of Innana (Ishtar), goddess of sex and symbol of fertility in nature. The procession to the akitu house is a kind of wedding procession, full of singing, music, and revelry. And the king, now fully confident of his continued and successful reign, will enjoy a night of conjugal bliss to ensure the renewal of life in nature and agricultural abundance for his kingdom.

Finally the entourage returns to Babylon, and the gods' statues depart to their home cities and temples. Very possibly, at some point in the Babylonian festival, an enactment of the episodes in the "Creation Epic," with the king himself taking the part of Marduk, was performed, though this is not certain. But what is certain is that confidence in the renewal of state, society, and nature was at its highest level in Babylon at New Year's time. For the rest of the year, the omen takers would be busy trying to fathom what was in the minds of the gods who lived in their midst.

FURTHER READING

James, E. O. *Myth and Ritual in the Ancient Near East.* London: Thames and Hudson, 1958. See pp. 53–58.

Kuhrt, A. "Usurpation, Conquest and Ceremonial: From Babylon to Persia." In *Rituals of Royalty,* 20–25, ed. D. Caundaine and S. Price. Cambridge: Cambridge University Press, 1987.

Decoding the Hammurabi Law Code

One of the most famous names in Near Eastern antiquity is that of Hammurabi, sixth king of the Old Babylonian Dynasty, who ruled Mesopotamia between 1792 and 1750. Although Hammurabi is well known by historians for his military and administrative skills, his reputation is highlighted by his issuance of a long series of legal formulations, 282 in number, in the second year of his reign. These follow a long paean of praise in which Hammurabi declares that Anum, the sky god and head of the divine pantheon, and Enlil, Anum's chief administrator, had commissioned Hammurabi to "cause justice to prevail in the land to destroy the wicked and the evil, that the strong might not oppress the weak" (prologue, 2.31ff.). Following the presentation of the legal prescriptions of the Code, a long epilogue lavishes praise on those who are guided by them, especially future kings, while those who ignore the statutes, or distort or alter their words, are mightily cursed. The stone stele, on which the text was incised, had been carried away from Babylon as booty by Elamite raiders at the end of the thirteenth century. Taken to Susa, in Iran, it suffered considerable damage but was retrieved by French archaeologists in 1801–2 and subsequently removed to the Louvre in Paris. The damaged parts of the inscriptions were restored from later copies of the Code.

When we think of a law code, we imagine that some authority—whether a sovereign, legislature, or judicial body or some other official group within a society—has commissioned a group of legal scholars and jurists to compile regulations for the maintenance of good order in the country, along with penalties for violations. The regulations may embrace customary, criminal, administrative, civil, and many other areas of concern to the society in question or to its ruling elite. Modern examples are the Code promulgated by Napoleon in France and that by Kemal Ataturk, using the French Code as a model for the new Republic of Turkey after the defeat of the Ottoman Empire following World War I. The most famous ancient Code of jurisprudence is that of the

Roman emperor Justinian (527–565 AD), who commissioned an editorial board to collect and analyze works of earlier Roman jurists.

Was the Hammurabi Law Code a work of this type? Was a Babylonian council of lawyers and jurists responsible for the document? All available evidence points to the negative. A comparison of actual court cases from the Old Babylonian period with provisions of Hammurabi's laws shows no correspondence between them, and the instruction to any petitioner to consult the Code for legal guidance is mere hyperbole.

What, then, is this fascinating document? The answer must be that it belongs to the genre of literature celebrating the image of Hammurabi as "King of Justice," a ruler who keeps the society in balance and good order in his role as surrogate of the gods. Any Mesopotamian king was the foremost personality of his realm. He functioned as an intermediary between the people he ruled and the gods who ruled the universe. As sovereign he was praised as a war leader; in peace he was the benefactor of his people. In historical documents, he was the central subject as builder and sustainer of temples and overseer of ritual and rite in religious affairs. In legal matters the king was, of course, the final judge. But as overseer of his society, the king had to act when his people were threatened by natural disasters.

One of the most pressing duties of a Mesopotamian king was to oversee the economic balance between the rich and the poor in his country. Normally, the relationship would find its own level. When, however, the Tigris or the Euphrates River flooded the adjacent farmlands and destroyed canals and cache basins because of violent and irregular storms, crops might be destroyed or fields prepared for plowing might be severely damaged. As a result, the struggling farmer would need to purchase seed and animals from creditors and would risk becoming a debt slave because of inability to pay. To keep such things from occurring, the king would issue an act of *misharum,* a Babylonian Semitic term that means something like "restoration of economic balance" or "period of payment remission." These acts took such forms as price-fixing or reduction of interest rates. The misharum act was designed to serve for a defined period of time, not permanently.[1]

If the provisions of the Code are not the calculated products of a legal commission, how should they then be understood? Perhaps the best description is that the entire collection is a compendium of customary law—for example, those provisions dealing with family and other human relationships, "traditional" punishments for assaults and other crimes, and restitution for damages to property and farm animals, practiced as normal in the region from much earlier times.

But what we call price-fixing regulations may indeed reflect the misharum acts instituted by Hammurabi when he came to power. In the provisions relating to captured soldiers and feudal responsibilities relating to veterans (nos. 26–41), we appear to have current rather than "traditional" concerns. We cannot forget that the time available for the issuance of all the Code's provisions was very short—the whole collection, we need to consider, was presented in Hammurabi's second year, which suggests that bits and pieces of previously known legal collections were "cobbled" together for the king. There is no consistently logical division of subject matter in the Code.

Outline of the Hammurabi Law Code

Sections	Contents
1–7	Proof, perjury, incorruptibility of judges, contracts
8–14	Thievery, lost property, kidnapping
15–20	Harboring fugitive slaves
21–25	Break-ins, robbery
26–41	Captured soldiers and feudal responsibilities
42–65	Renting and cultivating of fields
66–97	Loans to individuals
98–107	Loans to traders
108–11	Regulations of wine sellers
112–26	Business contracts and safekeeping
127–94	Men-women relationships, marriage, legacies, dowry, adoption
195–214	Assault and battery
215–40	Responsibility of professionals and workmen (malpractice)
241–67	Injuries to hired animals and thefts
268–82	Fixed prices for goods and fixed wages for work and services

Of the 282 provisions in the document, six of the first seven clearly establish principles of judicial procedure. The opening regulation emphasizes the importance of proof in accusations and penalties for lying (the example given concerns only murder). The third and fourth provisions establish the penalties for perjury in capital cases and in lesser matters. The conduct of judges who change their decisions is dealt with in the fifth provision, while the seventh establishes the need for contracts and receipts in matters of safekeeping and in business dealings. The only provision of the first seven listed in the Code that does not pertain to courtroom procedures is the second, concerning accusations of sorcery. Here the ordeal by water is required, and proof of an accusation is established by whether the accused drowns or comes forth alive from the river. Barring the section on sorcery, the opening of the Code concisely establishes those legal principles that lie at the base of any system of fair dealing between the accusers and the accused.

The nature of the Hammurabi collection appears to be inclusive for an agricultural society. Fully 25 percent of the provisions deal with family law and male-female relationships (nos. 127–94); nearly 20 percent deal with the rental and cultivation of fields and with injuries to animals (nos. 42–65 and 241–67); loans to individuals, including traders, and rules governing business contracts occupy about 20 percent (nos. 66–107 and 112–26); and price-fixing regulations for hire and for workers' wages, as well as regulations of wine sellers, make up about 7 percent of the list (nos. 108–11and 268–82). So far we have accounted for 72 percent of the Code's interests. Another 5 percent deals with the assignment of agricultural lands and their upkeep as feudal responsibilities of soldiers, one of the earliest historical examples of a "veterans' administration" at work (nos. 26–41). The rest of the Code, approximately one-quarter of the total, deals with major and minor felonies and misdemeanors, malpractices, assault and battery, and break-ins and robbery. While the scribes had succeeded in itemizing most of these regulations designed to keep a society in good order, they seem to have adopted an overall helter-skelter approach. Except for the succinctly and admirably stated principles of courtroom procedures stated in the first seven provisions of the Code, there is no compelling organizational structure of the rest except in the gathering together of more or fewer items under the same general category.

A feature of the Code worth noting is its use of "casuistic" phraseology in the provisions. The phraseology is characterized by the terminology "If . . . then." It basically deals with resolutions of specific situations. Its opposite, apodictic phraseology, is a statement of command, for example, "Do not enter this property." If you have been seen to enter the forbidden territory, the verdict is incontestable. You are per se guilty. The first casuistic phrasing assumes that a certain action might have taken place, but a process of inquiry must determine this, complete with evidence presented, proof established, and so forth. An apodictic approach forbids one from doing a specific action or requires a specific action to be done. In the Hammurabi Code, the emphasis is chiefly on legal process.

The existence of the Hammurabi Law Code signifies more than a simple attempt to ensure that right order and due process prevail in Babylon. It allows us to reflect on a major change that began to take place in Mesopotamian society at the turn of the second millennium. Under earlier Sumerian control, the region had exhibited a predominantly theocratic autocracy. The basic economy was dominated by the temple, which owned most of the land. A de-emphasis of temple control of the major civic concerns of life saw the beginnings of a separation between church and state, a situation accelerated by the entry of Semitic Amorites into the area. By the time of Hammurabi's reign within the First Dynasty of Babylon, the palace organization, with an independent king as propagator of civil law, had been fully established. The concerns of the temple were essentially restricted to sacred things. The Hammurabi period further reflects the emergence of fully free property-owning individuals whose interests were both protected and regulated by the rule of secular law, as were the interests and obligations of various classes of slaves and half-free individuals, whose social status is still a matter of considerable debate. Although the legal collection has a rudimentary organization, it is still possible to marvel at the range of legal principles and individual prescriptions taken up within it.

A Speculation on the Composition of the Hammurabi Code

We can only surmise on the accession of Hammurabi to the throne of Babylon that the following may have ensued, although the process must remain speculative.

1. An order would have been issued to the royal scribes to prepare a monument celebrating the king as lawgiver in accordance with time-honored tradition. This would have galvanized the scribes into action to collect samples of jurisprudence from previous regimes.

2. Just as today we might say "work increases to fill the time available for its completion," an appropriate parallel in reference to ancient scribal schools should be "the size of a text on a found object, and its

contents, in the case of the Hammurabi stele, a standing stone of a certain length and girth, depends upon the space available to be inscribed upon." The scribes preparing the Hammurabi Law Code had four areas to plot out: (1) space for a pictorial representation of Hammurabi standing before the sun god, Shamash, as he receives the laws from the "God of Justice"; (2) space for the introductory and laudatory text about Hammurabi as lawgiver; (3) space for the provisions of the laws themselves; and, finally, (4) space for the curses on those who would violate the provisions of the Code.

3. The compositional problems facing the scribes and stonecutters were the same as those facing modern-day printers, who must tailor a customer's text to fit the size of an available poster or page. Accordingly it is legitimate to ask, How much of the *contemporary* legal traditions of Babylonia have come down to us? And how much has been drawn from earlier legal compilations not now known to us?

On the Lighter Side of Mesopotamia

A Glimpse into Sumerian Palace
and Temple Household Life

One could easily infer, from the hundreds of thousands of religious, economic, jurisprudential, and other materials having to do with life in ancient Mesopotamia, that all was serious and focused on affairs of the "Great Institutions" like palaces and temples. For the most part the records we have cast a no-nonsense veil over the affairs of the civilizations we study. It is therefore very refreshing to come upon a text from the period of Ur III (2100–2000) in Sumeria that gives us a glimpse of the lighter side of Mesopotamian life. This text is part of the British Museum's collection of Babylonian tablets, cataloged as BM 14618 and studied by I. J. Gelb in 1965. It lists various classes of musicians and singers, including types of entertainers, connected to royal and temple households located in seven main cities and towns in the province of Lagash. The total number of individuals listed is 242; two-thirds of the total are musicians, singers, and entertainers; the rest are cult chanters, cantors, or the like. As members of royal or temple households, all these people would be given rations, according to their function and experience. Such rations would normally include barley and wool or cloth or items of finished manufacture.

From a technical, philological study of the tablet in question, and by a comparison with other Sumerian tablets listing names, professions, and rations, Professor Gelb was able to describe the composition of a typical Sumerian temple household and royal household. These included men, women, and children, all workers at various jobs, including smiths, carpenters, weavers, millers, and shepherds, and officials such as scribes and foremen of such occupations as weaving. Added to these, and extending the list of occupations known from similar types of tablets, were personnel identified as secretaries, cupbearers, gatekeepers, guards, milk carriers, and potters, their positions ranging from senior and important in the household administration to menial.

Focusing once again on the British Museum tablet in question, within the category of singer/musician, different varieties occur. Some of the players perform on stringed instruments, while some are probably percussionists, drummers, or "bones" players. Doubtless, these musicians also sang to the tunes they played. Professor Gelb also notes that singers/musicians were often blind, which allows him to refer to the blind musician in the *Odyssey* who plays his lyre and to the "Great blind bard Homer himself." He also refers to the later Babylonian period (ca. eighteenth century) to cite, in one instance, the case of a blind girl who was apprenticed to learn singing and to the circumstance that blind girls and female singers and musicians were known at Mari in Syria. In addition to their functions at royal entertainments in the palace or in cult ceremonies in the temple, the singers/musicians could also perform at funerary rites, where they could be hired in smaller or larger groups as wailers over the departed. This practice can still be observed in various parts of the modern world.

Quite fascinatingly, the category of singer/musician includes the snake charmer and the dancing-bear specialists. These certainly were favorite entertainments of both kings and priests. But far more, they were also popular in the courtyards and streets of a Sumerian city. We have all seen the snake charmer in motion pictures playing a seductive tune on his woodwind instrument, while a hypnotized snake, usually a cobra, sways sideways and forward before an equally hypnotized audience. The sight of a trained bear "dancing" to the beat and rattle of a tambourine must also have mesmerized an appreciative audience. It is a philological impossibility to know whether the bear keepers and handlers/trainers were also clowns or jesters, though this seems likely. While some bears were doubtless captured and trained from a half-grown, perhaps even a full-grown, state, we do have tablets indicating that bear cubs were received by individuals who were trainers and exhibitors, for further development. Nor was the commerce in bears occasional or sporadic. Professor Gelb cites references both to single bears and to bear cubs in numerous administrative texts. In one of these, 457 bears among 384,344 "domestic and feral animals" were received in the animal park during a twelve-month period during one dynastic reign of Ur III; in another, 164 bears among 62,203 animals were counted; a third text counts 15 bear cubs.

The reader should not think of these ancient Mesopotamian animal parks as equivalent to modern zoos. Of course the animals had to be managed to some degree, but the idea of the park was to allow the king to hunt on his own private preserve. His favorites were allowed the same privileges as hunting companions. An interesting document from central Anatolia from about 1750 tells us that Anitta, king of Nesa (Kanesh), while warring against and conquering neighborhood kingdoms, brought wild beasts, including lions and leopards, to his home city, clear proof that the custom of collecting wild animals for hunting or display purposes was a widespread familiar feature of royal activity. It is ironic that, long after the great city of Babylon was destroyed, all that could be identified of the site was the probable ruins of its game park. In the fourth century AD, the Roman emperor Julian (the Apostate), during his war against the Sassanids, in Iraq, arrived at a wall enclosing an area known as "The Royal Game Park." The emperor broke down the wall and partly killed, partly liberated, the game within. Although the name of the place was not mentioned, the description of the area by Zosimus, his historian, strongly suggests that it was Babylon.

Wild Animals and Game Parks

M en and animals have commingled since the beginning of time, mostly to man's advantage as hunter. But at the same time that he killed for food, the hunter could not fail to be impressed by the beauty and grace of his prey, the power and the apparent magic inherent in their forms and movements. The superbly drawn animals on the cave walls of Altamira and Lascaux from early prehistoric times capture the pragmatic and the aesthetic together. In the ancient Near East numerous birds, animals, and marine creatures might even have been considered gods, as most notably in Egypt and relatively so in other contemporary cultures. When the earliest settlements of the area developed into agricultural and trading centers, those wild animals that were domesticable, such as oxen and donkeys, became beasts of burden, while those that roamed free in the wild state were pursued or killed if they threatened human life or were captured for display and the entertainment of kings and courts.

When we think of the terrain of the Near East we visualize deserts, rough rock formations, mountains, dry wadis, and the precious few river valleys. We assume that the animal life of the area, besides the ubiquitous camel and the legions of sheep and goats, consists primarily of small animals and reptiles. This certainly would fit with our own experiences of the American Southwest, which often appears to mirror the terrain and climate of the contemporary Near East. However, conditions in the ancient world were considerably different and would seem to be possibly astonishing to the modern reader.

We are aware, of course, that the Near East in ancient times already possessed the environmental elements that would allow what is described as the first "food-producing" revolutions in history. By the sixth millennium inhabitants of northern Iraq had learned how to plant crops instead of merely harvesting wild grains and to produce flocks of sheep and goats for a dependable supply of meat and milk. In the mind's eye, one can see the development of the Near East into agricultural lands bordering nomadic herding areas and huge areas of wasteland. What we don't perceive is that the area was also inhabited by many species of ferocious wild animals, numbers of which still inhabit the jungles and open lands of Africa and India.

Consider first the western edge of the Near East, the Palestinian corridor. In addition to the bones of wild ungulates found in excavations—wild boar, roe deer, gazelle, and the wild species of modern domestic sheep—bones of hippopotami and crocodiles were found in the marshland along the Jordan River. Brown bear ranged the hill country and forests of the territory, along with other carnivores, such as lions, leopards, cheetah, jackals, and wolves.

While an ancient Near Eastern king had to concern himself with affairs of economic and military import and matters of international diplomacy, he also was concerned about his image as ruler. He was head of the religious establishment, chief hero in battle, dispenser of justice to his subjects, and direct conduit, so to speak, to the divine world; he was also a figure of strength, ability, and bravery, as promoted by his propagandist scribes. War annals repeatedly celebrate the king as victorious in battle, while embedded in such reports are notices of the numbers and identities of wild beasts killed on a campaign or in a royal hunt. It was common for a ruler to establish a game park of large dimensions within which he could stage controlled hunts led by himself with guards or also with palace favorites and captive kings. Assyrian palace reliefs of the seventh century vividly show realistic reliefs of lions about to be released from wooden cages, while the king, weapons in hand, awaits their charge. Other scenes show the animals in their death throes.

How dangerous was the open country in the ancient Near East? Very much so, according to a number of letters from officials in village and towns to their superiors in administrative districts or even to the king at his royal residence. At Mari, in central Syria, texts recovered during excavations show that not only did lions attack and devour domestic animals, such as sheep and oxen, but they also killed human beings—in one case some children who had strayed away from their homes. Beyond such attacks outside an inhabited area, the animals were bold enough to sneak into unguarded or only lightly guarded villages and snatch men, women, and children. From some of the letters it appears that officials of the king had a standing responsibility to capture a marauding lion and ship the animal to the royal court or another administrative center. It leaves much to the imagination to think of an official having to secure a cage from a neighboring town or village if there was none in his own jurisdiction, or having to build one, and then transfer the animal, which might have been temporarily shut up in a silo or other farm or village building, into the new, cramped enclosure. Not to mention the shipment of this cargo overland by wagon or by barge on a river or canal.

But it was not only the settled inhabitant who was at risk. As ancient Near Eastern states grew in territorial size, and as diplomatic activity increased between motherland and conquered territory, more and more was it common that couriers and ambassadors had to set out into unprotected territories to fulfill their missions. From the corpus of Egyptian literature we have a document known as "A Satire of the Trades," whose theme is to show that the best of possible professions in ancient Egypt is that of scribe. The relevant portion of this document, while still maintaining the thesis that the scribal profession was most preferred, offers the following opinion:

> the courier goes out to a foreign country, after he has made over
> his property to his children, being afraid of lions and Asiactics.
> . . . He does not return happy of heart.[1]

It was inevitable that mishaps involving wild animals would be reflected in legal disputes. We have evidence of this in the Hammurabi Code. Consider the case of a man who hired an ox for work in his field (Code 244). If a lion killed the ox in the open, the ox's owner had to bear the loss. On the other hand, and according to customary law as applied to a shepherd in whose fold either a hired or entrusted animal died of natural causes or was killed by a lion, then the shepherd had to clear himself by an oath and testimony before the statue of a god, and the animal stricken in the field would be returned to the owner (presumably as food).

A final glimpse of leonine activity takes us to Palestine in biblical times and to biblical narrations involving Hebrew heroes and prophets. The Bible gives us vivid examples of the dangers that lions could produce among peaceful pastoralists or farmers. In 1 Samuel 17:31–32, David, the future king of Israel, is introduced to us as a young man, a shepherd, who volunteers to do single combat against Goliath, the Philistine warrior, who has challenged the forces of the then Hebrew leader, Saul. Saul tries to dissuade David, to which David answers:

> Your servant used to keep sheep for his father; and when there
> came a lion, or a bear, and took a lamb from the flock, I went after

him and smote him and delivered it out of his mouth; and if he arose against me, I caught him by his beard, and smote him and killed him. Your servant has killed both lions and bears; . . . And David said, "The Lord who delivered me from the paw of the lion from the paw of the bear, will deliver me from the hand of this Philistine."

In 2 Kings 17:24–28, lions play a part in creating an environmental problem. The time is in the late eighth century, after the Assyrians had conquered Samaria, the small breakaway northern territory of a once united Hebrew monarchy. Under the Assyrian policy of removing their captives to far-off places and transplanting foreigners to the conquered regions, the newcomers to Samaria encountered severe difficulties with lions. Here is the biblical account:

And the king of Assyria brought people from Babylon, Cuthah, Avva, Hamath, and Sephar-va'im, and placed them in the cities of Sama'ria instead of the people of Israel; and they took possession of Sama'ria, and dwelt in its cities. And at the beginning of their dwelling there, they did not fear the LORD; therefore the LORD sent lions among them, which killed some of them. So the king of Assyria was told, "The nations which you have carried away and placed in the cities of Sama'ria do not know the law of the god of the land; therefore he has sent lions among them, and behold, they are killing them, because they do not know the law of the god of the land." Then the king of Assyria commanded, "Send there one of the priests whom you carried away thence; and let him go and dwell there, and teach them the law of the god of the land." So one of the priests whom they had carried away from Samar'ia came and dwelt in Bethel, and taught them how they should fear the LORD. (2 Kgs 17)

It is understandable that lions would attack flocks of sheep or invade vacant fields, and in the absence of security patrols on the roads, travelers were also always at great risk. An example of this is the fate of a Hebrew prophet who disobeyed the Lord and was met by a lion on the road, which summarily killed him (1 Kgs 13). Difficult as it might be for us to envisage the territories of the ancient Near East above Egypt as areas through which man-killers roamed, it is even harder to think of

such beasts as now associated with equatorial habitats in Africa as elephants, hippopotami, and crocodiles inhabiting regions of Palestine and
Syria. Literary references to the hippopotamus and the crocodile appear
in the biblical book of Job (chap. 41) as "Behemoth" and "Levianthan"
respectively. And although elephants became extinct in western Asia in
the early centuries of the first millennium, they were exploited, along
with the hippopotamus, primarily for the ivory of their tusks. Work in
ivory had been produced from as early as the Copper-Stone Age in the
Negev of Palestine.

The native artistic genius of ancient Near Eastern peoples manifests
itself far more in small inlaid items than in the more common massive
and overpowering sculptures created by the imperial Assyrians at the
height of their power. The skill of ancient work in ivory is brilliantly displayed in the hoard of items recovered through excavation at the site of
Nimrud, near modern Mosul in northern Iraq. Here thousands of items
dating to the ninth and eighth centuries were retrieved. This was the
period of Late Assyrian imperialism, so we cannot be absolutely sure that
all of the objects found at Nimrud were made on-site or were received
as tribute from vassal countries or booty from military campaigns. What
we have are exquisite examples of the ivory carver's art. The hoard
includes figurines, inlays for furniture or panels, decorated boxes, and a
variety of personal items such as combs and other cosmetic accou-
trements—hair decorations and palettes.

On a much more impressive scale, Phoenician kings would embell-
ish their thrones with exquisitely carved figures that figure prominently
in the Hebrew Bible. Solomon's building activity in Jerusalem after he
became king of Israel included two buildings built for him by Hiram of
Tyre. In Solomon's House of the Forest of Lebanon stood an ivory
throne that the king himself had commissioned. We also learn, to refer
back to our previous discussion of lions, that two lion figures stood
beside the arm rests of the ivory throne and "twelve lions stood there,
one at each end of a step on the six steps" (1 Kgs 10:19–20). In
Solomon's temple, ten bronze wheeled stands were highly decorated
with lion figures along with figures of oxen and cherubim (1 Kgs
7:27–28). All in all the power and terror manifested in the lion image
and the constant representation of these animals as symbols of power
and terror truly fitted the royal image at the same time as they evoked
a picture of freedom and dominance that the king demanded for himself.[2]

FURTHER READING

Borowski, O. *Every Living Thing: Daily Use of Animals in Ancient Israel.* Thousand Oaks, CA: Alta Mira Press, 1997.

Firmage, E. "Zoology." In *Anchor Bible Dictionary,* ed. D. N. Freedman, 6:1109–67. New York: Doubleday, 1992.

Van Buren, E. D. *The Fauna of Ancient Mesopotamia as Represented in Art.* Rome: Pontificum institutum biblicum, 1953.

Archaeology

The "Cold Case File" of the Historian

Here is the "corpse" in front of us. Investigation confirms that it once was a human habitation. This is known because evidence of pottery fragments is convincing. Where do these fragments come from? We must appreciate that the earth is alive, moving, always shifting, however slightly; it brings stones and boulders into a farmer's field each planting season. In our example, it nudges fragments of dishes and other similar objects upward from a long-lost village, town, perhaps even a city.

Were it not for this evidence of human habitation, the casual traveler would simply have assumed the presence of a grass-covered mound in an extended landscape of low hills and valleys, a part of the natural landscape. Several hundred years ago educated travelers, seeing evidence of human life in a remote area, would have written an account of their observations to their home historical societies and developed plans for further exploration.

An account of the history of archaeology, or how it is done, is not my purpose in this account. My particular purpose is to show the reader what must be considered when a mound is excavated. Excavation becomes an integrated scholarly enterprise that requires experts from a number of disciplines to succeed.

The Preparatory Phase

Once a decision is made by a university, a museum, or another certified scholarly institution to excavate a particular site, several necessary arrangements must be made. Unlike the early days of exploration and discovery in the Near East, when a traveler could personally arrange to haul away artifacts from a site to his or her home country, present-day excavators must have their plans referred to and approved by the particular ministries of culture involved. Earlier agreements granting permission to dig in a particular Near Eastern country were usually generous: the finds were divided between the host country and the visiting excavators. Today, nationalistic interests restrict this practice or eliminate it entirely. The time available to complete an excavation may depend on the host country's willingness to allow it to continue as much as on the resources available to the excavators.

Let's return to the mound that stands before us. The reader may ask: how and why did the mound become a mound in the first place? Let's go back to the time when the earliest inhabitants decided to settle in a particular place. They chose an open site adjacent to, or near, a source of water. They built their first shelters and storage facilities; manufactured their first tools and domestic utensils; and settled into a simple, and doubtless efficient, mode of life. At some point they may have been forced to leave and settle somewhere else. Perhaps the source of water failed or an enemy destroyed their settlement, perhaps even destroyed the possibility of a return because the land had been so thoroughly ravaged as to make it unproductive for generations. Wind-blown silt and sand would soon cover an abandoned place. With the passage of time, a new population might choose the site as its home, especially if some written or oral tradition defined it as a sacred place, or descendants of the original settlers might have returned. When the last population disappeared, the mound became a "living tomb" for the modern excavator.

What must be done before the actual digging begins is to create an accurate description of the site's geographical location. It must be surveyed. Indications of altitude, climate, and especially the amount of rainfall and its frequency must be determined so that its ecological setting may be fixed. If the site contains more than one mound, each of these must also be surveyed and described in detail.

How does one approach the actual digging of a mound? The interior of the mound has been built up by a succession of occupants. Each period of inhabitation has left evidence of its occupiers, and as time has passed, the remains of all these occupations have been compressed into strata, or layers. A popular and useful analogy is a layer cake. For one to discover what has been baked inside the cake of our analogy—the nuts, raisins, chocolate bits—without damaging the cake entirely, one would carefully cut and strip a section off its side. This would allow you to see how many layers there were and what lay hidden within. So too would you do with a mound: cut a series of step trenches to get an idea of how many strata were concealed within. Another method is carefully to dig a shaft through the mound for the same purpose. Once the test cuts have been made, the excavators can ascertain where the strata divide, determine how many there are, and get a sample of artifacts that lie within. What follows has to be a very careful and lengthy process of uncovering artifacts and recording the discoveries. These must be numbered, measured, identified by location, described in detail, and carefully cleaned and stored in collection boxes after their find spots have been noted on the descriptive maps of the excavation's surveyors. Organic materials may, for the most part, be dated by radiocarbon (C14) analysis. Analyses of strata will show whether the mound has had a homogeneous development or whether some shifts or changes in the developmental sequence have taken place. Events such as fires, invasions, or natural disasters, as can be discerned through careful analysis, must also be noted.

Once the preparatory steps have been completed, and matters such as surveying and area mapping of the sections of the mound to be initially dug have been established, the enterprise becomes essentially specialized. The director of the excavation has a staff of academic personnel at his or her disposal—specialists in architecture, ceramics, metallurgy, small crafts, and, if texts are found, document analysts—to assist in the analysis (these specialists may not all be present at the dig site). What types of finds will have to be analyzed?

Architecture

The following types of questions about houses will be asked.

Are there different plans? How are they situated? Open? Packed together? If there are different styles and sizes, does the placement suggest random selection of building sites or deliberate concentration, and for what possible reasons? Are there similarities of room plans, for example, sleeping areas, cooking and living areas, work areas? What of residences with different room sizes? Can anything be inferred about differences of functions? Considering construction features, what are the walls made of? Are they reinforced by timbers? Do the house foundations rest on stone foundations or on bare ground? How is entry gained into the typical house? How are the house walls joined? Reinforced? Are they of pressed mud or plastered over mud brick? Have the walls been painted? Do the houses have courtyards? Are the residential quarters separated from other communal areas; if so, what might this mean? If other larger and more imposing structures exist, as perceived by foundations plans, can these be identified? Both the entire residential plan, which will be drawn on maps and charts, and detailed drawings of individual house designs are needed. One must also be aware of changes in house plans over time and the possible reasons for these changes.

Concerning a Settlement's Subsistence

If evidence of animal and plant remains exists, tests must determine whether these are of wild or domesticated forms. If the plants are native to the area, the settlement's source of diet can be identified, but if not, the question of the food source becomes more complicated: Where did the items originate? Were they regularly imported, or were they chance commodities acquired through trade or other means? As for animal remains, the majority may be the normally expected domestic dogs, sheep, goats, and cattle, while bones of wild cattle, deer, wild sheep, asses, and other small stock would indicate hunting activity of some frequency by the settlement's inhabitants.

Concerning a Settlement's Inhabitants

If an excavation is fortunate enough to discover documents inscribed on clay tablets or on stone, these can provide direct information about the inhabitants and their customs, as well as, perhaps, chronological information. For preliterate periods we must rely on experts such as physical anthropologists, ceramic specialists, and other specialists for help. For example, burial remains can often reveal reasonable conclusions of a people's thoughts about death from an examination of objects deposited in graves, not to overlook what can be learned from scientific analysis of actual skeletal remains.

Concerning a Settlement's Work Activities

Beyond the activities of farmers and builders in an ancient community, there is usually ample evidence of hand-manufactured articles in a variety of techniques. We can divide these activities by craft.

Pottery

We may think of fired or unfired earthenware as humankind's earliest experiments in containing liquids and solids. Actually there is a long period of experimentation that precedes the manufacture of ceramics. Solids and liquids were stored or carried in containers made from natural products such as large, thick, but flexible leaves that could be shaped into containers; horns of cattle; carved wooden bowls and boxes; and especially animal skins. The recognition that clay could be molded into container shapes of all types, that leakage of liquids could be prevented by firing the clay, and that the objects produced provided a means for long-term storage produced a revolutionary change in how people could engage in all sorts of activities, such as extended travel, monumental construction projects where water and food could be kept on-site, and military campaigns. Individual decorative patterns incised or painted upon ancient pottery have enabled archaeologists to identify the work of specific peoples.

Metallurgy

The presence of locally manufactured objects in a dig, usually made of lead or copper but occasionally of silver and gold, sufficiently indicates that an advanced technology was employed. Metals found in an excavation must be distinguished by point of origin, if possible—whether locally made, acquired through trade, or relics of invasion and conquest. Early copper work was cold-hammered into ornamented products such as beads, rings, or pendants. Evidence of weapons, such as spearheads, swords, daggers, or helmets, implies a more sophisticated smelting and molding process.

Textiles

While textiles deteriorate or disintegrate in the course of time, traces of cloth and decorative patterns on them can be scientifically analyzed to reveal the origins of the materials used and the techniques of manufacture. Local or imported goods may then possibly be revealed.

Tools

An analysis of the means of production at an archaeological site is the key to understanding the inventiveness of a particular people. The tool kit of an early society is as much a key to its quality of life as is an accumulation of documents that speak directly to us. These tools can show centuries-long development from baked clay to sophisticated objects of copper, bronze, and iron, and each new technique will surely have suggested the manufacture of new types of objects and instruments.

Jewelry, Leather, and Leatherwork

Human desire for distinctive objects to wear for personal display or recognition of status ensured that precious stones would be highly prized and that jewelers would gain a special social status. Items like hairpins, necklaces, armbands, pendants, buttons, and beadwork, as well as buckles and elaborate headware, were manufactured for those whose status in society demanded it or who could afford such luxuries. Those items discovered in a dig may also include specimens acquired by trade or brought home by conquest—all of which must be decided by the analysis of the excavation's specialists.

Trade Goods

Before archaeologists can determine the number and type of trade goods in a site, they must, of course, know which are the natural materials to be found in the region they currently are excavating and which appear to originate elsewhere. Imports of materials external to the region may then be categorized. For example, if a few items of marble appear in a region where no natural deposits of the raw material exist, one might infer chance contacts with an outside source; if, however, many examples of such items appear, and over an appreciable period of time, it can reasonably be assumed that some regular importation of the raw material, or even the finished products, has occurred. The next step would be to search for the possible origins of the imports and to fix the resulting information into a larger picture of economic activity. Such investigations can be stimulated by finds varying from the agricultural to the manufactured. An especially fortunate situation would be the discovery of documents of bills of sale, orders, inventories, and the like, such as we have from Old Assyrian times, which document interregional trade between Assyria and Anatolia (see the vignette "An Old Assyrian Trading Enterprise in Asia Minor").

Cultural Artifacts

Cultural artifacts are usually figurines or paraphernalia used in religious contexts. Examples, and typical for early sites, are images of male and female deities. These are often identifiable by symbols attached to the images themselves—for example, items found within temples, including representations of sacred animals and ceremonial objects used in ritual contexts.

EGYPT

Theme and Variations
on Herodotus's Statement That
"Egypt Is the Gift of the Nile"

No more accurate statement has ever been made in describing any country than the description of Egypt by the "Father of History" dating from the fifth century. The Nile is enclosed by rocky cliffs backed by deserts on the east and west. It flows through a kind of geological slot that is sometimes straight, sometimes curved. The natural limits of the country are a series of rocky cataracts to the south and a verdant and marshy delta, triangular in shape, that opens onto the Mediterranean Sea to the north. Inside this quasi-rectangular box, the ancient Egyptian lived permanently at the mercy of a benevolent river whose regime was gentle, for the most part, and whose regular and predictable rhythms of flood and recession set the stage for Egypt's economic, political, and social life for millennia.

Variation I

The first theme to be considered is the nature of the river itself.[1] On its flow to the Mediterranean from central Africa it carries enriching silt, which will nourish the fields on its banks as it floods the valley floor. Below Khartoum, two great branches, respectively the Blue Nile and the White Nile, combine into a single stream, which expands owing to spring rains and summer monsoons on the Ethiopian Plains. As often happens when two imposing rivers combine into one, the single stream can be rapid and rough; in contrast the Nile remains gentle. Just as important is that, unlike the Tigris-Euphrates system of Mesopotamia, whose floodwaters are alkaline and therefore destructive to inundated fields, the Nile brings nourishing elements that renew fertility. It is an additive force provided by a benevolent nature.

Yet natural gifts require management if they are to be beneficial to human life. The Nile flood essentially dictated the yearly calendar of Egypt. The inundation season lasted from July to October and inaugurated three months of *intensive* agricultural work. The first month found the valley submerged. Previously prepared catch basins, dikes, and channels for irrigation stood ready to retain the gently expanding waters. The effect of too much water was to damage the irrigation systems. On the other hand, and disastrously severe, too little water could produce famine. These possibilities spurred the invention of the nilometer, a device much in appearance like a vertical measure, with markers for height cut into rock, and located most notably on Elephantine Island at the First Cataract and also northward toward the old capital at Memphis. The inundation season comprised three months by Egyptian reckoning: the month of the actual flood; the month of the receding flood or the land's drying out; and the month of seeding the new fields. The harvest of wheat, barley, emmer, and other crops came in the spring. In sum, the agricultural year found the farmer-peasants intensively occupied with managing and controlling the flood through restoring the fields; repairing artificial channels, dikes, and basins; and harvesting the spring crops. It is easy to forget that Egypt is not really an urban society. Rather, it is a series of landed estates, temple and tomb complexes, and small villages. Ultimately these were forty-two habitation complexes, or administrative districts (nomes), which served as the skeletal structure of administrative Egypt. They were amalgamated after two thousand years or longer into two kingdoms—that of Upper, or southern, Egypt, with twenty-two nomes, and Lower, or northern, Egypt, with twenty nomes—and finally, after 3000, into a single administrative unit under a ruler called the pharaoh. At whatever level of administration—single nome, regional, or national—the government was required to engage itself as surveyors of newly established fields in order to adjust tax rates.

This quick overview of Egyptian agricultural basics was undertaken to emphasize that the ground base of Egyptian civilization was the Nile River; from its rhythm evolved the entire basis of Egyptian existence as a nation throughout its history.

Variation II

A closely related theme is the organization of Egyptian life by administrators of nome or kingdom beyond the needs and strictures of the agricultural periods determined by the Nile flood. In the nome,[2] the ruler, or nomarch, was both the political leader—for example, in matters of war and peace—and the administrator of the food supply. His position allowed him both to establish and maintain an administrative cadre of irrigation supervisors, agricultural inspectors, and tax collectors, as well as to function as administrator of the grain supply, which (speculatively) must have allowed him to be seen as a kind of sustainer of life as well as the putative owner of his nome. Each nome, of course, had its central temple and priestly cult, so that a subtle integration of economic, attendant political, and, above all, religious concerns coalesced to erect a framework of servility over the lives of ordinary Egyptians. The agricultural year of sowing and reaping left vacant months in the yearly calendar, and these months were put to efficient use by nomarchs and pharaohs alike. The nine months remaining after the three months of intensive agricultural work were organized into a state labor force—a corveé—during which the serfs were fed and forced to live in barracks in return for their participation in all sorts of massive construction projects. From such organizations doubtless emerged the idea, along with religious justifications, that rulers were divine and owned the land. In effect, in addition to the expected use of labor for the building of palaces, temples, and sundry other civic and religious structures by an autocratic series of regimes, something unique to Egypt in ancient times was its devotion to mortuary cults and the construction of tombs.

Variation III

Part of the life cycle of the ancient Egyptian was the obligation he felt to preserve the bodies of the dead and to house those bodies in secure tombs.[3] In the earliest to medial periods of Egyptian history, this privilege was reserved for the highest classes of Egyptian society, beginning, to be sure, with the nomarchs or the pharaohs and their families. Already in earlier prehistoric times the dead were buried in rectangular or oval pits dug in the sand. The body was placed in a contracted position wrapped in a reed mat and accompanied by personal possessions of the deceased. The intention here was that the deceased was about to journey to some sort of spiritual realm. Hot sand might also have provided a natural preservative effect on the body. However, sand is poor protection for a burial and is likely to blow away. Some early graves were lined with wooden boards lashed together, which suggests an interest by the survivors in protecting the body within its primitive grave.

By the beginning of the Dynastic Age, about 3000, superstructures of sun-baked mud bricks were being built to enclose graves. The Arabic word for this type of structure is *mastaba,* meaning "bench," because it resembled such, although it was engulfed by sand. The earliest known such structure belonged to the king Aha of the First Dynasty. His grave had been roofed with timber and divided into five compartments. Beside the king's actual resting place, four adjacent compartments held the king's personal possessions. Above all this was a brick superstructure with numerous storage areas for food offerings, wine jars, and the like. Still in the line of prehistoric graves, it foreshadows the coming immense development of massively built tombs and pyramids. The main idea of future funerary construction was the essential model of the private house and its rooms.

It is not my purpose here to offer a developmental history of funerary architecture. There are at least eighty pyramids known from the west bank of the Nile and numerous tombs dug into the rock surfaces of the Valleys of the Kings and Queens in central Egypt. All these constructions throughout the millennial history of Egypt were made by gangs of *fellahin,* ordinary farmers of Egypt, and doubtless also by prisoners of war and other unfortunates. The direction and provisioning of such a labor force for duty every year required a massive administration of skilled overseers, scribes and accountants, and messengers to coordinate activities.

Variation IV

It is perfectly clear that to sustain the agricultural-economic system previously described in this vignette, and to regulate the use of time made possible by a nine-month hiatus in the year, a power point at the center of the country was needed. The nomarch served as such in his smaller jurisdictional area, but from the benchmark of about 3000 and the conquest of the north by the southern ruler, Narmer, Egypt's destiny was to be ruled by a succession of dynasties, not all, however, from native Egyptian stock. An Egyptian priest of the third century named Manetho wrote a history of his country in which he divided rulership into thirty dynasties. Manetho's work has been lost in the original but preserved in references of later writers.

The drama of the earliest days of Egyptian history, encapsulated in the reigns of pharaohs from the Third through the Sixth Dynasties, a group collectively known as the Old Kingdom, placed its imprint on all subsequent reigns in Egyptian history. For during the Old Kingdom the patterns of rulership—its position, rights, and privileges, as well as the cosmic bases of its authority—were established. It is this cosmic basis as it became interactive with political necessity that made of the pharaoh both a political leader and a god in his own right.

To attain his political position the pharaoh had to supersede his nomarchs in power. The details of this victory in general are shadowy. What is clear is that once-independent nomarchs were then incorporated as subrulers of districts and as faithful retainers of the pharaoh, who rewarded them with gifts, benefices, and promotions. The pharaoh was the donor of estates, tombs, rank, and wealth. Such donations as royal lands, temple lands, estates for nobles and veterans, and village services all had to be allocated along the banks of the Nile. Beyond these donations and gifts, grants for mortuary purposes, especially, and the need to reward new beneficiaries produced growing tensions between the nomarchs and the pharaonic government because the demand for benefices became larger than could be satisfied by the supply. In this way a rivalry between nomarch and pharaoh evolved, which led to the first great crisis in Egyptian history—the breakdown in the long initial six-hundred-year period of internal peace and security of the nation. We could point to the inevitable demands made to sustain the mortuary traditions as critically responsible for this crisis.

Variation V

The evolution of the Egyptian state was based on the universally accepted idea that the pharaoh was both god *and* man. This was a radical departure from the normative system in the ancient Near East wherein the ruler of the state was deemed to govern through his appointment by the chief god of the cosmos and, as is illustrated by the Babylonian system, theoretically reappointed each year during the New Year's Festival. In a sense, just as the Nile was forever performing its function as the yearly replenisher of Egyptian life, so too was the pharaoh the permanent director of how things are and ought to be in the land. His authority was theoretically not seen to have been derived from popular consent of his subjects or from power cliques but from an allegedly unbroken line of descent from cosmic entities (conceived also as humans or as mixed human and animal figures) into the realm of earthbound humanity. The pharaoh was the current ruler thought to be directly, that is, genealogically, descended from the sun god. Hence his rule was part of the entire system by which the universe operated, and stability both in human affairs and in the cosmos was deemed to be inseparable.

The immensity of this idea was doubtless already taking shape in pre-historic times and was fully effectuated at the dawn of dynastic government about 3000. The pharaoh, as a god, had overwhelming power of command and was thought not only to give but also to take back life, prosperity, and health. Just as the Nile, with its gentle and predictable regime upon which Egypt's very survival depended, became a symbol of regularity and abundance, so too did the pharaoh, who supervised the administration of the country and became the intermediary between earthly and cosmic affairs. And as the Nile could be depended upon to sustain life and allow its people a generally optimistic view of the survival of the nation, so too must the optimism it fostered have been the buttress of further views about the destiny of the life essence after death. The overwhelming dominance of mortuary cults throughout Egypt's life as an ancient society testifies to its belief in the ongoing unity of life and death as part of a renewable cycle of existence.[4]

Variation VI

At the same time that the Nile within its protective valley provided safety and isolation from Egypt's immediate neighbors in northeastern Africa and southern Palestine, especially during its formative period, the river also allowed Egypt to experiment with discovering the world to the north. Unlike a river whose estuary is broad and inviting to the outsider, and hence one that invites exploration and its concomitant dangers from outside, the Delta extension of the Nile provides both a protective barrier of safety and an opportunity for cautious exploration of the Mediterranean littoral. The Delta is both a morass of swampland and a navigable set of channels and streams. The Nile flows into the Mediterranean in two streams, on the eastern and the western sides of the Delta. These provided the opportunity for the Egyptians to develop their ship-building skills, for boats and barges that were sufficient for navigation on the Nile were inadequate for use on the open ocean. Once contact had been made with Phoenician ports, a steady trade in timber from Lebanon allowed Egypt materials for enhancing construction projects at home. Egyptians also learned about the proficiency of Phoenician seagoing vessels, which they called "Byblos Ships" and which gradually allowed Egypt to become a naval power in much later times.

If the Delta access to northern territories in Palestine and Syria in middle and late periods of Egypt's history thrust it into the tangle of international politics of the region, from earliest periods the avenue provided by the Delta into the heartland of Egypt allowed regular visits of itinerant nomads from the Fertile Crescent regions of Mesopotamia. These usually sufficed to allow pasturage for domestic flocks and a normal return of the immigrants to their seasonal itineraries. Two memorable incursions by outsiders into Egypt involved first a mixed invasion of Semites and Asiatics, called Hyksos, and later a routine visit of Hebrew tribesmen during the reign of Rameses II, during which they were enslaved before escaping to Palestine and their future home.

Summary

Altogether, in this short excursion on the idea of a river that is the heart of Egyptian life and experience even in our own era, I have tried to treat this natural feature as a theme that seems to me to have vitally affected the psychological and symbolic state of ancient Egypt's inhabitants, as well as the economic and political outlook of the country.

FURTHER READING

Andrew, Carol. *Egyptian Mummies.* Cambridge, MA: Harvard University Press, 1984. Paperback. Additional reading list on p. 70.

James, T. G. H., and W. V. Davies. *Egyptian Sculpture.* Cambridge, MA: Harvard University Press, 1983. Paperback. Additional reading list on p. 69.

Kees, Hermann. *Ancient Egypt: A Cultural Topography,* trans. Ian F. D. Morrow, ed. T. G. H. James. Chicago and London: University of Chicago Press, 1961; Phoenix ed., 1977. Paperback.

Murnane, William J. *The Penguin Guide to Ancient Egypt.* Harmondsworth, Middlesex, England: Penguin Books, 1983. Paperback. Additional reading list on pp. 357–58.

Stead, Miriam. *Egyptian Life.* Cambridge, MA: Harvard University Press, 1986. Paperback. Additional reading list on p. 71.

On the Essential Cosmic Rhythms
of Ancient Egyptian Life

This short vignette seeks to reflect on the core of the ancient Egyptian's "cosmic" existence, where the artistic and the poetic merged with the pragmatic to celebrate a fusion between the Nile dweller's earthly existence and his cosmic environment. Many observers, in my view, have failed to appreciate that the land of Egypt was, in itself, a thousand-mile-long artistic palette, whereon the colors of nature daily enclosed its inhabitants as if within a vast cosmic painting. Consider the ancient Egyptian homeland (and, indeed, the modern as well) as an aesthetic phenomenon. It presents the observer with an ever-changing pattern of light hues and tones. From dawn to dusk the Nile reflects an infinite variety of browns and blues. Narrow strips of cultivated land along each bank of the river provide vivid green borders during the growing season and serve to separate the narrow bankside fields from the larger deserts to the east and west. At midday, the hot sun adds a strong, illuminated cover over the earth base; and toward sunset all the colors of earth and sky become blended and muted. The journey of the sun through a cloudless sky each day subtly illuminates the vast array of colors and shades of colors, which are also enhanced by the vivid stands of flowers in riverside gardens and memorial estates.

Such colors were consciously employed by ancient Egyptian painters within the temples and tombs that proliferated throughout Egypt. The interior colors, used as backdrops or borders around scenes of ordinary life portrayed on walls, statues, and reliefs, sometimes appear as fresh as though they were applied just yesterday. The natural impulse of the artists was to duplicate in their own work the impressive colors of nature, which they routinely encountered each day. The sun, so central and dominant, enhanced everything in nature as it journeyed through the sky. It was seen as the author of all things because to the Egyptian it had originally emerged from limitless primeval waters—that chaos that contained the essence of all things in the universe. As the illuminator of all activity, the sun never relinquished its foremost role in Egyptian religion, although contrary notions of a dark underworld developed early and climaxed in the Osirian religion and its shadowy manifestations.

In a most interesting sense, the ancient Egyptian found himself at the center of two essential cosmic rhythms. The first was the circular journey of the sun on its path from dawn in the east, through high noon, and then into dusk as it began its nightly disappearance in the west, into the dangerous subterranean realms, before it reappeared as the symbol of a new day once more in the east. The circularity of the sun's orbit may be considered to be matched by a second, a seasonal, orbit created by the Nile River, flowing from south to north, and the rise, flood, and retreat of the waters that nourished the soil each year. The constant presence and interaction of these two so essential elements in Egyptian life may be visualized as a kind of navigational instrument. The outer circle of this instrument, vertical in placement, represents the sun's course from east to west. A second, horizontal, circle represents the yearly action of the Nile. At the center of our hypothetical instrument exists the ancient Egyptian. The sphere of his life encloses him in its regular occurrences.

Within the center of the cosmos where we have located our ancient Egyptian, the vantage point for his observations on how the operations of the universe took place, we now highlight his abilities artistically to interpret the world and poetically to describe it. There is, of course, ample evidence of the ancient Egyptian's abilities to understand the world from a pragmatic point of view. He knew how to build houses, tombs, and pyramids and how to deal with the practical requirements of life. But in my view his greatest accomplishments are to be seen in the ways he used his mind to produce poetic conceptions about his environment. Consider, for example, how he conceived of the sun as it moved through the sky. It is never just a hot, multicolored ball. It is a traveler beneath the earth. It is also the eye of the sky. It can be a glittering hawk or a passenger in the celestial boat. In human terms, it can be conceived of as a youth or full manhood or an aging man. As animal, it can be a calf, born from the womb of the sky, from the celestial cow. It can also be thought of as a cosmic "pellet" pushed along by the dung beetle, or scarab. The use of simile and metaphor is never far from the ancient Egyptian mind.

In the sphere of social and personal affairs, the operation of metaphor is also amply illustrated. Consider the idea of "justice," which was expressed as *ma'at*. Ma'at basically describes a flat-surfaced platform. Whether the range of abstract ideas associated with ma'at came first, before its symbolization as a solid foundation or a straight surface, or the reverse, it is clear that the word expressed a comprehensive idea in that it also denoted the idea of "right order" and "correctness" in all things, from personal behavior to the eternal order of the universe. In effect ma'at came into being at the moment of creation and remained effective forever. The absence of ma'at in human affairs was understood to be "evil."

How did the Egyptian appear to think of this pervasive concept? Not, certainly, through any rigorous and formalized statement of analysis or definition. To understand it for himself, even to explain it to others, he had to resort to artistic and poetic imagery. For example, ma'at was perceived and depicted as a woman wearing a large ostrich feather in her hair (the feather alone can suffice to symbolize her). Her antiquity is noted by an element representing the primeval mound upon which Aten, the creator god, emerged and which is embodied in the hieroglyphs of her name. She can be conceived as assisting the sun god Re in traveling through the sky and is also celebrated as participating in the judgment of the dead in the underworld. There are also subtle variations to her primary role as sustainer of order. She is often depicted as an "offering" to other gods to allow their association with the essential order of the universe. The principle here is the flexibility with which ancient Egyptian thought could understand the cosmos as being subtly fluid yet unified and constant.

If the cosmos is sustained by ma'at, this is no less true in the realm of human affairs, where the original definition of base or platform, signifying "levelness," is further developed into "uprightness" of various sorts: "truth," "justice," and "order," whose meanings depend upon context. Ma'at represents a concept of unity, a single base that is the totality of all positive value in nature and society. Within the latter, the citizens themselves maintain order both by good social acts and obedience to the governing rules and through proper religious observance.

In response to what appears to be the dominant judgment about Egyptian religion—that no coherent synthesis is possible—I would instead propose that it is poetry entwined in a gigantic, although sometimes confusing, fugue. It defies systematic categorization and rigid analysis because it offers immense opportunities for subtle characterizations and shifts of ideas and behaviors, which have been created to suit particular moments in Egyptian religious history. The underlying concepts are familiar in all the ancient cult centers despite the adherence to local traditions.

A brief example of this proposal may be offered through a comparison of the so-called Cosmology of Heliopolis with that of Memphis. In the former, Nun, as the limitless primeval waters, already contains the power to engender all the life forces of the universe. Nun brings forth Atum-Khephrer (two phases of the sun) and later Atum-Re, also a solar god, who continues the act of cosmic creation by spitting out Shu, the god of air, and Tefnut, the goddess of moisture. This creative act took place on a hill in Heliopolis, where Atum-Kheprer (the sun in its phases) was also symbolized as the *ben*-bird of the *ben*-stone, which was located in the *ben*-house, or sanctuary, at Heliopolis. Atum-Khephrer activated the newly created cosmic elements by putting his *ka,* his animating spirit, into them. Thereafter other divine entities were created—Geb, the earth; Nut, the goddess of the sky; the divine figure Osiris; the goddess Isis; the god Seth; and the goddess Nepthys. As a group these nine gods, known as the Ennead, represented at Heliopolis the original nucleus of divine entities in the universe.

At Memphis, by contrast, the traditional god of the region, Ptah, was held to embody in himself the essence of the other known created gods, so that the primeval waters there were known as Ptah-Nun, who begot Atum. Atum also has a mother, Ptah-Naunet. And it is Ptah-Nun, the Memphite begetter of all the other gods, who transmits life to them all. Ptah-Nun further animates them through conceiving of their inner spirits, or *ka*s, in his mind and activates them by his commands.

It is not that one statement of cosmology should permanently exclude another but that different adaptations of basic themes from these cosmologies can be constructed and intertwined to reflect current religious and social realities. It is as though different scenes might be written for the very same religious-historical play without any rejection of the fundamental ideas of the civilization.

As for the fate of mankind, humans were presumed to have been created equal, not necessarily with all social rights and privileges but in opportunity. Atum-Re did make the annual inundation so that the great and the poor could each benefit. He made the four winds so that all alike could breath. He allowed men the choice of leading a good reverent life. He also placed in their hearts the desire to share in a blessed afterlife through divine offerings to the gods of their respective nomes.

In sum, the Egyptian had the greatest ability to take the physical world as he found it, and the intellectual world as he created it, and to continue to elaborate and adjust each realm as he saw fit according to his spiritual visions and his temporal needs in any period in his history.

THE PALESTINIAN CORRIDOR

The Seagoing Phoenicians

The territory of Phoenicia, both because of the physical topography and for the fact that it alone had good coastal ports, was the only region in Palestine that could develop significant sea trade. Subsistence agriculture for the Phoenicians was impossible. Commercial life in Phoenicia depended on the sea, since its territory, small in size and bordered by mountains on the north and east, was off the main caravan routes of the Fertile Crescent leading to Mesopotamia and beyond. Its chief trading partners lay to the south in Egypt and to the west in the Mediterranean islands or along the North African coast. From its port cities of Tyre, Sidon, Byblos, and Acco, Phoenicia sent its greatest natural products—cedarwood and cypress—for the building projects of Egyptian pharaohs from as early a period as 2800.[1]

As used by historians of antiquity the terms *Canaanite* and *Phoenician* are, with further definition, practically synonymous. The Greeks called Palestine "Phoenicia" from their own word *phoinix,* meaning "purple," because its inhabitants produced a purple dye that was much in demand for the manufacture of fine garments.

The language of the Phoenicians is a northwest Semitic dialect and is closely related to Hebrew and Moabite. Phoenician was spoken for a millennium and a half, although actual inscriptions from Phoenicia are few and late (fifth to second centuries). Outside Phoenicia, inscriptions fall within the same general period. Phoenician remains have been found in Egypt, Greece, and Cyprus, but by far the greatest number of these come from the colonies that mainland Phoenicians founded in the western Mediterranean coastal territories of North Africa.

There is no doubt that Phoenician colonization in the eastern

Mediterranean antedates 1000. The question of Phoenician expansion in the west is more difficult. The traditional date of the founding of Carthage is given as 814, thirty-eight years before the first Greek Olympiad. Estimates derived from archaeological results also generally support a late ninth-century date. The Phoenician colonization of the North African coast probably was stimulated by the rise of Assyrian imperialism at a roughly equivalent time as much as by natural trading explorations. A view of the great mercantile city of Tyre in the sixth century comes to us from the prophet Ezekiel in the Bible (Ez 27), not in praise but rather in lamentation. (Tyre did not fall until 332, and to Alexander the Great, not to the Babylonians of the sixth century.) Phoenician colonial policy usually provided temporary havens on off-shore islands or peninsulas for their merchant ships. The majority of Phoenician colonies were for long periods small and poor places, depots for supplies and shelters for their traders. It would appear that the chief aim of these traders was to acquire tin, for the manufacture of bronze, from Gadir (Roman Gades, modern Cadiz). On the Mediterranean, Phoenicians became serious rivals of Hellenic traders. The two great Greek epics—the *Iliad* and the *Odyssey* of Homer—give a hint of this rivalry. Although Phoenician arts and crafts are mentioned in the *Iliad* the Phoenicians are seen as evil traders in the *Odyssey*.

As briefly mentioned previously, Phoenicia had long supplied Egypt with wood for ongoing construction projects of tombs, temples, palaces, and pyramids. Egyptian cargo ships so regularly plied the waters of the eastern Mediterranean coast to Phoenician ports that they were called "Byblos ships." We have a fascinating document from Egypt, popularly known as *The Tale of Wen-Amon,* which recounts the difficulties encountered by the title character on a wood-purchasing expedition to Byblos in about 1100. Whether it is an adventure story for the enter-tainment of homeland Egyptians or is based on an actual event is not known precisely.

The story can be summarized as follows:[2]

The power of the Egyptian empire had passed, and by 1100 the country had broken down into regional jurisdiction, with a ruler named Heri-Hor, high priest of Amon, installed at Thebes in Upper Egypt, and Ne-su-Ba-neb-Ded, the ruler of the Delta, who governed at Tanis. The occasion of Wen-Amon's journey was the desire to refit the ceremonial barge of Amon. In the glory days of Egypt's imperial power, a single pharaoh, a Rameses II, for example, would have authorized and financed the trip to Phoenicia, provided royal credentials, and sent troops to protect the expedition. A king of a Phoenician port city would have been quick and happy to comply with a great pharaoh's wishes and to receive the purchase price. Now, however, realizing that Egypt and its rulers were significantly weakened, the formerly subservient Phoenician trading partners were able to assert themselves while still keeping a sharp business eye on completing commercial transactions. So it was that Wen-Amon, having collected funds from Thebes and Tanis and with references from the basically weak rulers of a fragmented Egypt, set off to acquire wood. His ship was captained by a Phoenician.

The first port of call was Dor, whose prince sent a small welcoming present of wine, beef, and bread. Then a major catastrophe occurs: one of the ship's crew steals the gold and silver that was to have been used to purchase the timber. Wen-Amon makes the argument that the prince should reimburse him, but his appeal is rejected. The prince, however, asks Wen-Amon to tarry for a few days while his men search for the thief. Nine days later, the money still has not been recovered. Wen-Amon decides to leave after an apparent argument with the prince.

At this point there is a lacuna in the papyrus on which the story is narrated, but the following can be reconstructed from the surviving bits of text: After leaving Dor, Wen-Amon arrives at, and then leaves, Tyre and proceeds to Byblos, whose prince was Zakar-Baal. On this leg of his journey he somewhere encounters people of Dor and robs them of an amount of money almost equal to the sum that was stolen by the thief of his ship. Although the victims protest, Wen-Amon rejects their pleas until his original finances are found and returned to him.

Now having docked in the harbor of Byblos, Wen-Amon finds himself having to deal with an angry prince. (The course of this anger is not explained in the text. Was it because of Wen-Amon's robbing of the prince of Dor's subjects to replace his stolen money?) In any event, and without initially receiving Wen-Amon, Zakar-Baal orders Wen-Amon out of his harbor, not just once but eighteen additional times! What finally allows Wen-Amon to interview the prince is the fact that Wen-Amon has brought with him on his journey a small statue of the god Amon, whose alleged power caused one of Zakar-Baal's young functionaries to be seized with a spiritual frenzy. This impressed itself on the prince, who rescinded his order to expel Wen-Amon, though the latter had already found an Egyptian ship to carry him home. The prince, at the long delayed interview with Wen-Amon, regards the Egyptian with deep suspicion: Where are the letters of confirmation that should accompany his mission? Why did he sail with a Phoenician captain and crew, who might have tossed him overboard? Further wrangling between Wen-Amon and the prince of Byblos seems about to end in either a stalemate or a complete wreckage of Wen-Amon's mission, until Wen-Amon offers to send a message with the prince's secretary back to Egypt to acquire more payment for the prince. This done, and the payment received and delivered to Zakar-Baal, the prince has the wood cut from the forest and lain on the shore.

When Wen-Amon arrives at the place where the logs have been deposited, he sees eleven ships of the people he had earlier robbed in order to restore his own previously stolen money and realizes he is going to be arrested. Zakar-Baal's strategy was to have the pursuers capture Wen-Amon at sea, after he had sent him away, so that the god Amon, Wen-Amon's protector, would not punish the prince himself. Wen-Amon is thus sent off, pursued by his enemies, but is shipwrecked on the island of Cyprus. The princess of the town calls her people together and allows Wen-Amon to spend the night.

We do not have the end of our story because at this point the papyrus on which it is narrated breaks off. Is it too far-fetched to surmise that after further adventures our hero somehow gets back to Egypt to recount his tale of misfortune and his safe return?

Skilled as the Phoenicians were as seafaring colonizers, traders, architects, and craftsmen, perhaps their most memorable achievement was the transmission of alphabetic writing to peoples of the western regions of the ancient Near East—most significantly the Hebrews and the Aramaeans—and to the Greeks. It is clear that alphabetic writing was slowly evolving from the more cumbersome syllabic forms of writing over a long period of time and cannot be attributed solely to Phoenician ingenuity. More specifically, the Phoenicians transmitted this most convenient form of written communication to their neighbors, who made their own adaptations.

The idea of an alphabet is to have a system by which each written sign represents a sound in the language at issue. This insight appeared at the close of a longish experimental process in the ancient Near East in which the attempt to capture speech in a permanent form on portable material went through a number of phases in different areas of the region. Suffice it to say in this brief vignette that the process progressed through phases of pictographic, then syllabic, and finally alphabetic writing. The best recent book I have discovered on the subject of ancient writing, equally useful for the student and the general reader, is *Reading the Past: Ancient Writing from Cuneiform to the Alphabet,* a collection of six fully descriptive and explanatory sections on cuneiform, Egyptian hieroglyphics, linear B, the early alphabet, Greek inscriptions, and Etruscan written by outstanding experts.

Although the Phoenicians rank as one of the smallest societies of the ancient Near East, they contributed significantly to the region's economic activities and its international outreach as architects, builders, and foresters; and as sailors the Phoenicians were unmatched in the ancient world of the Near East.

FURTHER READING

Harden, Donald. *The Phoenicians*. London: Thames and Hudson, 1962.

Wachsmann, Shelley. *Seagoing Ships and Seamanship in the Bronze Age Levant*. College Station, TX: Texas A&M University Press and London: Chatham Publishing, Gerald Duckworth, 1998.

Wright, Ernest, ed. *The Bible and the Ancient Near East: Essays in Honor of William Foxwell Albright*. Garden City, NY: Doubleday, 1961. See appendix I, "The Role of the Canaanites in the History of Civilization," 328–62.

From Tribal Coalition to
Statehood in Ancient Israel

U nless you are a classics scholar with a serious interest in political theory, you will never have heard of the ancient Greek term *amphictyony,* whose translation is "those living around" or "near neighbors." This word is the key to understanding the genesis of religious leagues, states, and imperial formations of the ancient Near East. Tribes, cities, and states of the time standardly rose, expanded, and fell with predictable regularity. Vanquished tribes could be decimated, captured, and impressed as slaves or exiled away from their homelands; the same fates befell urban centers and clusters of villages. One of the central questions to be asked is how the defeated and displaced continued to survive and regenerate religious and political stability. Enter the role of the amphictyony.

To define the term functionally, an amphictyony is a group of social units—tribal or civic—that honors a central shrine; worships the shrine's god or gods, as well as its own; and contributes to the upkeep of that shrine and its personnel through regular contributions of money, other valuables, and agricultural and other natural products. It is governed centrally, from the shrine, in collaboration with the decision-making bodies of the individual members. In the case of tribes, it travels together as a group, its members may or may not wage wars in association with the group, and they can also decide to merge with the larger group permanently for reasons of safety or religious conviction. Connections are further strengthened through marriages and other social links.

In this vignette I will illustrate, however briefly, the movement from loose tribal associations to the establishment of a territorial state under a monarchy. The best-documented examples of this development in the ancient Near East are found in the Hebrew Bible in the books of Genesis through 1 Kings. For the moment ignoring those passages having to do with theological interpretations of historical events and concentrating on political realities only, we can glimpse in a reasonably general way how a group of covenanted tribes turned itself into a state.

We must begin by asking who the most ancient Israelites were. Originally they were an amalgamation of various Semitic clans, extended clans, and small and larger tribal units. The term *Semitic* simply, and only, means speakers of a language, with its dialects, that scholars classify as having a common grammar, vocabulary, and modality of expression. For example, Semitic speakers are wholly different in language usage and traditions from Indo-European speakers.

Modern Semitic languages include Hebrew, Arabic, Aramaic, Syria, and others. Modern Indo-European languages are chiefly derivative from classical Greek and Latin and include most of the European groups. From a strictly linguistic point of view, ancient Hebrew is but one dialect of a common West Semitic spoken in Palestine, Jordan, Lebanon, and parts of Syria.

The ancient Israelites were speakers within the general Semitic-speaking area of the Palestinian corridor who were also partly bonded by blood (as family clans); bonded through intermarriage with other clans or tribes; bonded with other groups through travel (e.g., for raiding, war, trade, protection, or common herding necessities); and bonded by political or territorial interests into loose temporary associations or tighter, more enduring associations.

Generally the clan and tribal components of earliest Israel cohered or dissolved according to prevailing circumstances at any given time. The practice that cemented temporary or more permanent associations between strangers was the exchange of covenants, or oaths, between the groups.

Most members of the earliest groups, which were eventually to form Israel, were seminomads. They lived and wandered in grazing areas between populated centers. They were shepherds, small-stock raisers, and small farmers. Given the climatic peculiarities in the Near East, they had to follow grazing patterns that kept them constantly on the move. They inhabited oases and followed the routes that led to wells, small tributaries, and rivers (in season). Their annual roving or migration extended from the Egyptian Delta through the Palestinian corridor to the Euphrates River in Syria, thence into upper Iraq, down to lower Iraq, and back again. And they also moved from the lower valleys in winter to the high pastures in summer. In the off-seasons, herding groups would retire to villages, which were usually located as far from city centers as feasible.

Generally, then, the earliest components of ancient Israel were loosely associated coalition members, bound by blood, marriage, or covenant, who were usually on the move all during the year and who could split off from any group arrangement as they wished and when they wished. A contemporary parallel would be the composition and activities of the American Plains Indians. Former friends could become enemies, not encounter each other for years, fight each other, and then, maybe generations later, enter into newly covenanted associations.

The intent of all these seminomadic groups was to stay out of the reach of city-kingdoms in Palestine, whose armies would capture their women, take animals as booty, impress males as slaves, and steal children. The cities were controlled by other Semitic speakers we know of in the Bible as Canaanites.

Essentially, ancient Palestine from the earliest inhabited periods (3000 and earlier) was divided into two hostile camps: the permanent city-kingdoms and their opponents, the impermanent associations of semi-nomadic herders.

According to several reports in the Bible, most of ancient Israel consisted of "a rabble and a multitude," some members of which had been slaves, some victims of powerful city-armies, some vagabonds and gypsies. A core group were adherents of the god Yahweh (not Jehovah, as is traditionally written), and many others flocked to this core group and covenanted with it. Thus, by leaps and bounds, over several centuries, this group, which was finally victorious over the urban Canaanites, came into being.

The oldest mention of Israel in a nonbiblical source dates to the twelfth century and appears on an Egyptian stone victory stele of the pharaoh Mernepthah. He states that his armies (on a foray into southern Palestine) defeated several cities and implies that Israel had been destroyed. That there is no city hieroglyph before the name of Israel in the stele suggests that the pharaoh had defeated a *people,* that is, a group with no fixed residence area. Probably the "victory" was a series of successful Egyptian skirmishes or even a giving of booty to the passing Egyptian troops by the tribesmen.

The Hebrews were latecomers in the roster of national groups in the ancient Near East. Full-blown civilization had existed in Egypt since 3000, in Iraq since 3100, and for the Canaanite city-state system since about 2000. All around the Near East, therefore, nation-states and city-state kingdoms had existed anywhere from eighteen hundred to eight hundred years before any mention of Israel appears in any ancient document outside the Bible.

The reason, perhaps, is that the seminomadic groups that coalesced together and fought together had not done so as a large covenanted group known as "Israel" much before the twelfth century. Before then they were merely known by their individual clan or tribal names, such as Judah or Ephraim or Benjamin. In this very early period, there were many more than the eventual twelve tribes of Israel. (The process by which Israel became fixed as twelve tribes will be discussed later. It really belongs to a later period.)

The states of the ancient Near East had developed writing and used it for a couple of thousand years before Israel came into existence. The groups that formed Israel were illiterate herdsmen; when they had to learn how to write—that is, when they defeated the Canaanites and took over Palestine as a territorial state and had to *administer the country* for the first time—they learned the art of writing but also employed Canaanite scribes who had worked for Canaanite kings in the conquered cities. This is doubtless why there are so many strains of Egyptian and Mesopotamian literature in the Bible.

At first Israel was a loose association of herding and raiding allies, as noted earlier. Each of the association members practiced a *version* of Palestinian religion common to all herders and agriculturalists of the region. These practices were Canaanite and reflected those of the Canaanite city-kingdoms. In the cities, fully developed pantheons of gods, literally scores of them, represented the Canaanite view of how the universe was organized. The whole system was used to underwrite the authority of a king as the legitimate choice of a divine council. The main emphasis of urban religion was to support the king and, through him, the state. There was very little emphasis on the individual, and there was little connection of what we call ethics with the religion.

With the herding groups, there was a significantly different emphasis. The god who led the group in question was considered to be a member of the group, and persons were intimately connected to the god through the group. But still, religion was considered to be pertinent to groups rather than to individuals. The great breakthrough that the Israelitic confederation made was their assertion of, and allegiance to, a new god, a single god, who protected them, guided them, fought for them, and demanded an ethical approach to life as well as complete fidelity and obedience.

This god, called Yahweh among the Hebrews, is traditionally associated with saving a small number of Israelite clans who had been impressed into slavery in Egypt in the thirteenth century.

Moses is credited with teaching the religion of Yahweh to the first members of the Israelite confederation of allied seminomads. Since his father-in-law was a Midianite priest, it is highly possible that Yahwism was known to the Midianite seminomads before it was transmitted, via Moses, to the Hebrews.

Yahweh had demonstrated his efficacy by rescuing enslaved Hebrews from Egypt. This meant that they had a divine leader who could, in fact, hold his own against the Canaanite gods of the land and who could defeat them. Wars were considered to be "gods versus gods," not simply armies versus armies. One followed a god who had demonstrated his effectiveness by being victorious in battle.

The Canaanite city-state system was falling apart at the end of the second millennium, both through internal revolts in the cities and through constant wars between the cities. It seemed possible that the Hebrews with their growing numbers of non-Hebrew allies could take over the "land of milk and honey"—that is, the agricultural, grazing, and wine-growing areas of central and northern Palestine—and also gain booty through successful operations against the weakened city-states.

A key to Israel's separation from previously allied groups is found in Joshua's speech to the assembled confederation army before Jericho in Joshua 14. He tells those who did not want to stay with the successful group any longer that they should leave and return to their old areas and old ways and serve their old gods instead of the new and successful war god Yahweh.

The early Israelite confederation war was the first great recorded guerrilla war in history—a kind of ancient Vietnam. Despite numbers of early failures, the Israelite confederation was occasionally blessed with excellent war leaders, such as Joshua, Barak (see the Song of Deborah in Jgs 5), David, and a host of individual tribal fighters whom we call "Judges" (see the book of Judges).

Subsequently, under Saul (a loser) and David (a winner), foreign mercenaries in Palestine supplemented the Israelite confederation armies. Note the presence of the Philistines in the Gaza Strip—they could have stepped right out of Homer's *Iliad*. Also note the battle of David versus Goliath, an Aegean warrior with iron weapons. The key battle that put an end to Canaanite domination in Palestine is described in the Song of Deborah in Judges 5.

Once the Hebrew confederation under Joshua had defined itself by excluding temporary allies in the amphictyony and had broken the Canaanite opposition in the pivotal battle described in the Song of Deborah, the then masters of the land faced new and unfamiliar challenges.

Formerly roving tribes now had conquered territory to occupy permanently. Within the clans and tribes, two great divisions appeared: the first was a southern combine of two tribes—Judah and Benjamin; the second, in the north, was a group of ten tribes collectively called "Israel." At this critical point in the history of the Hebrew amphictyony, the Bible tells us that many people agitated for the selection of a king, but not, however, without opposition. The opposing arguments well describe what ancient Near Eastern kings were like (1 Sm 8). Eventually a compromise was attempted with the selection of Saul as chief—his title in Hebrew is *nagid,* which signifies a kind of military/administrative leader, not a king.

The biblical account of Saul's "reign" is intermixed with the story of the rise of David, who, in fact, became Israel's first king. Saul had the misfortune of being opposed by a strong army of Philistines drawn from the five cities they had founded in southern Palestinian coastal areas. The whole area of the eastern Mediterranean, islands and mainland alike, had been ravaged by the so-called Peoples of the Sea, who were set in motion as raiders during the twelfth century. Elements of those were able to attack Egypt. They were finally repulsed by Rameses III. Defeated at the Delta of Egypt, they either rebounded to the Palestinian shores or, as defeated prisoners of Egypt, were planted as colonists by Rameses. What the Philistines brought to the Near East was Iron Age weaponry and military technique. The famous combat between David and Goliath (1 Sm 17) shows David with his slingshot defeating Goliath, who might have fought, in his iron weapons and shield, before the walls of Troy. The Philistines defeated the Hebrews in several battles, even capturing the Ark of the Covenant, the sacred symbol of Hebrew religion.

The obvious need among the survivors was for a military savior. This was to be none other than David, whose rise from shepherd boy to king is told in a tale that too often takes on the guise of a historical romance in the Bible (1 Sm 16–1 Kgs 2:10).

David first had to put down a bid for leadership of Saul's supporters and then launch a successful campaign against the Philistines and other local opponents, although he himself had earlier been a raider-ally of the Philistines. This done, he chose the formerly Canaanite city of Jerusalem to be his capital. Jerusalem would be the site of the future House of Yahweh, the great temple to the Hebrew god.

So far leadership over the Hebrew tribes had been either experimental (with Saul) or the result of military necessity. David's successor, Solomon (961–922), was an autocratic model of what ancient Near Eastern kingship could be like. He *inherited* his position and so was in a different political position from either Saul or David. He was "palace bred," whose accession to the throne resulted from connivance between his mother, Bathsheba; Nathan the prophet; probably also Zadok the priest; and Benaiah, soon to be the new commander of the army. His reign began with a bloodbath in which potential rivals to the throne among his peers were conveniently eliminated. His main tasks were four: to resettle the restless tribes of the traditional Hebrew confederation into permanent districts; to build the temple to Yahweh; to ally himself, through treaty marriages, to the plethora of major and minor kings bordering his new kingdom; and to build his kingdom into an economic force to be reckoned with. Fortunately for these designs, no threatening political power stood in Solomon's way. By the tenth century in the western regions of the Near East, Egypt was no longer a great imperial power. The Phoenicians on the north had never been a united land power. Across the Fertile Crescent Assyria and Babylonia had not yet become aggressive imperial powers with military aspirations in the west. So, fortuitously, Solomon was able to lay the foundation of a powerful economic empire, ranging from control of Syria to southern Arabia and beyond.

Solomon first divided the population and settled them into twelve administrative districts that cut across the older tribal boundaries. Herein lies the origin of the notion of "the twelve tribes of Israel." From different tribal lists in the Hebrew Bible we know that the original number of Hebrew tribes was never fixed exactly at twelve. The number twelve represents a system by which each new administrative district supplied provisions for Solomon's palace during the year, one for each month (1 Kgs 4, 7). The requisition list for *daily* provisions for Solomon's court is given in 1 Kings 4:22–23. Since the new administrative boundaries broke up the solidarity of intratribal allegiances, Solomon made primary allegiance to the crown paramount.

The marriages of Solomon were legion. His harem included many a princess from tribes and small kingdoms both close by and far-off but, significantly, included also a daughter of his contemporary Egyptian pharaoh and a princess from Phoenicia. All these marriages, as has been already noted, tended to cement relations with the most powerful of his neighbors. Solomon's proverbial libido, while doubtless pleasurable to him, served serious political purposes.

The single most vivid and symbolic work achieved by Solomon was his building of the Temple of Yahweh in Jerusalem. Indeed his subjects did most of the physical work, but as forced and hired laborers. The Phoenician Hiram, king of Tyre, supplied cedarwood and cypress and skilled craftsmen for the project, in return for yearly payments in huge supplies of wheat and oil. The temple itself was built on a Phoenician plan and is fully described in 1 Kings 6–8. The completion of the temple gave the Hebrews a fixed center for their religion and became the visible symbol of connection between Yahweh and his people.

By virtue of the Hebrew kingdom's location between Asia Minor and Egypt, the king was able to control and profit from commerce between these areas. Trade was widely internationalized at the beginning of the first millennium. The usually expected ship cargoes and pack trains bringing clothing, metals, and pottery were now supplemented by goods of a military nature. Anatolia was a natural breeding ground for fine horses, while Egypt had developed excellent chariot makers. The horse (quaintly called in Akkadian texts "donkey of the mountains") was early attested in Anatolia and is mentioned, though infrequently, in the Old Assyrian trading colony texts of the nineteenth century. Hurrian/Mitanni sources of the middle of the second millennium mention *maryannu* warriors, charioteers from the Indo-Iranian areas, which reflect Hurrian origins. A remarkable Hurrian text describes how to break a wild horse using a longe line, a technique still used today in the American Southwest. The trade in chariots and horses between Egypt and Anatolia allowed Solomon, as middleman, to build up his own chariot forces. At Megiddo, archaeological remains of stables lend support to the biblical statement that "Solomon also had forty thousand stalls of horses for his chariots and twelve thousand horsemen" (1 Kgs 4:26), although the numbers listed may be suspect.

Yet all of Solomon's successes led not to a flourishing and united Hebrew kingdom but rather to a revolt of his northern provinces in 921. Eventually the northern group split away from Judah and Jerusalem and existed as a rival kingdom to Judah, under the name of "Israel" and, much later, "Samaria." In sum, what had begun centuries earlier as a collection of disparate clans and tribes, and had produced a viable territorial state, tragically found itself divided into two rival and hostile kingdoms.

Ancient Persia and a Tale of Two Cities

Athens and Jerusalem in the Fifth Century

The twin springs of Western civilization flow from Greece and Palestine. The former gave birth to our dominant philosophical, scientific, and aesthetic views of life; the latter to our religious traditions derived from Hebrew and Christian teachings. Two cities—Athens and Jerusalem—can be thought of as originating or enhancing these traditions. Historically, each city was affected by actions undertaken by kings of the Old Persian Dynasty (550–331), either against them or on their behalf. Remarkably, people of Iranian origin had interacted with their Mesopotamian neighbors as early as preliterate periods in the areas adjacent to the southwestern corner of Iran. By about 1500 they had created substantial kingdoms in Asia Minor, but the story of major Iranian participation in Near Eastern political life belongs to the period after 1000 with the emergence of an independent Median kingdom.

This kingdom was founded by Deioces in about 700, with its capital at Ecbatana. Previously the Medes had been vassals of Assyria, but now they began their own drive toward imperial power. Under Phraortes (650) the Medes invaded and conquered southern territories in Iran occupied by the Persians, and so was formed a great Iranian state extending from the Persian Gulf northward to the Caspian Sea. Phraortes' successor, Cyaxeres, allied himself with a new Babylonian dynasty to deliver the deathblow to Assyria. The fall of Nineveh, Assyria's capital, in 612 found the new allies dividing the Assyrian Empire between them. Babylonia now ruled lower Mesopotamia as far as the borders of Egypt, while the Medes took over Assyria itself and the territories Assyria had previously conquered in Asia Minor. The Assyrians had earlier instituted an imperial policy of carrying off elite strata of the societies they conquered to regions and cities far from their original homes. They settled the exiles in Mesopotamian areas close to Assyria or in their Iranian possessions. One of their earlier conquests, in 721, had been Samaria, the territory in Palestine occupied by the kingdom of Israel, the northern breakaway of the once united monarchy, which had included Judah and its capital, Jerusalem. A century later, Babylonia, following Assyrian patterns of conquest, ravaged Judah and transported captives from Judah and Jerusalem to Babylon and neighboring cities and territories. They left behind the ruins of the great Temple in Jerusalem. Whole territories in Palestine were now to be occupied by non-Hebrew aliens.

The lot of the Judean exiles in their new homes was not overly harsh. Small communities of Jews established themselves in various places. Individual entrepreneurs became successful merchant traders, skilled craftsmen, even functionaries in high places. Earlier, the Babylonians had removed the Judean royal house and court and had sustained them in Babylon. So adjusted had some resettled captives become to their new homes that they preferred not to return to their previous settlements when the possibility presented itself. Since the captives were allowed to practice their own religions under their own priests, some sort of continuity of traditional worship preserved older customs and beliefs. For the pious Jew who would hope one day to return to a ruined Jerusalem, the restoration of the Temple in Jerusalem was the highest priority.

The alliance between Mede and Babylonian, between Cyaxeres and current Babylonian rulers, continued in force. Once the submission of the former Assyrian possessions was assured, the Babylonian Nebuchadrezzar turned to beautifying his capital at Babylon. So successful was he that Babylon became a showpiece of architectural wonder to visitors, including travelers from Greece. For his part, Cyaxeres, the Mede, concentrated on probing into western Asia Minor. Reaching the center of the country at the Halys River, Cyaxeres and his army encountered the forces of Lydia, a country on the far-off western coast. On May 28, 585, the two armies joined in battle. In the midst of the fray, an eclipse of the sun darkened the battlefield, which caused the combatants to conclude a peace. The boundary between Lydia and Media was established at the Halys River. The eclipse had been predicted by Thales of Miletus, who is reputed to be the first philosopher in Western civilization!

Now, for the first time, a Near Eastern imperial force had staked out a frontier near the edge of Europe. Soon after, in 550, the previously subordinate Persians under the leadership of Cyrus the Great overthrew their Median overlords. Cyrus's army repelled a thrust by Croesus, the current king of Lydia, who sought to extend his own territories beyond the Halys River and eastward into Cappadocia. Marching into Lydia, the Persian army captured Sardis, its capital, and turned the country into a province, or satrapy, of the Persian Empire. Numbers of Greek cities—

former Lydian colonies of such places as Athens and other Hellenic communities on the Greek mainland—now fell under the political supervision of a Near Eastern Persian Empire whose center was hundreds of miles to the east.

Inevitably, conspiracies against Persian rule developed, even though the Persians in Ionia, as the Asiatic coastal strip was known, were not oppressive. In 498 Sparta, the strongest military power among the mainland Greeks, refused to join an uprising against the Persians. The Athenians, however, sent twenty ships and, with their Eretrian allies, marched against Sardis. After the Greeks succeeded in occupying the former Lydian capital, now the center of Persian provincial rule, a fire broke out, and the city was destroyed. This incident marked the beginning of the great war between the Persians and the Greeks, which resulted in the ultimate rise of Athens to imperial power in its own right by the middle of the fifth century.

Eight years later (490) the Persians, sent by Darius, attempted to invade Greece but were thwarted at the Battle of Marathon. They retired to prepare a second invasion. A decade later the Persians crossed over into the Greek mainland once again and succeeded in reaching Athens, where they besieged and then defeated the Athenian garrison. The invaders burned the old temples on the Acropolis but found a city that had been evacuated beforehand. In two great and pivotal encounters, the Battle of Salamis at sea in 480 and the Battle of Plataea on land in 479, the Persians were beaten and were forced to retreat back to Asia Minor.

The defeat of the Persians had a radical effect on the political development of Greece. Athens had organized a navy that played a vital role in the defeat of the enemy. Preparation was necessary if Persia were to invade again. Thus was formed the Delian League, an alliance of islanders settled throughout the Aegean who contributed to the defense against a possible recurrence of the war. The league's treasury was located at Delos; members could contribute either ships or money according to their means. The Persians, having been confined to Asia Minor, were now no longer a land threat to the Greeks. The Aegean had also been swept free of enemy naval forces. The Delian League treasury was taken over by Athens and gradually converted to its own uses.

Let us examine now the work of Thucydides, the greatest historian of war and politics who ever wrote, for his account of a speech by Pericles, which is known to us as the "Funeral Oration." It was delivered on the occasion of the return to Athens of the bodies of the Athenian soldiers after the first year of a war against Sparta—the great Peloponnesian War (431–404). In presenting this speech, Thucydides discusses the virtues of Athens as a democracy. These virtues are worthy of being taught in every school as a model of democratic behavior. I have extracted the most critical points of his speech, which captures Pericles' view of the greatness of Athens as a model of democratic society. That model includes the following characteristics of the Athenian citizen and his form of government:

Versatility in its citizens to meet any emergencies

A constitution which favors the many rather than the few

Equal justice to all

Opportunity for all to serve the state based on merit

Freedom of individual action and opinion

Obedience to both written and moral laws especially protection of the injured

Multiple opportunities for the mind to be refreshed

Celebration of games and sacrifices all year round

Cultivation of personal taste in private establishments and as a counter to distress

International interest in commerce to share in world luxuries

In military matters, Athenians open their city to the world and allow foreigners the opportunity of learning and observing, although an enemy may occasionally profit from their liberality; trusting less in policy than in the spirit of our citizens

In education Athenians live exactly as they please, and yet are ready to encounter any legitimate danger

Cultivation of refinement without extravagance

Wealth for use rather than show: poverty must be struggled against not denied[1]

This very compacted attempt may give the reader an understanding that to its Western side the Persian Empire had found its limits of military expansion, which allowed Athens to flourish. Its military policy, its routinely desirable policy of war making, had been checked by the Greeks. Persian kings now sought allies within the Hellenic sphere and pursued a policy of diplomacy in order to advance their goals. By contrast, Persian armies within the territorial Near East were eminently successful. Cyrus the Great was able to conquer his erstwhile Babylonian ally in 539 and take over the territories that for several centuries earlier had been subject first to Assyria and then to Babylonia. Whereas the Assyrians and the Babylonians had carried off captives, the Persian rulers exercised a policy of allowing captives to return to their former residences. In addition, the Persians also granted financial assistance to the returnees to rebuild their sacred institutions.

The Hebrew Bible gives evidence of Persian rulers allowing four returns of Jewish exiles to Palestine and Jerusalem over a period of a century and a half or more. The first return took place under Cyrus the Great (about 538); here a start was made on rebuilding the Temple of Jerusalem, which the Babylonians had earlier destroyed. A second return occurred during the reign of Darius I (521–485) when the temple was completed. A third took place during the reign of Artaxerxes I (464–423), when the wall of Jerusalem was rebuilt despite the opposition of local Persian officials and non-Jewish townspeople, who had moved into the depopulated city after the Jews had been taken into exile. A fourth and final return is attested under Artaxerxes II (404–358) and was led by the priest-scribe Ezra.

Although Western estimates of the ancient Persians and their rulers as oriental despots traditionally color our views of Old Persian culture, we should remember that the Greek term *barbarian* means one who is "not a Greek," not necessarily a person who is uncivilized or primitively savage. We forget that the religion of the Persians was highly ethical. It had evolved from primitive Indo-Iranian beliefs into a system that divided the universe into an arena in which the followers of light and truth constantly confronted the followers of darkness and the lie. The prophet of this religion was Zoroaster, and it seems most likely that the Persian rulers were Zoroastrians. We may reasonably assume that their willingness to allow the Jews to return home and rebuild their temple stemmed from an attitude of toleration to those who believed in a god whose demands were ethical in the highest. In the Hebrew Bible, Cyrus the Great is called the "Messiah," the only non-Hebrew to bear that title.

If we allow our imaginations some free play, we can assert the following: in Athens of the fifth century the idea of self-determination in life was asserted and fully practiced as a daring proposition; in Jerusalem, in the same century, an ancient Hebrew religion founded by Moses almost a thousand years earlier was able to regenerate itself after being threatened with disintegration. In the case of the Athenians, Hellenic success against Persian military might ultimately have established the conditions under which Athens became the seed ground of Western intellectual development.

Can we not imagine Socrates walking and discoursing in the streets of Athens during the same years, months, even days as Nehemiah, in Jerusalem under the same skies, might be urging his associates to complete the walls of the city? Or, stretching chronological accuracy a bit, can we not visualize Pericles' speech to the Athenians about the greatness of their city and Ezra, almost a contemporary, speaking to an assembly of Jews in Jerusalem who stand in the rain as he tells them to put aside their foreign wives and remarry within the faith (Ezr 10:9–10)? Behind the assertions and confidence of the one and the determination of the other looms the shadow of the Persian Empire.

On Nomads and Nomadism

My reader most likely resides in a settled community of some sort—a village, town, or city—and views the ancient Near Eastern world primarily as a world of societies rooted in fixed territories, where the means of survival, such as available water, cultivable land, and favorable climate, allow permanent settlement. Forgotten in this scenario are those whose lives are lived always on the move. In groups they travel along regular routes during the year unless interrupted by hostile armies or natural disasters. We usually think of them as symbolized by the camel nomads of the deep, sandy deserts.

Camel nomadism in the ancient Near East is attested late—from the end of the second millennium throughout the first and thereafter—even though the camel itself is attested archaeologically somewhat earlier. The assumption has to be that its habitat remained the deep deserts of what is now Saudi Arabia until camel nomads appeared on the edges of Mesopotamia and Palestine about 1200. The camel is an ideal animal for life in the deep desert. It needs little water, can survive sandstorms, and is efficient transport. The circuitous routes taken by camel nomads are often hundreds of miles in length. Their social lives are conducted at oases or wells, and often the smaller tribal groups join larger federations of tribes for protection or other benefits. There is a veritable community of life, governed by strict traditional observances in the desert, and contact with villages or towns may be minimal or completely absent.

The more common types of nomadism in the ancient Near East include activities of nomads who live in the mountains and mountain steppes and the most normative type—dwellers on the desert edges. These nomads may look and act like their deep-desert neighbors and also live in tents, yet their entire pattern of life is significantly different. They are sheep raisers, sometimes also cattle raisers. Sheep and cattle do not have the stamina of camels. They require different grasses to feed upon, and they need water more often. Sheep and cattle herders find water and grazing far more easily available to them than do camel nomads. Their traditional journeys from lowland in winter to summer pastures in the uplands are regular and attainable in relatively easy stages. The herders can also buy and cultivate land and live in villages.

In the Bible, stories about the Hebrew patriarchs and their kin do indeed mention that camels were familiar to the early Hebrews. For example, in Abraham's brief sojourn in Egypt, the pharaoh gives small stock and camels to him (Gn 12:16) and then he leads away Rebecca, who "rode upon the camels and followed the man" (Gn 24:10–61). Jacob is recorded as having large flocks, asses, and camels (Gn 30:43); and Jacob gives a present of many goats, rams, cows, bulls, and asses, but also thirty camels and their colts, to his brother Esau (Gn 32:13–18). Further, on his way to Canaan from Paddan-aram to visit his father, Isaac, Jacob sets his sons and wives on camels and drives away "all his cattle, all his livestock which he had gained, the cattle in his possession" (Gn 31:17–18); there is also the caravan of Ishmaelites coming from Gilead, with their camels, to whom Joseph is sold by his brothers (Gn 37:25).

While these examples might suggest that the early patriarchs were indeed camel nomads, they clearly indicate that large numbers of small stock comprised the chief elements of their possessions, while camels appear to be additionally useful but not absolutely essential to the mode of life the patriarchs followed. The environment of the deep-desert nomad *required* the camel; that of those who lived on the edge of the desert was more forgiving.

Historians usually describe their type of existence as seminomadism, but as Michael Rowton points out, such a description gives a false impression of what the realities are. It is not that the seminomad spends his time between living in fixed territorial residences and then migrating with his flocks and herds, but rather "the pastoral land was *encircled* by urban settlement, either partly or completely; the grazing lands visited by the nomads constituted enclaves partly or completely *within* the sedentary zone."[1] This means that many tribes were already integrated with permanent settlements while still retaining their full tribal characteristics, as opposed to the situation where a tribe might be part-time sedentary and part-time nomadic. The "integrating tribe" would then become participants in a variety of economic and political activities and decision-making processes of the combined population of villagers, or townsmen, and tribesmen.

Let us return momentarily to the most extreme form of nomadism—the camel nomadism of the deep desert. Unlike their sheep- and cattle-herding cousins, the "Lords of the Desert" lived in isolated circumstances and had little or no political or economic interaction with settlements. The integrated or enclosed tribes, whether single or confederated, had (as Rowton points out) "a more rewarding mode of life," where, for example, farmers and herders could routinely interact. The rhythm of that interaction was usually self-regulated when governments were weak. Strong government usually tended to be threatening to tribal peoples. We need also realize that just as strong governments impinged on tribal authority, so also did large confederations of tribes tend to threaten the autonomy of single tribes or smaller confederations of these.

According to Rowton, studies of relationships between tribes and villages or towns in Mesopotamia show that the richest and the poorest within the tribes tended to settle down. The poorest lost their affiliations with the tribe, while the richest retained their influence and provided important linkages between the town and the tribe.

Since the tribe or confederations of tribes "enclosed" in certain territories followed the needs of their animals, their calendar, so to speak, differed from that of a sedentary group. Seasonal migrations were usually directed by tribal chiefs, but where such leaders were effectively subordinated, a village or town headman or a city king would then have to involve himself in the migrating affairs of the tribe. Rowton points out that in such cases the camp, tents, animals, fodder, and supplies, as well as the persons associated with these, "formed part of the ruler's domain in just the same way as the towns and villages did"—thus, the ruler's, or his governor's, sense of responsibility for the safety and good management of the nomadic group. The ruler, or his representative, often accompanied a tribal group on its usual migrations.

The role of enclosed tribal groups in military affairs was quite significant. Whereas the Hebrew tribes, as typically depicted in the Bible, sought to stay out of the reach of Canaanite city rulers or their district commanders, Mesopotamian enclosed tribes either voluntarily supplied contingents for royal armies or for militias in subdistricts of a kingdom or were impressed into such service. Military problems could emerge from raids by tribes outside the control of a king or governor in which the enclosed tribes were located or from hostile armies against the dynastic center itself. Similarly, hostility could routinely emerge between farmers and the migratory tribes, whether or not the tribes were under control of sedentary officials.

ANATOLIA

An Old Assyrian Trading Enterprise
in Asia Minor

The image of early commerce in antiquity that modern readers hold is often of single, sometimes chance, encounters between isolated peoples, whose ventures are simple exchanges of small stocks of merchandise and whose capital resources are relatively insignificant. Certainly no lending facilities, no credit arrangements, no companies of entrepreneurs in business associations, no regular means of transport, and no long-term regulation of business affairs by the traders or political overseers. And yet from the evidence of a hoard of thousands of clay tablets emanating from central Anatolia (Turkey) and dating to a period of about 160 years between 1900 and 1740, we encounter a highly organized international trading enterprise shipping goods from the early Assyrian capital at Assur in northern Mesopotamia to settlements on the high plateau of Asia Minor in exchange for locally available commodities.

What is especially interesting about this Old Assyrian trading system is that it signals a major development in economic organization for early Mesopotamia. Traditionally, the palace institution along with the temple of a city's principal god together functioned as foci for essential economic functions. Each held substantial agricultural and grazing lands on which the large majority of the city's population worked, while smaller numbers of specialized craftsmen served the needs of both institutions. Payment for services was given for the most part in rations of grain and other natural or craft products. This kind of system is known as a "redistributive economy," where the produce of the land comes to an institutional center and is then doled out to individual workers according to their rank and the type of service contributed. Under this system, temple and palace were from earliest times landlords, employers, and storekeepers in the ancient Mesopotamian city.

As such they naturally required large staffs of officials to administer their services and reckon their accounts. Because of the apparent magnitude of these interests and operations, they inevitably became bureaucratic, to the extent that special associations of functionaries and workmen began to appear among the citizenry. Each of these associations was directed in its work by a foreman, and one of them, the association of the dam-kar (Sumerian)—the professional trader—is of special interest to us.

The importance of the dam-kar in the economic life of ancient Mesopotamia may readily be seen if we consider how ill-suited the region is for anything but agriculture. It is an alluvial country, nourished by deposits of sediment brought down by the Tigris and the Euphrates Rivers. It contains no deposits of stone or metals, nor is there good timber available for building. From the earliest times in the country's history, the inhabitants of the Mesopotamian river valleys had to import vital materials from neighboring countries, for which they paid by exchanging products of the soil. In the development of interregional commerce, the professional merchant was all-important. He became the prime mover in intercity and international trade. That he received an allotment of land for his services to the community indicates the degree of his importance in the life of the ancient city.

Primarily an employee of the temple in early periods, the dam-kar was able to build up a store of capital for his private commercial use. No doubt this was possible because he was able, much like other landholding members of the community, to accrue surpluses over and above the produce he owed the temple at harvest time and to use these surpluses to make loans at interest to less prosperous citizens. Further, he could finance private trading enterprises and reap profits from his participation as creditor, as well as claim special commissions for particular services to other businessmen.

From the time of the Old Akkadian Dynasty to the brilliant Third Dynasty of Ur the hold of the temple upon the economic life of the Mesopotamian city appears to have loosened to the extent that more and more contracts between private individuals appeared. This was also the period in which political power was more concentratedly centralized in the secular rather than the religious institution. The effect of this shift of emphasis is seen in the emergence of the palace as an important entrepreneur, as important, perhaps, as the temple. The dam-kar now was seen to serve both institutions, and accounts were kept for him in both. But he continued to serve his own interests as well, and he functioned, then, both as government trader and as private entrepreneur.

The Hammurabi Law Code of Old Babylonian times (ca. late eighteenth century) shows us the dam-kar (Semitic: *tamkârum*) not only as an itinerant trader but also as one who employed agents in his business. He also appeared as a capitalist par excellence and as a moneylender. He was fully emerged as a "public trustee," whose services were offered both to government officials and to private citizens and whose activities were regulated by law. As a public trustee, he functioned both as a citizen of his city and as a member of the professional group, the association of *tamkârû*.

To attempt to further trace the development of private trading enterprise would be irrelevant to our purpose, but during the Old Assyrian period, in Assur, a great number of trading companies existed. These were organized most often as family enterprises and were headed by patriarchs. It is not entirely clear from our sources that these companies were composed of tamkârû exclusively or seen, for that matter, primarily, for the role of the tamkârum in Old Assyrian trade is obscure. He was, to be sure, a necessary functionary, but the most important entrepreneurs are rarely reported to be tamkârû. Rather, it was the entrepreneur who made use of the tamkârum in his operations.

Whereas in earlier periods of Mesopotamian history the amount of private enterprise was restricted and rather marginal, in the Old Assyrian period, by contrast, it was significantly enlarged. The entrepreneur's activities still fell under public supervision, and he continued to serve the interests of palace and temple, but now most of his trade was what might be called "company trade." Yet, as we shall see subsequently, there appears to have been a great deal of cooperative enterprise between companies.

The background material just presented prepares us for a visit to the site from which the vast majority of texts revealing the extent and complexity of Old Assyrian interregional trade have been excavated. These texts are written in cuneiform and are conveniently called "Cappadocian Tablets" because of the historical name of the larger region in which they were found.

On the central Anatolian Plateau of Turkey stands a ruin mound called Kültepe, or "Mound of Ashes," located not far from the modern city of Kayseri. In ancient times its name was Kanesh. It was the seat of a small kingdom that stood at the hub of intersecting trade routes in the region. It also served as a center of international trade with a Mesopotamian kingdom called Assur, located in northern Iraq. This trade connection lasted for about 160 years before it petered out under the pressure of internal wars in Anatolia. What is intriguing is its duration and its complicated structure. That an interregional trading venture of so many years could be conducted between peoples of vastly different languages, customs, and traditions, across great distances and difficult terrain and under the regulation and safeguards of treaties, is remarkable and completely unexpected.

We don't know how the Old Assyrian traders first contacted the peoples of Anatolia. The treasures that lay in the mountains to the northwest of Mesopotamia and the knowledge of finished products in textiles and jewelry circulating in Syrian markets must have lured caravaners to those far-off and little-known territories. Eventually they succeeded in establishing permanent residences with storage facilities. As treaty partners with Anatolian rulers they amply repaid their hosts not only by acting as commercial facilitators but also by introducing Mesopotamian cultural features into Anatolian life. Their scribes passed on the technique of writing on clay tablets, and as settled residents in Anatolia they introduced their language and religious practices to the region. Their caravans, plodding roads and tracks between towns and villages that previously had had but little contact with each other, fostered an awareness of the outer world that would allow later conquerors to create large kingdoms rather than simple municipal regimes.

We will first examine the excavations on the site of Kanesh. Turkish excavators have dug here for a half century and have recently uncovered the foundations of two palaces and other buildings, which may be temples, and also a large storage building. The older of the palaces is contemporary with the most flourishing period of Old Assyrian trade, the younger to the end of that time, when Kanesh was conquered by the king of a neighboring city, who then transferred his administrative center to the site. The "Palace Mound" is roughly five hundred meters wide and in the shape of a rough circle. It stands about sixty feet higher than the surrounding fields, where, on the northeast, the Assyrian residence quarters are located. The older palace at Kanesh clearly dominated the city landscape, so that the king and his officials and soldiers could keep a watchful eye on behavior in the lower city.

What's left of the older palace is a complex of room foundations clustered about open courts. A protective wall of stone and mud brick, reinforced at critical spots by wooden beams, surrounded the whole. According to the excavators it was a two-storied edifice with a flat roof. Materials from the upper level of the palace had fallen through to the ground as a result of a great fire that gutted the building. Also throughout the Assyrian residence quarters below the terrace, the same conflagration totally destroyed the multistoried dwellings. The business records, which have allowed us such insight into the lives of the traders, survived, as we shall see subsequently. Within the palace there were rooms for residential use, such as living and dining areas, kitchens and bedrooms, reception halls where royal business was conducted, and small shrines for worship. But the palace was not simply a residential complex; it contained rooms where goods received in trade and other valuables could be stored. In all, it was a commercial facility as well as a political center.

We can sense the lost glamour and wealth of the palace from objects salvaged through excavation. A wide range of pottery of many graceful shapes and qualities—bowls, goblets, cups, teapots, pitchers, jars, and fruit stands—comes to light. A small but interesting collection of metallic objects also tells of specialized crafts either practiced in workshops within the palace precincts or received from outside. For example, workmanship in bronze is represented by two swords, a pin, and a bracelet. There is also gold foil and a handle of ivory. These objects, though meager, speak of luxurious items that must have been plentiful in the royal residence.

On the flat land below the terrace were located the Assyrian trader districts, which were situated at some distance away from the center of local authority on the terrace. The Assyrians called their settlement a *karum,* a name carried over from the trading quarters of Mesopotamian cities. In Mesopotamia, the karum quarter described the harbor area along rivers and canals. The Assyrian traders simply transferred the name they were used to in order to identify their residential activities abroad.

A karum was far more than a place where only the physical equipment of commerce was provided. Well beyond storing and loading facilities, it was also a bank, an accounting office, and an information center for its members. It was a place of assembly for business meetings. Such meetings were run by an executive committee of the most experienced, influential, and prosperous traders. These groups set agendas and generally kept track of the community's business operations. Equally important, they represented the home capital at Assur in negotiations with local rulers. On particularly critical matters the entire membership in good standing of the karum was summoned. The tablets also tell us that the karum was a court, whose decisions could be appealed to the Assyrian prince and the city council back home.

We now know of a number of colonial settlements of the karum type, and of a smaller type called *wabartum,* and numbers of towns in which the Assyrians maintained resident committees to look after their interests. The list will expand as excavations continue. The karum at Kanesh was the administrative superior of the entire network in Anatolia and Syria. Its executive regularly communicated with the other colonies, whether sending its instructions and advice to them or passing on edicts from the home city of Assur.

As capital of the Mesopotamian Old Assyrian kingdom, the city of Assur was jointly governed by a sovereign called "the prince" and a citizen assembly called "the City." The chief activity was commercial. All the important citizens appear to have been entrepreneurs, investors in the commercial activities of the Anatolian trade. They collected goods from local and regional markets and workshops and financed caravans to deliver them to the distant emporia of Syria and Anatolia. These caravans also engaged in small transactions with buyers along their regular routes. In Assur, the "City-House," similar to the "Karum-House" of Kanesh, functioned as the home office for all transactions.

In the residential areas of Karum Kanesh, five districts of streets and houses have been excavated. The streets are snuggled between clusters of two- and three-floored houses. The status and wealth of the owners determined the number of rooms in each dwelling. Next to the Assyrian districts, a complex of houses belonging to Anatolian natives and also one of mixed Assyrian and Anatolian households shows that the different populations lived and worked together in close proximity. The different groups did intermarry, even though an Assyrian trader may have left a wife behind in Assur. The Anatolian woman would be considered a secondary liaison or concubine. In Assur, the sons and daughters of entrepreneurs combined to work in the family business. The young men often were sent abroad to oversee the family's fortunes. Only rarely do we gain an insight into the private affairs of trader families. One text shows that all was not sweetness and light. A letter from a wife in Assur to her absent husband bitterly complains that while he is living in style in Kanesh she does not have the wherewithal to celebrate a religious festival in Assur.

We would know nothing of Old Assyrian trade were it not for the many thousands of clay tablets that survived the conflagration that befell

Kanesh. The Old Assyrian tablets are small, pillow-shaped hunks of clay that fit the palm of a merchant-scribe's hand. He would incise the messages dictated to him on their surfaces with a stylus. The tablets would then be baked in a hearth to emerge hard as stone. The fire that destroyed the karum could not destroy these records, which were stored in large clay urns or vats, in clay boxes, or even on wooden shelves in the rooms that served as offices. When groups of tablets were shipped to a neighboring karum or to Assur, they could easily fit in the saddlebags or other containers in a donkey's load.

The Anatolian residences were equipped with workshops, where vanity items, funerary gifts, and perhaps objects for ceremonial use were made. The Turkish excavators of the karum have discovered that the dead were buried beneath houses, and from the graves and more elaborate tombs have come precious jewelry, though most graves had already been plundered near the time of the original burials.

The mechanism of Old Assyrian trade was anything but simple. The family entrepreneurs of Assur were both investors and exporters. As investor, an entrepreneur could commission a professional merchant, a tamkârum, to do business for him, or he himself could finance itinerant traders. Groups of entrepreneurs could form partnerships and collectively share in the profits. Where the main interest was return in money, business contracts were written to specify the amount of time a loan was given, whether years, months, or units of five days. Stipulations included what interest applied to the loan, how surplus profit was to be divided, and what penalties were forthcoming for delayed repayment. As exporter in Assur, the entrepreneur assigned his goods for delivery to his family representatives abroad. In turn, these could make additional contracts with caravaners headed for local and regional markets. Alongside larger combines of distributors, single peddlers or, more usually, pairs also functioned in the sale and delivery of goods, each serving as guarantor for the other. With a clay tablet record required for each transaction, we can see how the number of tablets would mount into the many thousands.

The goods exported to Anatolia from Assur were principally metals and clothing of local manufacture. Tin, in bulk, and smaller amounts of iron and silver, among other metals, appear regularly in the export lists, but gold and silver served chiefly as investment capital. The caravaners also used small amounts of loose tin for routine expenses such as food, lodging, wood for fires, and, when needed, forage for their animals. In return for the delivery of Mesopotamian goods, the traders collected supplies of copper and Anatolian clothing for shipment to Assur. A favorite garment in much demand at home was the *kutanu,* possibly the prototype of the classical Greek *chiton,* a tunic made of linen or wool.

Long strings of donkeys, whose capacity was about 150 pounds each, made up a caravan. Sometimes the Old Assyrian tablets give us a precise itinerary for a small journey, which is an immense aid in reconstructing routes for mapmakers and historians. The animals appear to have been sold off at the end of a journey so as to reduce maintenance costs. When needed again, they could be reassembled for further journeys. When crossing a major waterway, for example, the Euphrates River, a caravan would be ferried by barge or other type of freight-carrying boat. Sometimes in an area that was not patrolled by native police, or had broken out in revolt or other violence, a caravan was in danger of being raided, having its goods stolen, and having its personnel scared off or killed. One letter to a caravan leader from his boss gives instructions about how to proceed in a suspected dangerous area. First, he says, divide the caravan into three parts. Send the first part by route A. Then send the second part by route B. Finally, send the third part by whichever route is the safer. Two-thirds of a caravan getting through was better than a total loss!

Since the Old Assyrian government in Assur and the individual kingdoms of Anatolia were all major players in international trade of the early second millennium, they all sought to profit as institutions from the lucrative commerce. Before a caravan could leave Assur for Anatolia, it had to pay taxes and tolls to the government. When it reached Karum Kanesh in Anatolia, it had also to pay the karum treasury a small percentage of its worth. But even before the goods could be assigned to its recipients, the caravan had to "go up," as the tablets report, and assemble in one of the palace's courtyards, where the royal family and high officials exercised the right of first option to select goods from the entire shipment both as gifts due them and as purchases.

After the city of Kanesh and its Assyrian karum were destroyed in about 1750, traders did return after a generation and were active for a short period. But the political climate both of Anatolia and of Mesopotamia was changing. Soon a single powerful state we know as the Old Hittite kingdom would arise and control central Anatolia. The Old Assyrian kingdom, hundreds of miles to the east, would succumb to the pressure of local rivals. But the glimpse we've gotten of how international trade could flourish in the absence of military conquest in an early period of Near Eastern history is admirably enlightening.[1]

On Chariot Warfare

From the earliest indications of settled life in the Near East, we have routinely encountered evidence of military preparedness and activity. Many prehistoric settlements were enclosed by walls; by the end of the early Neolithic period, or New Stone Age, the site of Jericho in Palestine at about 9000, for example, already possessed substantial fortifications, including a probable observation tower made of stone. Excavators have discovered that Jericho's walls were rebuilt seventeen times during the next few thousand years. Similar types of massive fortifications have also been found at Anatolian and Mesopotamian sites.

The great majority of prehistoric and historic settlements could not, of course, match the defensive structure of a site such as Jericho. They were nonetheless usually encircled by mud-packed walls, later by sturdier brick structures complete with gateways and elevated defensive ramparts. Attacks against such villages and towns usually resulted either in demolition of the walls and massive slaughter of the defeated residents or in a new lease on life for the successful defenders. Brutal warfare was a regular feature of ancient life, and yearly campaigns were regularly mounted unless and until some city ruler was strong enough to impose peace upon a larger area under his control.

By the time line of about 2000, two features of human inventiveness combined to raise the effectiveness of warfare to new levels. The first was the knowledge of how to make bronze by the addition of regulated amounts of tin to the already familiar production of copper, so as to produce weaponry of greater hardness and durability than earlier; the second was the introduction of the horse and chariot to military operations.

We often underestimate how technological developments affect our understanding of history. Yet technological advances in society are vitally important to know if and how we are to understand the continuing challenges societies face, how those challenges are met or ignored, and the consequences of those challenges. Take, for example, the discovery that tin when alloyed with copper could strengthen the finished product. The strength added to copper through the addition of tin allowed a military force to be more effective in ground battles against an enemy than was previously possible. Arrow and spear points made of bronze meant that weapons could strike harder, with greater accuracy than traditional copper weapons, and could last longer. Bronze helmets and body armor could give greater protection to the individual soldier than leather equipment alone. Bronze fittings in construction provided more secure joints.

But even more than the innovations just noted, the introduction of the horse into the realm of warfare dominated Near Eastern military adventures on land and changed the face of battle for thousands of years thereafter, even as the introduction of the tank in World War I altered traditional modes of battle in modern times. The early ancient Near Eastern world knew three types of equids: the donkey; the onager, or wild ass; and, from about the year 2000, the horse. Horses had been known in the wild state in regions on the edges of western Asia and beyond long before this period. The donkey, more naturally servile than the onager, became the load carrier of farmers and traders. The onager was best used in wagon transport, although teams of onagers are shown in early Sumeria pulling a chariotlike wagon. The horse, however, did not function as a beast of burden. Horses were already documented in the Old Assyrian period between 1900 and 1750. Their purchase price was higher than that of the common donkey (they were, in fact, known as "donkeys of the mountains"). Also in the Old Assyrian trader texts, we find mention of an official whose title translates as "horse master."

Domesticating a wild horse is not a routinely simple operation. It will be useful to describe some of the operations involved. The horse breaker may decide to challenge the horse one on one, leaping on its back and trying to hold on until the animal gives in and submits. Early American western cowpunchers appeared to use this method, which routinely produced broken arms, legs, and ribs for the unfortunate riders. At the opposite extreme, the breaker may try a gentler approach, gradually getting the horse to accept his presence and leadership by softly talking or singing to the animal. This approach takes time and patience and may not prove to be effective even so. A more useful approach is to let the horse run in circles at the end of a long rope, which ultimately tires and gentles the animal. This method, still employed in the American West, is described in a Hurrian text composed almost four thousand years ago.

But breaking the horse is only the beginning. The ancient would-be horseman had other problems to solve before he could count the animal as his partner. How do you lead a horse? How do you make it respond to your wishes to turn, to stop, or to pull a cart or a chariot? And what do you feed it when it has been removed from its natural home into a human habitat? These and many more concerns must be addressed to stimulate further thought and experimentation. Soon enough a new "industry" must be born: the production of equipment to manage the animal and with it a new class of persons whose sole duty is to maintain the animal: the supply master, the breeder, the veterinarian, and not least the soldier.

Experiments in breaking and training horses doubtless began on the steppes of western Asia many centuries before the animal was introduced into the Near Eastern milieu. As late as 714 the Assyrian king Sargon II, in an account of his eighth campaign against Urartu (in the area of Lake Van in northeastern Anatolia), could still note that the Urarteans had the best-trained horses of any people. It was only natural that Anatolian peoples—Hittites, Hurrian, and Kassites—would be the first to use the animal as a regular feature of their military campaigns from about 1500 onward.

While the introduction of cavalry was a significant aid to the foot soldier, it remained for the development of the chariot to make previous organizations of battle obsolete. Chariotry is not a simple outgrowth of a people's early knowledge of how to use oxen, asses, or donkeys in order to haul wagons. A chariot must be light and maneuverable. Just as with the domestication and training of the horse, there is a special technology required to make a chariot. The maker must know the best kinds of wood to use for the different parts of the apparatus. For example, wheel hubs and spokes require hardwoods of different densities. Rims require flexible, straight-grained wood. Beyond this, new designs had to be devised for bridles and bits. The problem of how to hitch the horses to shafts extending from the chariot had to be solved, as well as the problem of how to swivel the axle of a chariot so that a fast turn would not cause an accident. Alongside the great inventions of ancient Near Eastern peoples, such as the introduction of writing, the development of metallurgy, and the ability to create monumental architecture, the role of the ancient engineers must take a foremost but as yet mostly unacknowledged place.

The use of chariotry in mid-second-millennium battles also required that new tables of organization and tactical plans be devised. Charioteers also rose as a new status class in urban life. The new chariotry was either directly or indirectly responsible for upgrading the weaponry normally used in battle. For example, a lighter, shorter, and easier to handle chariot sword had to be developed to accommodate use from a fast-moving platform. Similarly, pikes and spears had to be made more manageable than those used by ground troops. Other adjustments of a defensive sort had to be made: in defensive armor both for the horse and for the chariot and in the matter of the chariot's carrying capacity. Quite apart from the support cadre that kept the horses and chariots in good fighting condition, it was now necessary to assign three men to one chariot unit: a driver, a shieldsman to protect both the driver and the fighting man, and the archer-swordsman warrior. Beyond this, chariot warfare required careful attention to matters of choice of terrain over which the battle was to be fought and constant training for the concerted use of large numbers of chariots in a pitched battle. For evidence that extraordinary numbers of chariots could appear for a battle, I need only cite the report in the Bible (Jgs 5:13) that the Canaanite Sisera brought nine hundred iron chariots to attack Israel.

The Hyksos in Egypt

An excellent example of how the introduction of a new military technology could affect the course of a well-established society can be seen from the results of the Hyksos invasion of Egypt during the eighteenth century. The Hyksos, a name conventionally translated as "rulers of foreign countries," were a mixed group of Semites and Indic peoples originating in Syro-Palestine. They managed to infiltrate the eastern areas of the Nile Delta during the eighteenth century and conquered the Egyptians. They succeeded in establishing their dominance for about 150 years. Their rule was remembered in Egyptian tradition as having been barbaric. They were tribute-demanding overlords and are reported also to have destroyed temples.

To an Egyptian society that, for nearly a millennium and a half, had nurtured itself along the banks of the Nile without major interference from the outside world, the Hyksos invasion was a major shock. The success of the Hyksos was achieved through their own acquaintance with, and possession of, the new military technologies initiated by the chariot cultures of their northern Anatolian neighbors. The Hyksos introduced into Egypt a smallish, very lightly built horse that was not ridden, similar to the modern Arabian horse, and was not a draft animal. It tended to be sway backed. The chariot it could pull was also light. For personal armament, the Hyksos brought with them small shields, the composite bow, and metal arrowheads. They also introduced an important change in sword design. Their swords were cast in one piece for strength, with the sword itself being sharpened at both blades. These weapons could easily be used in battle, as could a two-handed saberlike weapon, which had an end piece to keep it from flying out of the wielder's hand. Further improvements included axe-heads, anchored in sockets instead of lashed to poles for greater rigidity, and the introduction of bronze scales and leather for body armor and helmets.

These improvements should be compared to the Egyptian army's equipment during the Old and Middle Kingdoms. Contingents of troops then used the long bow, which was cumbersome. Arrows were tipped with quartz or ebony. Rarely were quivers used. A warrior carried his own arrows and also primitive clubs, some with stone heads. Axes and dagger blades were made of copper. Protection for the warrior was a bull-hide shield, which covered all of his body and was very cumbersome to yield.

All in all, the import of Hyksos innovations in military armament had a powerful effect on the Egyptian psyche. It remained for the founder of the Eighteenth Dynasty, Ahmose I, to reorganize the civil and military structure of Egyptian society and bring it into the new world of the mid-second millennium in the ancient Near East. His successors of the Eighteenth and Nineteenth Dynasties subsequently made Egypt a powerful contender in the military and diplomatic arenas of the area for the next three hundred years.

The Assyrian Army at War: The Assyrian War Machine

The military potential of the new chariot army was brought to its fullest between 900 and 600 by the Assyrians of northern Mesopotamia. Although the Hittites had made excellent use of chariot warfare to establish a broad region of dependent territories in Anatolia and northern Syria, it remained for the Assyrians of the first millennium to gain a grip on the entire Near East through its swift-moving troops and its calculated tactics of terror. As though to anticipate modern war photography, late Assyrian kings decorated their palaces with friezes both of their armies in the field and of themselves while hunting. From such friezes we can get a glimpse of all sorts of soldiery, chariotry, cavalry, siege machinery, views of towns under attack, and opponents killed outright or captured. We must, however, always be alert to the sculptors' exaggerations in their portrayals of the size of figures and the equipment shown. A broad survey of the sculptures just mentioned allows us detailed views of the Assyrian army in action.

The Assyrian military establishment consisted of a permanent standing army supported by provisional troops under the control of the king. The troops involved have been estimated to number in the hundreds of thousands. The king was closely protected by a cadre of special bodyguards. Supplementary to these were special regular units located in the provinces, along with cavalry. Their quarters might be border outposts as well as fortified locations in potentially troublesome districts. In times of military emergency, a general draft could be established among the population. The Assyrian army, unlike armies of earlier times—which campaigned in specific seasons, governed by when the harvest ended, or the conditions of favorable weather—was a year-round military force capable of action at any time regardless of terrain or weather conditions. This was an army that was trained to march up to thirty hours without a major break (similar to modern-day elite ground forces) and to live off the land if its food supplies ran out on a campaign. At the approach of the central army, the territorial governors were also alerted to make supplies and other resources available.

On the march, the units of the Assyrian army included the following: cavalry, for scouting and advanced skirmishing; chariotry, for tactical mobility once battle had been drawn; ground forces, including spearmen, archers, and swordsmen; engineers; a supply corps; a "naval auxiliary"; and a host of native levies to round out the attacking force. We can visualize this army from the palace sculptures previously mentioned.

The King

Foremost in battle, the Assyrian king is depicted as larger in size than any of his troops. He wears what appears to be a metallic helmet, decoratively incised, with a kind of conical extension of the helmet rising above it. His features are heavy, his musculature massive. He appears to wear bronze or other metallic body armor. His bow is huge as he shoots arrows against the enemy. His horses and chariot are larger than those of his accompanying charioteers, all features signifying his preeminence in battle.

The Cavalry

Cavalry men are depicted wearing peaked hats, perhaps a distinctive unit identifier. Their horses are equipped with reins and bits and also with blankets on their backs.

Infantry

Foot soldiers in the palace reliefs carry pikes; they appear to wear upper-body shirts of protective armor. Some carry quivers of arrows but without bows. Each also carries a dagger or short sword for hand-to-hand combat. Their clothing is a shirtlike affair ending at the knee. Their helmets include a kind of earflap, with short, semicircular crests on the top. The spearmen carry chin-high, full-body shields that have a slightly rounded top. Many of these spearmen are depicted as barefooted. Their spears have fluted points. The spear appears as having been unit-cast instead of having an attached head. The spearmen appear on the march as a phalanx, their spears extending over head height. Some infantry units wear caps or caplets. One such unit appears to have bronze shields with defined rims and defined center decorations. These shields curve inward, are large and circular, and protect the body to chin height. This unit also wears legging shoes, seemingly of leather further protected by bronze. A third group does not wear caps or helmets but carries the round metallic shield; they wear leggings and tunics.

Bowmen

Bowmen appear to be protected by infantry spearmen marching in front of them. Bowmen carry a smaller body shield and wear a leather or bronze decorated shirt. They carry a short sword, wear a pointed cap, and walk barefooted. Their primary weapon is not the long bow, similar to the king's, but a shorter curved bow. They routinely carry quivers and may also wear flat caps.

Charioteers

The chariots depicted in the Assyrian reliefs appear to carry two or three persons—a driver and the fighter or these and a third spearman. The horses appear to be small, hence presumably fast, and wear armor protection over their chests, necks, and bodies. Of great interest are the differences noted between chariot wheels having six or eight spokes. The older style of four-spoked chariots, familiar in the Egyptian army, was very unsuitable for operations over rough ground, although they were eminently useful on the flat ground, where speed was required for pursuit. On rough ground the four-spoked chariot wheel could easily buckle, with disastrous results for the individuals in the chariot. By building eight-spoked chariot wheels along with their apparently normal six-spoked wheels, the Assyrians met the challenges of the mountainous territories in which they lived and fought. The twelve-spoked chariot in which the king rode was probably more useful in ceremony than as an aid in combat. Assyrian chariot wheels appear to have had wide rims, another asset for combat over rough terrain.

The "Naval Auxiliary"

Any land army fighting in territories through which streams and rivers flow must have the ability to ford them or will find itself stymied. The Assyrian army had boats available, probably commandeered on the march. One scene from the palace reliefs shows a crew of four paddling a boat across a river. Another shows a boat transporting a chariot across. Different types of oars are also depicted on boats, suggesting different functions for the various boat types. Most interesting are what might be called the ancient "seabee." A member of this group is shown crossing a stream by floating on an inflated animal skin, while another carving shows a fellow "seabee" inflating such a skin by mouth. There is also a most fascinating image of a trooper actually appearing to swim across the river.

Engineer Corps

As a necessary adjunct to forest and mountain combat, the Assyrians developed what we would recognize as a "pioneer corps," which would clear the way through especially difficult terrain by hacking down trees, cutting trails through otherwise impossible underbrush, and repairing weapons and other pieces of large or small equipment. Their main function was to design and operate effective equipment against massive city walls. To this end the Assyrian army was equipped with scaling ladders that allowed its troops to reach the high positions from which defenders were shooting arrows down on the besieging army. The idea of scaling walls with ladders was something of an improvement on the time-honored siege method of piling up soil to create a huge mound up which besieging troops could climb to reach the defenders on the parapets and so stand even with them in the assault. The siege ladder left the attackers in a very vulnerable position. The defenders could push the ladders outward and away from the walls with resulting catastrophe for the attackers, or the defenders could hurl down rocks or shoot arrows from above. Far better than the scaling ladder was the battering ram, which could smash through weak spots in city walls and gates. The Assyrians appear to have had two types. The first was a four-wheeled armored device with two extended rams. This device had a protective wooden or metallic raised wall attached to its top behind which bowmen could shoot arrows at the defenders. In addition to this style of ram, there was a six-wheeled version with a snub-nosed snout in front that could batter city gates, while a troop of protected archers could keep up a barrage of arrow shot.

The Assyrian army represented the culmination of what was militarily possible in the pre-Hellenistic period of the ancient Near East. The fall of the Assyrian capital at Nineveh to a coalition of Medes and Babylonians in 612 signaled the end of a regime whose military might and techniques of psychological warfare had terrorized both settled communities and tribes centuries earlier.

Some Observations on
Ancient Near Eastern Treaties

Treaty making has a long antiquity in the ancient Near East, but this vignette is not the place to offer a comprehensive survey. Instead, I would like to note four examples of unusual variety and interest: the trading treaty of Old Assyrian times (nineteenth and eighteenth centuries); the Hittite system (1550–1200); the Old Persian (sixth century to 330); and the Hebrew Covenant with God (thirteenth century).

To begin, the modern treaty is a secular instrument by means of which two or more states or other types of international communities agree to have binding relationships with each other for general or specific purposes. The force behind the treaty—that is, the *Authority* that theoretically guarantees it—is based on a tradition of international law as capable of being applied by various types of international tribunals. States change their contracted allegiances as it serves their purposes to do so, but the standing of the treaty signer can suffer severely in the eyes of the international community should he choose to disregard its commitments or resort to force. The realities of political life to the contrary notwithstanding, the treaty in modern times is still regarded as a potent regulatory force in the sphere of international relations.

In the ancient Near East a treaty was considered to be a compact ratified primarily by the deities of each side and only secondarily by the human agents, the kings or governors involved. The treaty thus represents the strongest assertion of the desire and the ability to perform promises that are guaranteed by solemn oaths to the gods and protected by the threat of invocation of curses that have been written into the treaty. In the deepest sense a Near Eastern treaty is the epitome of a religiously sanctioned relationship; in fact, there can be none other *but* such a relationship between two parties in international affairs or, for that matter, in internal affairs. However much treaties could be and were broken in the political arena, the earthly course of events was ultimately given a *cosmic* interpretation. Hence the expressions of great wrath and indignation that appear in reports of revolts in the royal annals of ancient Near Eastern states. The modern political analyst might conclude that the realities of power and its demands alone dictate the actions of rulers and that records of political actions taken usually amount to little more than rhetorical justification. But it would be a mistake to conclude that the kings of the ancient Near East were merely rhetoricians. By contrast, they were so psychologically dependent upon the "will of the gods" as inquired after and presented to them by their religious advisors—therefore so attuned to the necessity of operating within, and living up to, the religious or cosmic perspectives that defined both the destinies of their states and their own positions—that political action at home or abroad could not be seen except as conforming to a world plan intended by their patron deities. The consequence of this is that the violation of treaty relationships in the ancient Near East always had a religious—and not solely a political or military—dimension.

Basically, as Dennis J. McCarthy, SJ, has pointed out, treaty provisions were imposed under oath and placed under the sanction of divine witnesses. Curses for treaty violations were routinely imposed. The treaty, far from being a mere document, was a species of dramatic performance in that it represented the words of the king to the treaty partner, whether to a ruler of equal status or to a vassal.[1]

In our first example we encounter a situation in which native populations in central Anatolia and foreign traders from Assyria, in northern Mesopotamia, intermixed as trading partners, the Assyrians being able to establish numerous colonies adjacent to host cities. A host city would routinely be ruled by a royal personage with whom the resident foreigners had concluded trading pacts. In the course of time the trading colonies abandoned their settlements and activities under violent conditions both in Anatolia and their native Assyria, and central Anatolia became a territory in which rival princes sought to dominate each other by forming coalitions of vassals.[2]

It is from the Hittites that much of the information we have about treaties in the ancient Near East has come. The Hittites were an Indo-European-speaking language group who entered central Anatolia early in the second millennium perhaps from regions far to the east of Mesopotamia. They formed a kingdom that was centered on several traditional cities on the Anatolian plateau. By about 1500 they had emerged as an imperial force in the Near East and for the next three hundred years maintained a system of treaty relationships within and outside their borders that rivals the international systems we are acquainted with today.

From Mesopotamia they adopted the cuneiform system of writing their own language on clay tablets. Excavations at Bogazkoy in central Turkey, site of their capital city, Hattusas, have unearthed many documents of political and religious import, and from them we have gained insights into the nature of their internal and external political relationships. The Hittite state archives were discovered by Hugo Winkler.

From these records we have learned that the Hittites, far from being a monolithic and closely integrated state, were rather a federated, or feudal, entity. This can also be seen in their religious organization, where multitudes of weather gods, for example—each attached to its own village or city—functioned under the supervision of the national gods. In the international political sphere, a system of "equal" states and of "vassal" states was established. We are fortunate to have political instruments, or treaties, that illustrate each type of relationship maintained by the Hittites.

The treaty type relating to affairs between the Hittites and other powerful states is known as the "parity" treaty, in which the Hittite king wishes to establish a protectorate or a sphere of influence, at best. This type of treaty is more a matter of "noblesse oblige" than of force upon the recipient. Theoretically the Hittite king "grants" the treaty, though in the great example of a treaty between the Hittites and Egypt (about 1300), the Egyptian version stresses the "brotherhood" of the treaty makers. According to the Egyptologist John Wilson, the Egyptian text "was a translation, edited to give greater prominence to the role of Egypt in granting peace." Usually, however, and from the Hittite point of view, the treaty partner was the grantee of Hittite benevolence.

The clauses of such treaties as we have indicate that the Hittites calculated well in their international relations. They could ensure the future bonds between themselves and their opposite numbers by using their own princesses as marriage partners for the latter. This, of course, meant that successors in the ruling line of the treaty vassal would always be related to the Hittite royal family. While the terms of those parity treaties were less severe than those the Hittites imposed on lesser states, the protégé could not pursue an independent foreign policy but had to submit to the Hittite king's instructions about whom the protégé was allowed to communicate with. The protégé is an ally, does not pay tribute, and has no claims on territory previously lost to the Hittites in war. The protégé, further, must supply troops to the Hittite king in case of the latter's need, but only under specific instructions. Even the annexation of lands to his own realm by a protégé of the Hittites is regulated and supervised by the Great King.

Most severe terms were imposed on the weakest states by the Hittites. In the so-called vassal treaty, which was less a pact between two states, the arrangement called for a strictly defined personal relationship between the Hittite king and the vassal. What the vassal might or might not do in the political sphere was carefully specified. Rather than being treated as a quasi-ally, the vassal was kept on a much tighter rein.

All this suggests a smoothly operating ancient Hittite international system in the second half of the second millennium in the northern regions of Anatolia, Syria, and Palestine. Although many revolts did break out during Hittite domination of these areas between 1500 and 1200, the attempt to fashion and maintain an international system through negotiated treaties is a noteworthy achievement in the history of early political development. In roughly 1200 the Hittite Empire was destroyed by the "Peoples of the Sea," who invaded Asia Minor and even reached the borders of Egypt before being repulsed.[3]

While the treaties we have been discussing to this point resulted from and applied to pragmatic political situations—that is, the methods employed by a superior power to pacify and govern lesser powers—there is in my view another, entirely different, perspective in the ancient Near East. This emerges from the Old Persian (Zoroastrian) contract as a *metaphysical* element and in human affairs. The underlying concepts are those of Truth (*aša,* or Indian, *rta*) and the Lie (*druj*), both of which already appear in political contexts in the inscriptions of Darius I, the Achaemenid ruler at the time of Cleisthenes' ascendancy at Athens.

For Zoroaster and his followers, aša is not merely abstract; it applies in all areas of human activity. Including, as it does, the corollary meanings of *righteousness, order, the mean,* and even (in Sassanian times) *the Path,* it affirms a lasting opposition to druj, which as the Lie encompasses the concepts of *unrighteousness, disorder, deceit,* and *the non-Path.* There can never be reconciliation between the two. Truth combats the Lie forever. The followers of Truth, the *ašavans,* comprise an army that wars with the *drǝgvants* (var: *drvants*), the army or followers of the Lie. On the metaphysical side this reveals itself in the imagery of the forces of Light warring against those of Darkness.

The application of these concepts to human life is seen not only in the personal realm of ethical choice but quite specifically in the realm of government and its area of administration. For Zoroaster, Truth means the organization of affairs, particularly, "a peaceful agricultural and pastoral order." Zoroaster's doctrine is the "universalization of a concrete political and social situation," one that Zoroaster means to be achieved and defended by the sword. Similarly the Old Persian kingdom was destined to be in the hands of the followers of Truth. The Persian king, or more properly the "King of Kings," holds this kingdom on trust from Ahura-Mazda, who is the source and guardian of Truth and Order. As the source of Light (but not himself the Sun), Ahura-Mazda illuminates the reality of Truth. This reality is activated by "Good Mind" *(Vohu Manah),* the same Mind by which the Persian ruler controls his own impulsiveness in administration.

The Persian ruler, then, has his kingdom on trust and, as a follower of Ahura-Mazda and the Zoroastrian principle, is dedicated to the promulgation of Ahura-Mazda's law through "good mind," truthfulness, and appropriate rulership. Not that the monarch was necessarily a philosopher-king. Rather, his was the ubiquitous problem of all princes: to administer according to principles of *Authority,* which are seen as eternally valid in a world characterized by inconstancy and disruption.

For Zoroaster, druj, the Lie, is the essence of Evil, which violates the natural and the world order. It comes not from God, who, by contrast, chastises those who conceal the Truth. When wedded to *aešma,* "violence" or "fury," the Lie produces not only an offense against Truth but a violent assault against the established order. Doubtless Zoroaster was thinking of the nomads of his own time (ca. late seventh century) in his pronouncements, so that the Lie was understood to produce aggression. In Darius's inscriptions the Lie is equated with "rebellion," with those who subvert good government. Since followers of the Lie war against Ahura-Mazda himself, they must be either completely vanquished or converted.

The basis of this is naturally pragmatic as well as philosophical. The king must continue to reign. But another, crucial, aspect of Old Persian/Zoroastrian thought requires consideration: the Lie is a violation of the *contract* that embodies the Natural Law. In the internal and the external affairs of the Old Persian Empire there can be no doubt that (a) disruption of order through the Lie and its effects as internal rebellion and (b) violations of orderly relations in external affairs as affirmed through treaties, were treated as violations of the cosmic order. An examination of the basis of this assertion concerns the role of Mithra within the divine sphere of the Achaemenid Persians.

Although commonly known as a "savior" god and the object of a military cult to the later Romans, Mithra had a different character and function in the older Persian religion. He was a great war lord, to be sure. But he was also the deity who specifically ensured the sanctity of contracts between men. Even more acutely, Mithra represented in his own person the inviolability of *all* contractual relations. Mithra, ranked second only to Ahura-Mazda, along with Ahura, were seen as "pre-server-creators" as they must have existed before Zoroaster produced a spiritual revolution within the religion of Iran; as "bound together in closest union," the two gods "stood as guardians of Truth and Order [and] were united against the Lie." It is not necessary to enter here into the difficult question of precisely how the Old Iranian pantheon was built up; what is significant for our purposes is *the position of the divinity who ensures the sanctity of contract in human affairs at the top of the divine hierarchy.*

The importance of Mithra is nowhere more highlighted than in the Avestan hymn to this god, which is dated approximately to the second half of the fifth century and is the single extensive ancient Iranian source about him.[4] After the opening stanza in which Ahura-Mazda is represented as addressing Zoroaster to inform him that Mithra is equal in worthiness to himself and is to be worshipped and prayed to as to himself, the hymn continues (in the words of Ahura-Mazda):

> The knave who is false to the treaty, O Spitamid, [Zoroaster] wrecks the whole country, hitting as he does the Truth-owners as hard as would a hundred obscurantists. Never break a contract, O Spitamid, whether you conclude it with an owner of Falsehood, or a Truth-owning follower of the good Religion; for the contract applies to both, the owner of Falsehood and him who owns Truth.

Herewith, in a nutshell as it were, is a statement of tremendous importance in ancient Iranian thought and for the practical politics of the Persian rulers. The notion of the absolutely primary significance of contracted relationships is further elaborated in section 29.115–17 of the hymn and confirmed in the actions of Mithra against the treaty breaker in section 27.111.

There can thus be no doubt about the crucial role of the idea of contract in Old Iranian religious and political thought. It can be summed up in the form of an analogy: to the Order of the Cosmos upheld by Ahura-Mazda, Mithra, and other deities of the Indo-Iranian pantheon may be compared the Order of the Political State and the Empire upheld by the Persian king, the protégé of the Wise Lord, Ahura-Mazda. To the contract that holds the universe in balance may be compared those agreements that govern relationships between friends, fellow citizens, partners, husband and wife, fellow students, disciple and teacher, son-in-law and father-in-law, brother and brother, and father and son, and *in the international sphere, between two countries.* As the Old Persian Empire came into existence and expanded, the sense of earthly imperial order as a parallel to the cosmic order must surely have expressed reality to the Persian mind.[5]

Finally, the fourth type of treaty that emerged from the ancient Near East, one that has endured until now and will continue to be honored by the people who are party to it, is what I would call the covenant treaty between the Hebrew God, Yahweh, and his people. This treaty is in the form of a religious bond that is valid forever. It is not understood to be a pact between equal partners but has been offered by Yahweh to his people as a pact pledging fidelity by God for eternity in return for all the fidelity of his people. What is remarkable in this relationship is that the compact, or covenant, has no terminal date but moves forward throughout history until "the Day of the Lord" arrives and history is complete.[6]

FURTHER READING

Akurgal, Ekrem. *The Hattian and Hittite Civilizations.* Ankara: Republic of Turkey Ministry of Culture, 2001. Profusely illustrated.

Gurney, O. R. *The Hittites.* London: Penguin Books, 1990. Paperback.

When Princes Squabble

A Royal Dispute in Central Anatolia

This vignette consists of a single letter written by the ruler of a city-state called Mama, located in a south central region of Anatolia, to the ruler of Kanesh, a powerful city-state some two hundred kilometers to the north. During the period of Old Assyrian trader residence in Anatolia (ca. 1900–1750), Kanish had been the center of trader operations from which an extensive network of major and minor trading outposts was controlled. Each of these outposts had the status of a guest community in a native Anatolian locale governed by a major or minor royal personage. At about 1750 conditions in Early Assyria, as probably also in Anatolia itself, contributed to a termination of the previously vigorous trade between the regions, and Anatolia became a disputed territory for the ambitions of local rulers. This is the situation reflected in the letter now to be discussed.

The Anum-Hirbi Letter

The "Anum-Hirbi Letter" was discovered on the city mound of Kultepe (ancient Kanish) and was published by the Turkish scholar Kemal Balkan, in Turk Tarih Arkeologya ve Etnografya Dergisi VII, Seri No 31a, 1957. For the convenience of the reader I have taken some liberties with the visual presentation of this letter, which, in its technical form, might have been confusing to a general audience. Balkan's transliteration and translation of this letter also appears in my book *Assyrian Colonies in Cappadocia,* 97–98 (see the bibliography).

The Text

Lines

1–3   Thus says Anum-Hirbi, Prince of Mama: To Warshama, Prince of Kanish, speak:

96

4–16   You wrote me: "The Prince of Taishama is my slave; I take care of [control] him.

But do you take care [control] of the Prince of Sibuha, your slave?"

Since the Prince of Taishama is your dog, why does he argue with the other rulers? Is the Prince of Taishama to become a third prince [in status] with us?

17–34   When my enemy killed [defeated] me, the Prince of Taishama invaded my country and destroyed 12 of my cities. He carried away their cattle and sheep. He said, "the Prince is dead, so I have taken my fowler's snare [so as to catch the prey]. Instead of protecting my country and giving me heart [i.e., encouraging me], he not only burned up my country, but created evil-smelling smoke. [However] while your father, Inar, for nine years was besieging the city of Harsamna, did my land [i.e., people] invade your land? Did it kill an ox or a sheep?"

34–36   Today, you wrote to me saying, "Why do you not free the road for me?"

37   I will free the road.

[lines 37–48 broken and most incoherent]

[Anum-Hirbi continues:]

49–56   You wrote to me, saying: "Let us take an oath [conclude a treaty]. Is the former oath insufficient? Let your messenger come to me and let my messenger come regularly to you."

56–57   Tarikutana [the Prince of Kanish's diplomatic envoy] sealed up stones instead of [the expected] silver, and deposited them [in Mama as a diplomatic gift]. Are these things good [in the sight of] the gods?

This important letter from the Prince of Mama to the Prince of Kanish, to recapitulate, was found during Turkish excavations on the city mound of Kanish. Written in the Old Assyrian dialect, which Anatolian scribes had learned from their commercial guests, it not only supplies information but also allows important inferences to be made about regional political conditions existing in Anatolia in the period just prior to the period of Hittite domination.

Analysis of the Letter

Lines 1–3. Unlike our practices of writing "Dear Mr., Ms., Sir," or the like, in our salutations, the common opening line of a cuneiform letter reflects the fact that an author of such could not write and is dictating the message to a scribe who can. Thus the letter is literally a speech to the recipient. The reader of the tablet on the receiving end "says" to the person addressed what the writer has spoken.

Lines 4–16. The Prince of Mama's complaint to the Prince of Kanish: In an earlier letter, Warshama, the prince of Kanish, had affirmed to Anum-Hirbi, Prince of Mama, that another ruler, the Prince of Taishama, was his "slave" and that Warshama essentially controls him. But, does Anum-Hirbi control his own "slave," the Prince of Sibuha?

Anum-Hirbi now accuses Warshama of not really supervising the Prince of Taishama because the latter has been plotting with other rulers. Does Warshama want his vassal to rise in status and become an equal to the two of them? (The reader will note that vassals are referred to as "dogs" as well as "slaves.")

Historical Note

Although the rulers of Mama and Kanish, respectively, appear as equals in our letter, this state of affairs may not always have existed. That the Old Assyrian traders had originally established their main Anatolian outpost at Kanish suggests, in itself, that Kanish was a city that ruled over the entire central region, though this remains speculative. The town of Mama hosted a smaller outpost of Assyrian traders. This does not necessarily argue that the Prince of Mama was less powerful a regional ruler than the Prince of Kanish. Our letter certainly suggests that they were communicating as equals.

Lines 17–34. The complaint of Anum-Hirbi continues. Not only does the Prince of Taishama seem to be pursuing an independent series of talks and negotiations with other rulers, but he has already been guilty of having attacked the Prince of Mama's territories. After an unknown enemy had earlier defeated Anum-Hirbi, the Prince of Taishama then invaded Mama on his own, taking advantage of Anum-Hirbi's situation instead of giving encouragement and aid, as it is assumed he was obligated to do. The metaphorical use of the idea that the Prince of Taishama had "taken his hunting snare to catch fowl" captures the image of his having destroyed twelve of Anum-Hirbi's cities, captured sheep and cattle, and set the Mamaean territory ablaze. These lines represent Anum-Hirbi's attempts to put the best possible face on the situation. Did *he* attack Kanish when Warshama's father, Inar, was occupied for nine years besieging the city of Harsamna? Did he hurt an ox or a sheep? Anum-Hirbi displays himself as the injured and innocent party in his relationship with Kanish. The implied question is, Why did Warshama not control his own "dog" then?

Lines 34–37. "To free the road" in these lines means to establish communication by opening and protecting the roads for caravan trade, messengers, and other types of travelers. Anun-Hirbi's retaliation against Kanish has been to cut off relations with Warshama. Nonetheless he agrees to renew the relationship with Warshama.

At this point in the letter there are eleven broken and unreadable lines (37–48) except for an isolated reference to seventeen men.

Lines 49–57. Warshama, the Prince of Kanish, proposes a new oath between them. Whether this is a new treaty is not clear. In any event, Arum-Hirbi agrees to an exchange of messengers on a regular basis but asks whether the former oath (or treaty) was insufficient. The final indignity noted by Anum-Hirbi is that a Kanishean envoy, Tarikutana, was supposedly bringing silver to Anum-Hirbi, but instead of the silver he sealed up stones. The letter ends a bit wistfully—"Are these things good [in the sight of] the gods?"—considering that the gods were understood to be the guarantors of treaty obligations.

Subsequent decades will find the Hittites on the political scene in Asia Minor/Anatolia, where local rulers like Warshama and Anum-Hirbi would both become dependents of a new order or face their own destruction.

SOME LITERARY OBSERVATIONS

On the Greatness of Gilgamesh as an Ancient Near Eastern Epic

Ask literary critics to name the great epics of antiquity and they will quickly offer the Homeric *Iliad* and *Odyssey* and Virgil's *Aeneid*. A few might include the Old Babylonian *Gilgamesh Epic* but might suggest that *Gilgamesh* is primitive by comparison with Homer or Virgil, although it contains material of epic compositional worth. My purpose in this vignette is to celebrate the *Gilgamesh Epic* as a composition whose plot, structure, characterization, and literary devices merit a judgment that would place it among the foremost compositions of world literature, ancient or modern.

Assyriologists approach the epic almost purely from the standpoint of concern about how individual compositions about Gilgamesh and his companion, Enkidu, helped create the larger poem or how matters of chronology or philology need to be addressed in order to assemble the fuller portrait. These concerns, of course, are absolutely necessary for scientific analysis. But here I would like to take my reader through a literary analysis of the work to bring out how its plot, structure, characterization, and themes function as a whole in the epic. For convenience I offer a brief synopsis.

Gilgamesh, described as two-thirds god and one-third man, appears as a tyrant-king of Uruk in lower Mesopotamia. He rules his city autocratically and with unbridled licentiousness. The citizens appeal to the Council of the Gods for help. In response, Enkidu, as a "double of Gilgamesh," is created to divert Gilgamesh. At first Enkidu roams freely in nature, living with the wild animals; but after being seduced by a temple harlot from Uruk sent to ensnare him, Enkidu is rejected by the animals who were his companions. He is led by the harlot into the city, where he encounters Gilgamesh, wrestles with him, and is accepted by Gilgamesh as his friend. The two companions now decide on an adventure to attack Huwawa, the monster who guards the Cedar Forest. Having killed Huwawa, Gilgamesh and Enkidu return to Uruk. Gilgamesh's victory attracts the lustful attention of Ishtar, patroness of her great temple within the city. But Gilgamesh sarcastically rejects her as a treacherous lover. Enraged at Gilgamesh's insults, Ishtar cajoles, then threatens, Anu, her father and chief god of the pantheon, to create the Bull of Heaven to kill Gilgamesh. Gilgamesh and Enkidu, however, kill the bull, and Enkidu, in a fit of hubris, hurls the Bull's thigh at Ishtar from the wall of Uruk. This act dooms him. His subsequent death stimulates Gilgamesh to embark on a great journey to seek immortality. He sets out to visit Utnapistim and his wife, the only survivors of the Great Flood, which wiped out human life at the beginning of time. In this quest Gilgamesh becomes like Enkidu as he wanders the steppe. His journey takes Gilgamesh through magical terrain, in which he encounters persons and creatures who try to dissuade him from completing his quest. Finally Gilgamesh is ferried across the "waters of death" by Urshanabi, the boatman, to visit Utnapishtim and his wife. Utnapishtim recites the long tale of the Flood and proceeds to prove to Gilgamesh through various tests that he cannot attain eternal life. The defeated Gilgamesh returns to Uruk, and the epic ends.

Since a major work of literature validates itself by exhibiting various kinds of unities and integrations of thematic and structural elements, I should like to begin my analysis with some observations of the way our epic deals with matters of space and time. The city of Uruk with its protective walls becomes the focal point of the two great adventures in the poem: the expedition of the companions against Huwawa and later Gilgamesh's journey to the abode of Utnapishtim and his disappointed return. The city is the geographical "compass point" that lies at the center where earth and the realms of the divine meet. The life of Enkidu after his creation begins in a pure and natural way until his corruption by the harlot and his introduction to the licentious life that characterizes

Uruk under Gilgamesh's rule. After Enkidu's death, the poem has Gilgamesh roaming the steppe as a double of the life Enkidu led, though without the innocence of his lost companion. A key observation should also be made about the walls of Uruk. At the opening of the epic the reader (in its own time it was heard, not read, except by scribes for teaching purposes) is asked to contemplate the greatness of Uruk and its walls, the very same thought that Gilgamesh expresses to Urshanabi, the boatman, as they later return to Uruk. We recall that the motivating incident of the second part of the epic takes place upon the walls of Uruk, where Enkidu, in wild excitement, hurls the thigh of the Bull of Heaven at the goddess Ishtar. In all, then, the city of Uruk and its walls serve as an anchor for the events of the narrative.

If we consider how time is used in the epic, the work appears to have an elementary "straight line" plot development. After the nobles of Uruk, having been oppressed by Gilgamesh's misrule, pray to the gods for relief, the plot appears to advance through interlocked episodes, yet the poet has a few surprises in store. He employs the "dream" to build anticipation within the work. Although he might simply have had Enkidu brought face to face with Gilgamesh and proceeded from there, he builds suspense by having Gilgamesh experience two dreams, which Gilgamesh does not understand and which allow the introduction into the story of his mother, Ninsun, to interpret. This episode directly anticipates the arrival of Enkidu and the harlot into Uruk and sets up the confrontation between Enkidu and Gilgamesh. The use of the dream device is further developed in the scene in which Enkidu realizes his own death is imminent. He sees that the gods have gathered in council and wonders why. A second dream allows Enkidu to see a view of the underworld, the destination of the dead and soon of his own. The effect of this vision on Gilgamesh is to strengthen his resolve to attain immortality.

As readers, we do not ordinarily investigate how authors plan out their works to produce the effects we admire. But it will be useful to spend a bit of time on the imaginative world that the writer produces and that the reader (or hearer) encounters. It has to begin somewhere, with the author's choice. But no author can begin without a vision of some idea of where his or her story is going. Many, even most, authors will say that they had just the vaguest general idea of what will happen once they embarked on their tale. Some writers say that a story somehow seems to have a life of its own and really leads them to a conclusion they could not clearly predict.

In the case of *Gilgamesh Epic,* there already were episodes from early

Sumerian times that gave plot ideas and thematic materials to a later poet. Characters like the two heroes were already known, as were the standard divinities and other traditional characters and incidents. But no poet of Old Babylonian times could simply fit them together and produce the work that we have. It could not be, in modern vernacular, the equivalent of a "cut and paste" production. For each work of literary art has its own organic life, a completion, that makes it what it is and not merely a collection of separate pieces that somehow can be fitted together like a jigsaw puzzle. The poet of our epic certainly had a central theme, the doomed search for immortality on Gilgamesh's part. But there are also several other themes that the poet wished to introduce into his story. No less important than the search for immorality is the theme of Gilgamesh's failure to understand his role as a surrogate for the gods in administering justice for his people and accepting the balance of political structure within the city, where citizens and nobles had met in their assemblies from time immemorial. Additionally, the theme of fraternal love between Gilgamesh and Enkidu should be cited, as also the relationship between Gilgamesh and his mother, Ninsun. Beyond this we need to consider the connection between the earthbound heroes and the gods and the contrast between the purity of the primeval, natural world and the hedonistic world of city life.

All these themes had to be kept in mind by our poet. But what sort of plot could be devised that would allow the poet to introduce incidents that would emphasize these thematic materials while advancing the story to its final and necessary conclusion? And once, as poet, he could block out his episodes, what range of action did he need to get from one episode to another, and what kinds of characters did he need to carry through the progress of the story? None of this is automatic. As a writer, where do you start your story? And once you have decided on a start, where do you go from there? All the individual decisions that an author makes have consequences for the final success of the narration.

Including human beings, gods, individual creatures of bizarre characteristics, and groups, there are about thirty characters in the epic. Where and how to introduce them is a major part of the poet's task. The skill with which he accomplishes this task figures importantly in the "knitting together" of a believable plot. And from the creation of this plot we derive intense pleasure and satisfaction. Let's observe how the poet of *Gilgamesh* goes about producing his effects.

The opening eighteen lines of the epic (the rest of the introduction being broken off) is the poet's introduction to his audience. Gilgamesh (not yet named), the omniscient and omnipotent ruler of Uruk, returns to his city after a long and weary journey to tell the story of "before the Flood"; all his toil he engraved on a stone stele. Notice that the poet is saying it is not he himself but rather the hero of his story who is originally telling the tale. This is a clever way of bringing the audience directly in contact with the story's hero. The poet then invites his audience to consider the greatness of Uruk, Gilgamesh's city, and its impressive double walls, on which, or inside which, key incidents that motivate the plot take place. Not only "look at them" but "go up and inspect them for yourself," urges the poet. Much later when Gilgamesh returns to Uruk with his companion, Urshanabi, the boatman, after failing in his quest, he repeats the same sentiment as is expressed in the epic's opening, but now the expression is far more on the weary and cynical side. Where the poet removes himself from the story and turns it over to the characters in action is unclear, but it must be after Tablet I (ii) l.11, where the complaint of the nobles begins.

That the scene that motivates the action of the entire epic begins as a complaint against the king of the city signals a political motif. The nobles of the city ask the gods for redress against Gilgamesh's violations, and the divine answer is to create Enkidu, who immediately, but reluctantly, falls under Gilgamesh's wild plan to attack Huwawa, the guardian of the Cedar Forest. The reason Gilgamesh gives for undertaking the expedition is to eliminate evil in the land, but nowhere in the epic is this developed as a major cause. The real reason is to celebrate Gilgamesh's own prowess. Enkidu, who knows about Huwawa's power and ferocity, tries to dissuade Gilgamesh from setting out on the expedition, as do the nobles of the city and also Gilgamesh's mother, Ninsun. Realizing that Gilgamesh will not be dissuaded by their appeals, the Assembly counsels him to be guided by Enkidu. Ninsun offers prayers to Shamash and appears to place some sort of protective charm around Enkidu's neck. While the scene contributes to the anticipation and suspense of the impending departure, two comments—the first from the Assembly, the second from Ninsun—give us an important clue to the character of Gilgamesh: the elders say to Gilgamesh, "Childlike, mayest thou attain thy wish!" (III, v, 37), and Ninsun, in her prayer to Shamash (III, ii, 10–11, Assyrian version), says, "Why, having given me Gilgamesh for a son, with a restless heart didst thou endow him?" We should not forget these indications of Gilgamesh's immaturity.

An epic adventure requires epic preparation. Twelve hundred years before Homer was to write the famous eighteenth book of his *Iliad,* in

which the smith, Hephaestos, creates a great shield for Achilles as he prepares to fight Hector, the Trojan hero, our Old Babylonian poet wrote
an episode in which another smith and his workers cast fine weapons for
Gilgamesh and Enkidu to use in their combat against Huwawa! Also, the
use of the dream device in the battle against Huwawa was also effectively
employed by our poet.

The consequences of epic so often bring tragedy in their train. How
can the plot develop? If Enkidu is to advance or complete the mission
for which he was created, what action must ensue? Do you get away
scot-free after killing a creature belonging to the milieu of the gods? Presumably our poet could have created many scenes in which Enkidu
might have been killed, and in this way to introduce the motif of
"Death" and Gilgamesh's response to it, but he chooses to have Enkidu
die because of Gilgamesh's indiscretions in humiliating Ishtar. Stories of
Ishtar's treatment of her lovers were certainly part of the Mesopotamian
tradition, but why did our poet choose to have Gilgamesh humiliate the
powerful goddess? I believe he saw the following opportunities to
advance his plot: first, he was reminding his audience of Ishtar's fickle-
ness toward her lovers and her wild and treacherous nature; second, it
gave the poet an opportunity to create a magnificent scene in which
Ishtar, as a headstrong daughter, intimidates her father, Anu, who is
characterized as being able to be bullied by her even though he is the
head of the divine pantheon; and third, the creation of the Bull of
Heaven allows a last appearance of Gilgamesh as hero, but one that trig-
gers an unsuspected hubris in Enkidu, for which he must pay with his
life. The killing of the Bull and the assault on Ishtar are sufficient reason
to prepare the way for Enkidu's death, Enkidu's vision of the Abode of
the Dead, and finally his actual death. This causes Gilgamesh to panic
and sets him on the road to discover the secret of immortality. The center of the epic has been reached. It now remains for the poet to create
incidents that describe Gilgamesh's journey to the abode of Utnapishtim
and his wife. Before Gilgamesh sets out on his quest, Enkidu's role in the
epic must end, but one thing remains. Just before Enkidu dies, Shamash
speaks to him from the divine realm and says that Gilgamesh, who has
honored him in life, "will make Uruk's people weep over thee (and)
lament, will fill [joyful] people with woe over thee" (VII, iii, 45–46
[Assyrian version]).

In treating the episode of Enkidu's death and Gilgamesh's thoroughgoing grief, the unknown poet of the epic deserves the highest critical
acclaim. The scene is handled delicately; it is the most beautiful moment

in the poem. A deep sense of pathos, of irony, and of tragedy flood in upon the reader. The heavenly decision to create Enkidu culminates in the heavenly decision to destroy him. Between these two acts we have seen Enkidu being drawn into the corrupt Gilgamesh's orbit and have seen in the development of his own hubris the cause of his own tragedy. This is also the cause of the beginning of Gilgamesh's tragedy. For Gilgamesh, the loss of his friend is a blow that shakes his very nature. And it has been his own unnecessary act, the decision to engage Huwawa, that results in the destruction of that which he holds most dear. The suffering lament of Gilgamesh in Tablet VII is proof enough of the impact of the loss on the king.

If it has taken catastrophe to shake the character of Gilgamesh, is there any indication that the loss of Enkidu may stand at the beginning of a process through which Gilgamesh gains a greater perspective of himself and the nature of humanity and its responsibilities?

The dimensions of the episode are total in terms of what has gone before; they encompass all the major elements of the poem. Here in Uruk, whence the action sprang, Heaven and the Underworld are brought into sharp focus through the ominous dreams of the dying Enkidu. The major characters—Gilgamesh, Enkidu, and the nobles— are juxtaposed; the grief of the king is now poignantly related to those same leaders whose prayer for relief from their arrogant ruler was the motivating cause of all that has happened. King, nobles, and dead companion give us the tableau of grief that has flooded into the human realm of Uruk. It is another kind of grief than that which characterized the city at the beginning of the poem. Gilgamesh not only realizes the starkness of death's actuality but also is given to understand the terrible power of heaven that can claim its own and relegate humankind to oblivion. Both Enkidu and Gilgamesh have journeyed far by the close of the first half of the epic. It is for Gilgamesh to continue to journey in search of discovery, and it is this journey that leads to his final awareness of the limitations of his humanity and of the finiteness of human purposes in general, that occupies the remainder of the epic.

Tablets IX through XI represent Gilgamesh's odyssey in the same way that Tablets I through VIII represent Enkidu's. Enkidu has roamed the steppe before coming to Uruk; Gilgamesh will now also roam the steppe like a child of nature before he too will return to Uruk, a defeated king. There is calculated invention here. Yet the poem will not hasten its thematic conclusions. Gilgamesh has been shaken, but the death of Enkidu does not in itself produce insight in him. Rather, he is overcome by personal loss and vows to overcome death for his own salvation. The full realization that he too is marked for eventual oblivion will come only after he subjects himself to the utmost hardships in metaphysical realms. This is in keeping with that impetuosity of his nature, which we have already seen in the first half of the epic. The death of Enkidu has only begun the process of Gilgamesh's true education. It has plunged him into remorse and shaken his self-confidence. But the fear that this blow has produced is not yet seen by him as a truly decisive and valid fear. He is yet to learn that the quest for immunity against death is not in the same order of things as the quest to the Cedar Mountain against Huwawa. In the one, divinity may assist, even ensure, the victory. In the other, no divinity, however autonomously acting, can violate the laws set down for finite man. It is the one-third element of mortal nature in Gilgamesh that will chain him to the unalterable "other" realm, from which the divine elements in him constantly strive to escape.

The "structural geography" of part 2 of the epic is as divorced from the real world as part 1 was anchored in it. The sequence of places in which the episodes of the last two tablets take place includes first the steppe and then the mountain of Mashu, at the limits of the world, whose gates are guarded by the mythological Scorpion-men. Through this mountain's trail, never before traveled by a mortal, Gilgamesh will journey for twelve leagues in total darkness before arriving at a garden of jewels. Beyond this garden he will encounter Siduri the barmaid, who dwells by the edge of the sea, and then Urshanabi, who will ferry him across the Water of Death to his climactic interview with Utnapishim.

Besides satisfying the requirements of the poem that the hero undergo superhuman adventures, the choice of locales in which the concluding episodes take place effectively enforces the theme of education in the epic. For each encounter with the Scorpion-man, with Siduri, with Shamash, with Urshanabi, and finally with Utnapishim and his wife emphasizes the inevitability of Gilgamesh's failure and incidentally stresses the right and proper sphere of human concern. At first deceived by his visitor's goldlike appearance, the Scorpion-man is curtly reminded by his own wife that Gilgamesh is partly mortal. His subsequent warning to Gilgamesh stresses the impossibility of the king's proposed journey, but he adds a hope that Gilgamesh will travel on in safety. The interview with Siduri, the divine barmaid, reinforces the motif of humankind's finiteness. Gilgamesh, she says, will not achieve eternal life. She adds to her prediction a standard of human behavior that seems to emphasize hedonism, yet this is not the implied standard of the epic, although it may be taken as such. The advice Siduri gives is typical of her calling; it is the barmaid's view of life.

The second major climax of the epic comprises most of the eleventh tablet, which contains the famous account of the Flood and its hero, Utnapishim. Not only does this encounter between Gilgamesh and Utnapishim allow an opportunity for the telling of a grand story, but the story itself is a keystone in the edifice of instruction within the epic. It is significant that the Flood story gives no single reason for the Deluge; its purpose is not to stress an explanation of why death exists but only to satisfy Gilgamesh about the unique instance in which one man and his wife were granted immortality. He will not be satisfied in any other way; for throughout all the poem Gilgamesh has disregarded the obvious: that "when the gods created mankind / Death for mankind they set aside / Life in their own hands retaining" (X, iii, 3–5, Old Babylonian version). Even his successes in getting to the abode of Utnapishim have ultimately deceived him. In two instances while there he deceives himself about his ability to remain awake during Utnapishim's test and, later on, about his ability to keep the Plant of Youth. The key thematic lines in the entire episode are those that contain Utnapishim's rhetorical questions and conclusive statements about death in X, vi, 26–39 (Assyrian version). Gilgamesh's failure at this point to realize the futility of his quest leads only to the necessity of actual demonstration and to his final defeat.

Gilgamesh's return to Uruk accompanied by the boatman Urshanabi is a final instance of the epic's use of irony. At the height of his self-confidence Gilgamesh had set out impetuously to battle Huwawa and had even taunted Enkidu with the faint charge of cowardice. Little did he regard the cautioning advice of the elders to be guided by Enkidu's experience. Now he returns to Uruk with another companion, still heroic but also quite chastened. This, I believe, is the spirit in which we are to understand the last lines of the epic—the statement of the great Gilgamesh brought to a new sense of understanding, however much it has cost him. At the beginning of the epic we, the audience, are invited to consider the marvel of Uruk—its city and its king. At the end the *we* has become Urshanabi, who can indeed consider Uruk, as now can Gilgamesh, from the perspective of what it means to be human.

In closing, then, I offer the view that the theme of the *Gilgamesh Epic* is not simply that which reads it as a foiled search for immortality. The epic also is a survey concerned with the theme of the "education of a king," a theme of such central concern in the perspectives of Mesopotamia that it surely helps to account for the continued popularity of the

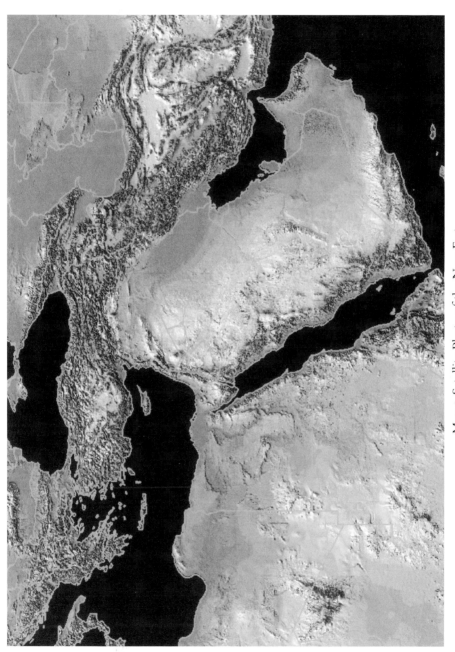

Map 1. Satellite Photo of the Near East

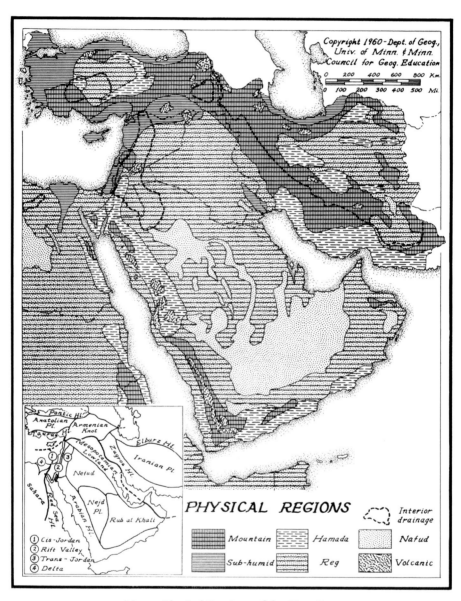

0   200   400   600   800 Km.

0   100   200   300   400   500 Mi.

Pontic Ht.
Anatolian
Pl.   Armenian
              Knot
Taurus Ht.   Elburz Ht.
        C.-J.   Mesopotamian
              Zagros Ht.   Lowland   Iranian Pl.
    ④ ① ③
        ②   Nefud
Sahara Ht.   Nejd
        Red Sea Ht.   Pl.
        Arabian Ht.   Rub al Khali

① Cis-Jordan
② Rift Valley
③ Trans-Jordan
④ Delta

PHYSICAL REGIONS

Interior drainage

Mountain	Hamada	Nafud
Sub-humid	Reg	Volcanic

Map 2. Physical Regions of the Near East

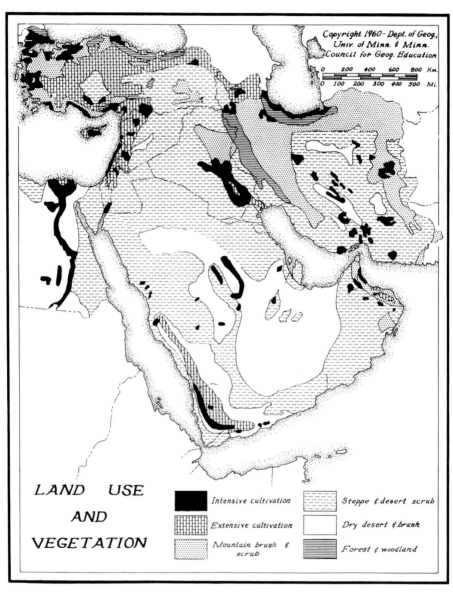

LAND USE AND VEGETATION

Intensive cultivation

Extensive cultivation

Mountain brush & scrub

Steppe & desert scrub

Dry desert & brush

Forest & woodland

Copyright 1960 - Dept. of Geog., Univ. of Minn. & Minn. Council for Geog. Education

0   200   400   600   800 Km.

0 100 200 300 400 500 Mi.

Map 3. Land Use and Vegetation of the Modern Near East

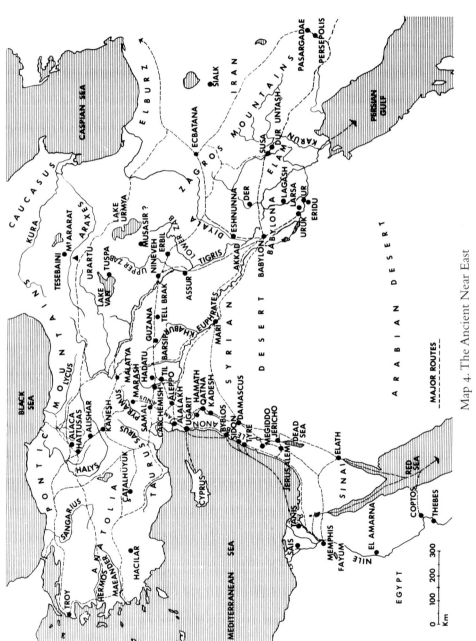

Map 4. The Ancient Near East

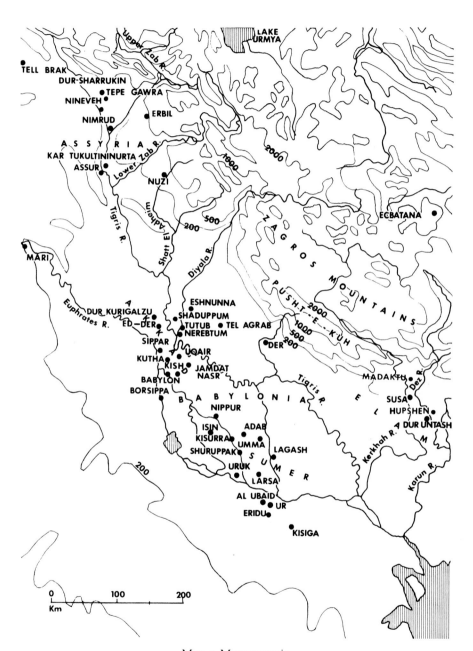

Map 5. Mesopotamia

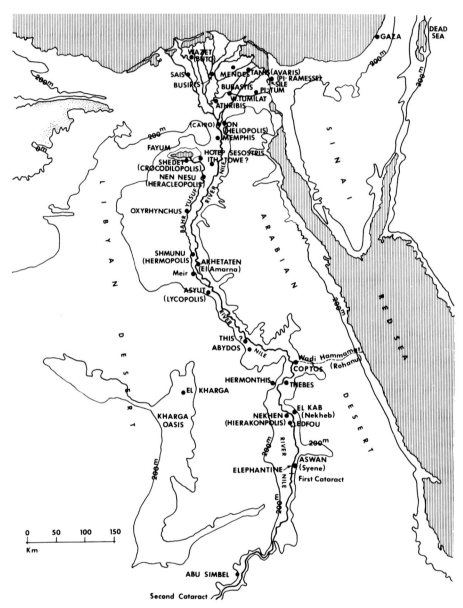

Map 6. Egypt

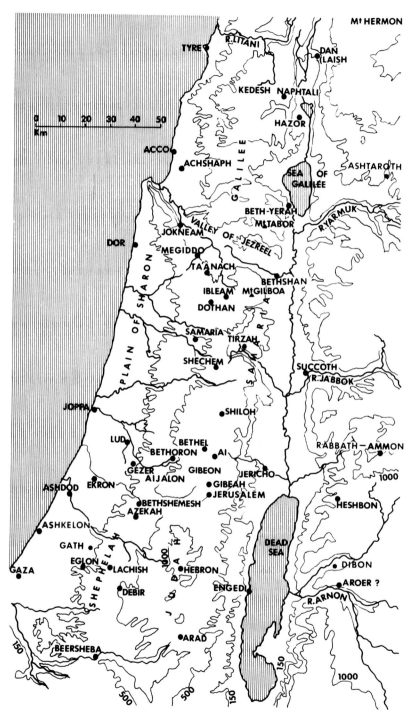

Map 7. Palestine

Fig. 1. Processional entryway to the Amun temple at Karnak, Egypt

Fig. 2. Temple of Bacchus at Baalbek, Lebanon (Roman period)

Fig. 3. Defile entryway (the Siq) to the rose-red city of Petra in Jordan, showing the Treasury (Nabataean–Roman period)

Fig. 4. Monumental Arch and colonnaded way at Palmyra, Syria (biblical Tadmor).

Fig. 5. Golden sarcophagus of Tutankhamun

Fig. 6. Mask of
Tutankhamun

Fig. 7. Tutankhamun's chariot

Fig. 8. Sphinx and pyramid, symbols of ancient Egypt, at Giza

Fig. 9. Tomb painting of an Egyptian noble and his wife hunting birds (Tomb of Menna at Thebes)

Fig. 10. Tomb painting of the god Osiris on his seat of judgment in the Egyptian underworld

Fig. 11. Tomb painting of workers on a noble's estate threshing grain

Fig. 12. Workers, all from the same village, excavating the site of al Fustat, Islamic Egypt's early capital

Fig. 13. Ancient Egyptian nilometer

Fig. 14. Typical setting of a contemporary Egyptian village along the Nile

Fig. 15. The Nile and its banks nestled against the desert

Fig. 16. Ancient Israelitic city mound of Beth Shan with Roman ruins in the foreground

Fig. 17. Example of a Palestinian "High Place" where Canaanites offered human sacrifices of children to their gods

Fig. 18. Phoenician temple site at Byblos, Lebanon, with Egyptian obelisks standing in its midst

Fig. 19. A nomadic encampment in southern Israel's Negev Desert

Fig. 20. Caves at Qumran, in Israel, where the Dead Sea Scrolls were discovered

Fig. 21. The settlement where members of the Qumran community lived and worked

Fig. 22. The Lion-Gate entry to the Hittite capital at Yazilikaya, Hattusas, near the present-day village of Bogazkoy in central Anatolia, Turkey

Fig. 23. The Hittite open-air religious gallery at Yazilikaya, Hattusas, in central Anatolia

Fig. 24. A line of twelve Hittite warrior gods in rock relief at Yazilikaya, Hattusas

Fig. 25. The Hittite king Tudhaliyas IV (thirteenth century) embraced by the god Sharruma in a rock relief at Yazilikaya

Fig. 26. Mount Ararat and cone in northeastern Turkey

Fig. 27. The Apadana (terrace platform) at Persepolis, the ancient capital of the Persian empire

Fig. 28. The Acropolis and the Parthenon, symbols of Athens's greatness in the mid-fifth century BC

Fig. 29. Part of the extant retaining wall of the Hebrew Second Temple, now popularly known as the Wailing Wall, the most sacred Jewish place of worship, in Jerusalem

Fig. 30. General view of the Ishtar Gate at Babylon

Fig. 31. A wall fresco of a prowling lion from Babylon

Fig. 32. Examples of cuneiform tablets, from the Kelsey Museum of Archaeology at the University of Michigan, Ann Arbor

Fig. 33. Irrigation ditches of the Euphrates

Gilgamesh story in all periods of Mesopotamian life. This, again, is not to say that other important and attractive elements are not equally present—the attractiveness of Gilgamesh as a half mythical hero; the exciting stories of his heroic adventures; the depth of friendship between himself and Enkidu. But if all these themes are present, they are nevertheless not present, as I have hoped to show, in isolation from each other, but rather they are carefully interwoven. Scholars will have much to do to complete our knowledge of the "facts" of the poem. But the epic nevertheless stands alongside the greatest epics of world literature because of a recognition of how its component parts stand together to carry through a great plot and great themes.

The *Gilgamesh Epic* and Tragic Vision

Tragedy emerges when humankind dares to exceed its limitations. Humankind's failure usually results from some misconception about the nature of human abilities or destiny and standardly involves errors of judgment, inability to bridle excessive emotions, and failure of will, on the one hand, or overcommitment of will, on the other. The result is dislocation, anguish, pain, and often death. As bystanders or observers, an audience of written drama or of one in real life becomes obsessed that something horrible will happen. Yet it does not flee but remains fixed in fascination, even as the participants in the events plunge on to defeat, however unknowingly. The tragic hero and his audience are indissolubly linked. It is as though, owing to the human condition, someone in life or in art will always dare to challenge the ordinary in an extraordinary way, while the rest of us, secure within our routine existences, respond from the depths of our being to what becomes an unequal struggle. The attraction of tragedy—and its greatest solace—is that a necessary failure will occur. In order to define ourselves to ourselves, to understand the nature of our mortality, we must (ironically) attempt to deny that very mortality. But through that denial we are allowed to reassess and reaffirm our common condition, though often with no better understanding of it.

The Greeks did not invent tragedy in human life, but only the first grand way of representing it. They perfected a type of drama in the fifth century that for the first time encapsulated before their citizen audiences a highly concentrated mixture of plot and internal (choral) commentary. These were garnered from traditional myth and epic actions that, as Aristotle observed, induced pity and terror in any audience. Audiences were able to grasp the essence of the tragic dilemma and make the effects, if not completely reconcilable with human aspirations, at least humanly acceptable. Tragic drama, organized by the Greeks as theater, became a mirror for all members of society within a defined civic context. It reflected no new, no impossible, solutions to the human dilemma. It did, however, present an imitation, a mimesis, of life, to be reacted to, repeated with variations, celebrated, and studied, in the life of one person, one family, one city.

What of tragic representation in earlier antiquity, especially in Mesopotamia? The usual opinion is that, where religious perspectives so pervasively dominate the institutions of a society as to smother individual initiative and personality, there is no room for recognition of individual tragedy. What is expected, what is required, is obedience. And where obedience reigns, the kinds of questioning likely to produce a genuine tragic vision are lacking. The peoples of Mesopotamia, like those of other areas of the ancient Near East, asserted the value of dependence upon unchanging tradition in which, as defined in myths of creation, an order of life was revealed. This order was to be followed faithfully for all time. The rebel against tradition by definition could be no hero. Rather, he was but a fool, one without knowledge.

Within the pervasive Mesopotamian religious system, the ceremonies of the ecclesiastical year, those inspired or necessitated by special occasions, as well as those routinely celebrated, affirm a momentary equilibrium between the concerns of the believers and those of the divinities that guide them. Alternatively, they urge the restoration of a previous harmony that may appear to have collapsed. Here, it is the entire community that functions as the collective actor in the imitation of life, the mimesis. The task in such a society is to celebrate success in accordance with the "Way" and to repent and petition for help and consideration where the "Way'" is assumed to have been violated. Religious ceremonies represent drama in Mesopotamian society; the many temples and shrines are the particular theaters. Onstage stand king and priest as chief characters—the one the embodiment of the society's symbolic understanding of itself; the other the effective instrument of divine communication and direction. In Mesopotamia genuine concern about the fortunes of a single human life, seen from a purely human and empathetic perspective, would appear to be lacking.

But no society, however pervasively religious, is without the potential for expressing its version of tragic vision. We cannot expect the Greek forms of tragedy to be the paradigm for tragic representation anywhere, however much it be that for us the word *tragedy* has become synonymous with the word *Greek*. In accommodating tragic vision—a universal—to the particular pageant of the play, the Greeks found an appropriate instrument for binding their past to their present and their future as a civic expectation. From the point of view of their perspectives of life and history, the Greeks succeeded in forging a specific cultural understanding of human limits and daring. The Mesopotamians, by contrast, created literary genres in which we can easily identify genuine human problems and emotions but also in which they failed to take the opportunity of close inner examination; the deepest anguish of the human soul is most often treated within a descriptive or lamentational style or, as often in the wisdom literature, within the context of cliché.

The notable exception appears in the Old Babylonian version of the *Gilgamesh Epic,* where for once, and if only for once, a Mesopotamian poet reached an epitome of statement about man, the natural creature, although dealing with a king. And in so doing he combined traditional elements of epic in such a way as to transcend the epic spirit itself and arrive at an authentic tragic vision. The *Gilgamesh Epic* did not give birth to a genre of tragedy in Mesopotamia; we cannot even know how the Mesopotamians reacted to the work. But we can celebrate the particular genius of one Old Babylonian poet who was a creative observer of his fellow man. Anchored essentially within the culturally bound limits of his theme, he was able, nonetheless, to touch the universal. He took two familiar Mesopotamian motifs—the search for fame through heroic adventure and meditation about the inevitability of death for humankind—and crafted into connected episodes a work that produces a completely unexpected insight. He introduced and treated in depth two profoundly human themes that inevitably contribute to tragic vision—the themes of companionate love and loss and of personal guilt and alienation.

FURTHER READING

Maier, John, ed. *Gilgamesh: A Reader.* Wauconda, IL: Bolchazy-Carducci Publishers, 1997.

Reflections on Ancient Near Eastern Myth

The dividing line between ancient and modern modes of thinking began to be drawn in the sixth century with the speculations of the Greek philosopher Thales. He sought to discover the simple substance that underlay the structure and functions of the universe. It does not matter that later Greek thinkers rejected his choice of water as that substance in favor of other substances, such as air or ether. What was crucial was that Thales introduced the idea of "proof through observation" of natural processes themselves rather than reliance on mythical expression for explanations of natural events. He well deserves his reputation as the founder of scientific method as the path to knowledge of the physical universe.

By contrast, the ancient world of the Near East saw the universe as "alive," populated by forces defined as gods who possessed domination over human beings, in a realm that was most often threatening and whose aim was control of human beings and their institutions. These forces had constantly to be propitiated. All activities of human life were touched by fear of impending disasters if proper rites and rituals were incorrectly performed or omitted. Even if rites were assiduously performed, the gods would still not always be placated. Houses (temples) were built as their earthly residences, and these were supplied by their own huge estates and maintained by large staffs of functionaries. Gods were actually believed to reside within their temples in the form of statutes, which had to be awakened in the morning; washed and fed; clothed; then, in ceremonies, carried around; and finally, at night, put to bed.

Who were these gods? What might have been the manner of their creation? It seemed logical to the ancients to suppose that phenomena in the universe capable of independent movement and will—all animals, birds, and fish—as well as invisible forces that controlled the weather, the movement of the stars, the renewal of harvest, and the like, were a decidedly special group of beings. The behavior and latent power of these beings were held to demand attention, respect, and obedience.

When early peoples tried to understand what the universe was and how it functioned, they brought into play the great propensity of the human mind for thinking in similes (comparisons) and metaphors. A simile simply equates two or more things: "this event is like that one"; "this range of objects is like that one"; "my love is like a red, red, rose," and so forth. An example from Mesopotamian modes of thought is the perception of the storm god, Adad. From the proposition that "the storm is like the power of a god," we can easily move to the stage of metaphor, where the comparison is transformed into an *identity*. Now "the storm *is* the power of a god," and finally, the storm god, conceived as a person, is, *himself,* the storm. Metaphorizing the mysterious processes of the universe personalized the universe and made it possible for humans to feel that a second set of living and active beings, far superior and infinitely more knowledgeable than they, controlled everything. These entities, usually but not always completely, were visualized in human form. They were thought to have organized their realms in the same way as did humans. Divine society thus could be imagined to have kings, assemblies, divisions of labor, and a wide variety of administrative functions. The gods were invested not only with human emotions and decision-making powers but also with a full range of human vices. Their adventures were modeled on human behavior.

The interaction of a divine realm with an earthly one allowed for ingenious interplay of a literary imagination. While the word *myth* is notoriously difficult to define to everyone's satisfaction, I would offer my own definition here: myths are perceptions set loose in the imagination that come to be identified as reality. At base, they are fantasies. They operate in every area of human endeavor and can concern single individuals or entire groups. My choice is to consider myth in its form as literary composition and leave to psychologists and psychiatrists the task of investigating its origins in the human psyche. What we have to consider are compositions whose characteristics involve either actions of the gods alone or interactions between gods and humans. Myths can take the form of single episodes, extended segments, or whole plots. They can also appear to generate varieties of stories about single or multiple characters. All these can be studied using methods of standard literary criticism. A cosmic myth, put another way, is a reading of the divine environment, a way of knowing something of significance about the universe, an abstraction that makes the environment intelligible and tradition meaningful. A kind of play. But it is not the reading, or the abstraction, of the scientist. Both myth and science produce "stories."

Both use symbols—the one in words, the other in numbers—that represent units of completed thought; for example, Hera is the wife of Zeus, and $2 + 2 = 4$; an adventure of a god, and $E = mc^2$.

But myth, being of the fabric of words, is also charged with connotation; its words and symbols contain overtones of meaning. In myth, images of life are captured. Yet these images may not in themselves be "logical." A living, pulsing universe is ever-changing. One mythic character can change into another. It can, if necessary, disappear in the twinkling of an eye. The drama of a mythic story is infused with magic.

Since myth and religion are traditionally linked, we need pause to consider their connection. In the ancient Near East basic human needs were tied to the existence of the powers, which could fulfill those needs. The primary concern, however, was the survival of the *group* rather than the individual. Contemporary critics of religion tend to stress religion as a force that subjugates human potential. Marxists see it as the "opiate of the masses"; Freudians see it as supplying the "father figure" authority. Rationalists conclude that religion keeps people from living life on its own terms, while others stress that in religious belief the individual intellect is subordinated to superstition. Lost in this mélange of modern criticism is the perception that before the emergence of the individual as a central concern of religion, as understood in the Judeo-Christian tradition, the ordinary person counted for little. The *social group as a whole* was the central object of concern.

The means by which the gods were approached were through recitations of many sorts—prayers, hymns, and incantations—and with appropriate ceremonies, which were normally accompanied by rituals. The question of the necessary recitation of myths along with rituals is open. Rituals, being traditional behaviors designed to influence the deities, were attached to all manner of procedures, even those beyond the purview of the religious establishment. While there were great religious ceremonies, such as the eleven-day celebration of the New Year in Babylon, many dealt with the most mundane matters, such as the cure of a toothache.

Our word *myth* comes to us from the Greek *mythos,* which the ancient Greeks used in two different ways: the first as indicating "anything delivered by word of mouth" (such as a speech in a public assembly), conversation, counsel, the subject of a speech, a design or plan, or a saying; the second as indicating a tale, story, legend, or fable, as opposed to a historic tale. Our modern use of the term derives from the second range of meanings, which even goes so far as to characterize myths as "lies" as opposed to propositions based on logical reasoning.

The attempts to define myth as a characteristic of human thought have been so fascinating a challenge that whole schools of modern interpretation—from the historical and anthropological to the psychological—have grown up as a matter of course. My approach, while eclectic, leans heavily on the literary and agrees with the definition offered in the *Princeton Encyclopedia of Poetry and Poetics* as "a story or complex of story elements taken as expressing, and therefore as implicitly symbolizing certain deep-lying aspects of human and transhuman experience." To this definition I add my own understanding of myth as "a story in the form of a plot accepted or selected for particular public or personal reasons, and given credence as reality." The story can be complete in itself; it can also appear as a scene in a larger narrative or as a scene fragment. It can even be elaborated with variations.[1] Myth, historically in religious societies, is routinely and often intimately tied to ritual but not exclusively so.[2] In our own times, psychological analysis has taught us also that each individual can be his or her own mythmaker.

It would be mostly presumptuous to attempt anything like a typology of ancient Near Eastern myths, were it even possible in space or time to do so in a book of this type and in the face of already published works by outstanding specialists in the relevant fields. What I can propose to do is discuss myth in its apparent nature, as I perceive it after a career of some forty years, and hope to stimulate some needed discussion of its essence and functions in the societies we study.

To begin with, *myth,* as it applies to societies as a whole, can be discussed as having some obvious functions. Most important of these is its function as establishing the basis of central authority for a society. It is a belief, or set of beliefs, that takes the form of a narration (in early societies) about how things in the universe were fixed into their final form—how the organization of the universe came about, who runs it, and what is the relation of human society to this cosmic order. In other places in this book I have spoken of this "authority" myth as the "constitutional" basis of the society in question. It establishes the "right," and usually eternally valid, basis for the development of life in general and specifically the validity of the society's government. We are used to labeling such accounts as "creation stories" or "myths." I prefer to see them as "political documents," not necessarily or primarily as the *only* certified versions in the society of how it believes cosmic events occurred.

A corollary role of myth is in its function as validation. Myths validate the positions of ranking authorities, as well as the establishment of all sorts of institutions and even changes in those institutions. Further, myths can be used as measures of personal behavior, as most vividly can be seen in, for example, Homer's *Iliad*. New behaviors in society can also be established by myth, as can the eradication or nonvalidity of older, now nonfunctional, ones. The educational function of myth is also notable, in that instruction for kings and priests, to mention but two instances, becomes viable and traditional. What is also true is that myths that are outdated and nonfunctional can continue to be revered in a society, so the task of the investigator of any historical period is to try to distinguish, if possible, the living myths from those that are no longer functional. Beyond this also lies the problem of studying any society, of analyzing behavior that is not formally displayed in literature or art yet is a true reflection of what is genuinely believed in the society in question.

We have merely touched on the many functions of myth in a society, but often we forget that a major use of myth in an ancient society, beyond its use in religious and political texts, was its value as entertainment. Our serious purposes as professional scholars or intelligent readers so often miss the fact that myth was part and parcel of an ancient society's literature and art. It served the literate as such. But it also served the vast numbers of nonliterates as popular theater. Surely the activities of the gods as embedded in official myths were recited by readers to crowds outside the temples or sung about by the musician singers who populated the households that functioned in temples and palaces of Mesopotamia and Egypt. Certainly such compositions contained adventures of individual gods; romantic alliances, as between Ishtar and Tammuz in Mesopotamia, where, in cycles devoted to them, they appear as husband and wife; courting lovers; and enraged or frightened personages. Victories of kings and warriors were also sources for oral and musical presentation for the masses of people celebrating sacred or other festival days or simply gathering for an evening at a party, tavern, or public square.

It is useful, as we continue on this fascinating subject, to speculate on the origins of written myth as a literary form. Certainly in the oral phase of an early society, individuals, such as priests, would have composed and recited tales about the gods. Oral presentation was subject to continual variation, all, in a religious context, within the familiarity of orthodox themes. Once writing was invented and used, earlier and freer forms of expression about happenings in the divine world became fixed and orthodoxy became standard, such that the formal recitations of central myths at religious ceremonies in their fixed forms may have differed (though perhaps not substantially) from the versions known in the street by illiterate people, who made up the vast majority of a society's population.

Conscious myth creation is subject to the same rules as those that govern any type of literary creation, myths being works of the human imagination. As with the works of single, private authors, a body of work may grow around early themes and change as needed in the maturation of the author or of the outlook of a society. Especially is this true in the development of characterization, if not of central ideas. Thus, in the case of a society's cast of religious characters, stories about them and their roles in the entire panoply of religious ideas can subtly change from region to region within a society's territorial boundaries.

It is important, as we continue to think about myth, not to confuse ancient Near Eastern myth with Greek myth, for what we generally know about myth at all begins with our reading of the latter in school. If, in their earliest stages, the stories of the Olympian gods were once reflective of a thoroughgoing religious reality among the Greek tribes, by the time of the fifth century, when Athenian democracy was born, earlier religious themes were transformed into secular drama in the tragedies of Aeschylus, Sophocles, and Euripides. Greek religion, though still reflective of age-old religion and certainly practiced or signified by ancient ritual at games and festivals, was no longer the dominant perspective of the Hellenes, though it certainly was still valued for its traditional meanings and appeal. But the new gathering of force was rationalism, and religion became a repository for stage effects and audience exhilaration. Greek religion had been captured, so to speak, by secular interests.

Fascinatingly, the Greek religious tradition became the backdrop, or screen, against which familiar epic heroes and heroines could be seen in action, and audiences could both be transfixed by the fate of these characters and wonder at the relevance of the myths used in dramatic productions to their own lives. Here myth bordered on the psychological, whereas in ancient nonbiblical societies of the Near East there was hardly any possibility of knowing how the individual related to the gods except that it was purely in the hands of the gods to deal out good or bad results according to their own, always hidden, designs.

Today, it is impossible to deal with myth without referring to psychologists' understanding of it. Generally they stress that those who believe in it enhance their self-regard and that myth allows individuals to express a variety of needs, especially those deeply rooted in societal tensions. Individuals become able to elaborate their internal images of thoughts, mental pictures, and daydreams, things they may not have fully grasped or tensions they may not have resolved, through stories and symbols, by means of which they gain confidence and security. Put another way, myths are symbols by which members of a society adjust to their environment. The nature and effectiveness of that adjustment, of course, vary from one society to another. The confidence about life and death displayed by the Egyptians in their inscriptions varies greatly from the uncertainties about the fate of humankind that characterized Mesopotamian beliefs throughout its history.

FURTHER READING

Frankfort, Henry, H. A. Frankfort, John A. Wilson, and Thorkild Jacobsen, eds. *The Intellectual Adventure of Ancient Man*. Chicago: University of Chicago Press, 1946.

Kirk, G. S. *Myth: Its Meaning and Functions in Ancient and Other Cultures*. Berkeley: University of California Press, 1970.

Kramer, Samuel Noah, ed. *Mythologies of the Ancient World*. Garden City, NY: Doubleday, Anchor Books, 1961.

Wisdom Literature

Among the major genres of ancient Near Eastern literature, "wisdom literature" allows us insight into what was considered to be a good life. Whether in Egypt, in Mesopotamia, or within the Hebraic biblical tradition, there existed a remarkable similarity of experience and outlook that can be observed. A special case, to be discussed subsequently, is biblical wisdom, where information for our theme is more fully available.

In its broad outlines, wisdom literature is characterized by advice to the recipient in the form of instructions issued by a sage or a high official, including kings, on how one should live in order to experience tranquility and profit. These instructions come not from the type of philosophical formulations that the classical Greeks might have offered but rather from life experience in which the official or the ordinary person has participated or should otherwise be aware of. The aim is to guide a person, especially a young man, through his youth, maturity, and old age, so that he will be well regarded and can also be considered as fit for attractive positions that a king or other high official might wish to fill. The authors of such texts might actually be renowned sages, or, if the advice is anonymous, the name of a traditional sage might be attached to the text. The content of such texts stresses pragmatic means to achieve personal, social, economic, and political ends.

Meditations on the meaning of life are reserved for a different type of exposition. This variety of the genre raises the question of the overall understanding of life, the answers to which are usually given in a pessimistic mode. Here, heavy emphasis is placed on the actions of the gods relative to the existence of mankind; such texts stress the inability of mankind to perceive and understand divine intentions relating to them. Usually this type of composition counsels obedience to divine wishes as established in traditional religious practices.

Egypt

We may begin with some excellent examples of Egyptian instructions. These surviving copies as collected, for example, in *ANET* (1969), represent but a small part of what must have been a favorite genre in Egyptian scribal schools. Wisdom themes were already being composed as early as the Old Kingdom (about 2500) and were persistently produced throughout Egypt's long history. For convenient reference in the text cited previously, we have instructions of, or to, three royal personages, one from a vizier, one from a father to his son, and one from an agricultural official named Amen-Em-Opet, some precepts of which bear a close relationship to material in the biblical book of Proverbs. All of these may serve as touchstones for further examples of the genres that were produced in neighboring societies of the ancient Near East.

Two main types of instructions will be discussed here: the first, instructions on how to treat elders, rules for courtiers, and those engaged in official business: the second, instructions in which a king or high official gives cautionary advice to a son and successor.

The "Instruction of the Vizier Ptah-hotep" sets out as an essay on public behavior and proper bearing in the performance of administrative duties. These include the ability to speak modestly and deferentially in performance of one's duties and to treat both the wise and the ignorant equally. As a leader, one must be just, for the strength of justice is lasting. If one is included within the hospitality of a more powerful man he should be yielding and humbly polite, and so he will be favored. Take people for what they are, not what they once might have been. A good son is correct and follows his father's way, but cast off the son who does not follow his father's wishes. Stay away from the lures of wanton women; instead found a household with a loving attitude toward your wife, which is a guarantee of a long marriage. Also, if you have attained importance, don't be miserly. Also be temperate in the treatment of your friends. The reward for obedience and moderation is a long and honorable life.

A more specific type of instruction advises how to maintain oneself in power as king. It is the "Instruction for Meri-ka-Re" and is attributed to his unknown royal father. Its background is an age of disintegration between the end of the Old Kingdom and the reestablishment of order with the rise of the Middle Kingdom. A short opening of twenty lines, which may have dealt with a prior rebellion in the kingdom, is broken. Immediately following is advice on how to deal with contentious rivals and with dangerous followers: kill them! Again, as in Ptah-hotep's advice cited previously, be a master of speech. Here, however, mastery implies strength and can forestall attacks. The king should be patient but should set up defenses on the boundaries and frontiers of the land. One should promote great men, for "great is a great man when his great men are great." There are further cautions against improper conduct in the administration of justice and against slaughter, which is of no advantage to the king. Additionally heed advice about what to do specifically regarding a rival southern kingdom, which should not be treated with evil intent. Meri-ka-Re's father has had to deal with enemies to the north and south, and the son is counseled to build fortresses in the north. The old king had earlier committed some errors of judgment in a difficult period of his reign, which led to warning his successor against repeating them.

The two examples of instructions just discussed stress matters concerned with specific levels of society, here the ruling classes and the king himself. The long tradition of instruction writing from Egypt was the concern of scribes who wrote on behalf of these classes. Their interests were to provide a set of rules for persons who naturally were going to attain important administrative positions in the society or who already occupied these. While it was true that the rich and privileged, indeed also the talented, were admonished to deal fairly with the poor and the untalented, we do not have in this literary environment a wide interest in speaking to, or about, "everyman." This eventually does develop, but toward the end, not at the beginning, of the enterprise.

Mesopotamia

The wisdom tradition of Mesopotamia is deeply embedded in Sumerian origins and continues into later Babylonian and Assyrian literary practice. The eminent Sumerologist Samuel Noah Kramer, in his short article "Sumerian Literature: A General Survey,"[1] alludes to two compositions of the wisdom type, the first known as "The Farmer's Almanac," which contains instructions of a farmer to his son, and the second known as "The Instructions of King Shuruppak to his son, Ziusudra," a compendium of advice to a royal heir. Kramer also refers to Sumerian proverbs in the hundreds, which include maxims, sayings, and short Aesop-like fables contained in ten to twelve scribal collections and which were used as textbooks in schools both in ancient Nippur and Ur.

Two texts especially worth mentioning in connection with Assyro-

Babylonian wisdom compositions are the "Dialogue of Pessimism," in Babylonian and Assyrian copies, and "A Dialogue about Human Misery." In the former, a master and his slave banter back and forth about such activities as dining, hunting, having a family, loving, and sacrificing, the style of the composition being first the master's desire to engage in the activity, followed by the slave's willing agreement, and then a sudden reversal of the decision by the master, also with the slave's willing agreement. After all the wavering indecision and negativism of the preceding dialogue, we arrive at the key question: "What then is good?" The master's answer is to have his own neck and the slave's neck broken and for both to be thrown into the river to drown. But the master says he would kill the slave first, to which the slave cunningly replies that the master would then not outlive him by even three days. The "Dialogue about Human Misery" presents a debate between a man reporting on his own wretched state and what he considers to be the social and religious platitudes of the society at large. His friend-adversary insists that the downtrodden complainer has failed in his religious duties, offering comment to the effect that his companion has failed to consult the god and that, if he does, his food supply will be constant and his losses will be recovered immediately. There is no deep examination of issues in this text but merely assertion that the mind of the god is remote and men cannot understand it. But above all, religious duty is still the answer where bad luck and undeserved hardships may afflict the sufferer.

Israel

The ancient Hebrew term for "wisdom" is *Hokhma,* which alludes to behavior that will aid mankind to achieve both a satisfactory and a profitable life. Its maxims, as earlier expressed, are drawn from actual human experience and tradition, and its aims are solutions to human problems through the exercise of behavior that is appropriate to a situation. The sages who taught such behaviors were not only schoolteachers and court counselors but also scribes working in the highest echelons of public service. As a group these sages represented the literate elite of ancient Israel. Perhaps originally they aimed their teaching at the upper classes, but eventually their counsel filtered down to the population at large.

A roster of books in the biblical tradition expressing wisdom themes are the Old Testament books of Proverbs and Job and fourteen psalms in the book of Psalms and the Apocrypha books of Ecclesiastes, 1 Esdras, Tobit, Baruch, and the Wisdom of Solomon. Also included are the Letter of Aristeas, Pirke Aboth ("The Sayings of the Fathers"), the Christian "Letter of James," and the Didache.

In the Hebraic tradition what was emphasized was respect for age and authority and a useful strategy of life. Ultimately in Israel the search for wisdom was linked to religious insights. It was Yahweh, Israel's god, who was acknowledged to be its originator and author; "wisdom" did not emerge from the experiential and rational instincts of mankind.

Israel was a latercomer to the written traditions of the ancient Near East. As a collection of tribes whose homeland was the Palestinian corridor up the borders of Mesopotamia, it had as yet no scribal schools such as existed in Egypt, Canaan, or Babylonia until it conquered Palestinian territory and established a sedentary kingdom under David and Solomon. Certainly possessed of an oral literary tradition long before this, the Hebrews now absorbed the written traditions of their neighbors, including wisdom texts. The oldest indication of Hebrew wisdom is embodied in the Book of Proverbs, in which there is clear evidence that the scribal author knew of the Egyptian "Instruction of Amen-Em-Opet" (see Prv 22–24).

In addition to verbal indications, there are several significant borrowings of images connected with wisdom taken from Egyptian materials as well—the biblical image, for example, of a royal personage as author (Solomon). In the Bible, wisdom can be personified as a prophetess (Prv 1:20–33, 8:1–36) but also as a hostess (Prv 9:1–6), as opposed to a foolish woman (Prv 9:13–18). Of special interest in this connection is the image of an ancient Egyptian sage, Imhotep, at the court of the pharaoh Djoser (Third Dynasty), who was venerated as a god after his death. In the Bible the designation of a secular sage as the creator of wisdom could not be made because the Hebrews believed that their god, Yahweh, was the sole author of all wisdom. Wisdom could be presented as a heavenly image, created by God, who stood at the side of God. Such a notion appears in Proverbs 8:22–31, where wisdom is said to have been created by the Lord "at the beginning of his work," just as much earlier in Egypt, *ma'at,* the essence of Justice, also came into existence at the creation of the universe. This idea finds expression in the abstract image of Sophia, as theoretical "wisdom," in the thought of classical Greece.

To close this brief summary, it is further important to note that, in Israel, wisdom did not remain limited to a class ethic. It came to instruct all who sought a curriculum for a safe and honorable life. It was intimately linked to religious perspectives in that it affirmed that the ultimate authority for a good life emanated from a knowledge of the divine will as was traditionally codified in ecclesiastical law.

Translating an Old Babylonian Poem

"Prayer to the Gods of Night"

Readers of all ages are perennially interested in how one works to translate texts written on hardened clay surfaces of ancient tablets to the written pages of modern publications. The short answer notes a three-stage process. First, the text must be meticulously copied so as to duplicate not only the signs but every other feature that is visible on the surface, or surfaces, of the tablet, such as linear divisions, unexpected spacings, ways in which the ancient scribe divided his writing surface, and the style of "handwriting" that is evident. The document must be measured carefully and indexed. And the breakages on the tablet that may exist must be carefully drawn in on the modern copy. One may ask, "Why not just photograph the tablet?" Some tablets are able to be photographed successfully, but most are not because of their crowded epigraphy and the fact that individual signs have not simply been scratched on the surface but indented into originally soft clay. What is left after the document has been baked in the sun, or fired, in antiquity is a stonelike object covered with three-dimensional signs, any one of which could represent either a syllable of a word, a whole word, or some other linguistic indicator. Only careful copying by hand can reproduce what the trained eye sees.

The second phase of the process, after transcription, is called transliteration. This simply means copying down, in their proper order, the sounds of individual syllables or the meaning of whole-word signs and other scribal indications as we know them.

The third phase is translation into our modern languages, which, of course, is based on dictionaries and grammars of the language developed since the original decipherment of the language at issue. My interest is to provide a *prayer poem,* not simply a clerical document. The reader who is not acquainted with problems inherent in translation will greatly benefit from the stimulating essays in Reuben A. Brower, ed., *On Trans-*

lation (Cambridge, MA: Harvard University Press, 1959; Harvard Studies in Comparative Literature no. 23).

The Translation

1. Since translation is never mere mechanical transfer of words (hence, ideas) from one language to another, we shall have to give over the metaphor, so dear to us, of translation as a "bridge." A bridge implies passage, haulage, as if foreign poems, their words and ideas, were discrete objects piled up on the opposite shore, waiting to be carted across deadweight and tabulated and stored on this one. Or as if, say, one or two or three Babylonian, Greek, Provencal, or Danish words *equaled* one or two or three English words, as though x in the equation equals $2y$ or $3z$. For a fact, we should not be bound too closely by mathematical method in translating. Rather, we are after transformations, living compounds, approximate equivalences in perception of idea and mood (for that is all we can hope for). Ultimately it is magic, not mathematics.

2. The English language ought not to be treated, again, as if it were a Babylonian, Greek, Provencal, or Danish *dialect*. It is itself, has its own constructions and idioms, and ought to be respected according to its own nature. Bad English will not render even ordinary Babylonian, except to render it asunder.

Our poem, a prayer, is written in cuneiform; its place of origin is unknown, but its style of writing identifies and dates it as Old Babylonian, composed therefore at the latest about 1600 but probably earlier. The clay tablet on which it appears contains forty-two lines covering front and back, but only the first twenty-four lines comprise the text with which we shall work. The remaining eighteen lines consist of two shorter prayers of the same type, addressed to the "Gods of Night," but they are too fragmentary for translation or use except here or there for purposes of comparison.

In addition to these two smaller variants we have one other prayer of the same genre and period, also of twenty-four lines. This text (which shall be referred to as *Variant* in the following discussion) is almost identical with our poem and can help us restore readings where our text is broken off or obliterated. In a few instances interpretations and emendations based upon this *Variant* are preferable, and in each case I will indicate why. Since the poem we are to translate is not a "private" creation, in the sense that a Babylonian Blake or Donne, *writing as an individual,* composed it, but rather a public prayer form composed under the auspices of temple ritual and established as liturgy through long tradition, we are justified in using variant readings to construct the "model" poem, the representative of the type.

For the Assyriologist or the student of cuneiform writing wishing to consult the transcription, the transliteration, or the (French) translation of this text (AO 6769), see G. Dossin, *Revue d'Assyriologie et d'archéologie orientale XXXII* (1935), 179–87 (text and commentary).

A Very Literal Rendering into English

1   They are lying down, the Grand Ones, the locks
     the bolts are placed
     The crowds the people are still
     open are closed gates (city-gates)
5   The Gods of the Land the Goddesses of the Land
     Adad and Ea Shamash and Ishtar
     have entered the (room? recess?) of Heaven
     not they judge judgment
     not they decide words
10   veiled Night
     palace sanctuary(s) very still
     the one who goes on the road implores Nergal
     and the one connected with the law (courts) is full of sleep
     The judge of truth the father of truth
15   Shamash has entered his (room? chamber?)
     Shining Gibil heroic Irra
     Elamite bow
     Pleiades Orion Dragon
     Chariot Bison
20   Gods of grandest night
     Stand by me
     In the ceremony I make
     the prayer I pray
     truth confirm (for me)

What is the sense of this? In line 1 we learn that the Grand Ones or the gods are in repose for some reason or other. At the end of line 1 the scene shifts quickly from heaven to earth, where the "locks and bolts" are now set, the people have quieted down, and the gates are shut. So that in lines 1–4 we are introduced to the notion that the cessation of heavenly activity is paralleled by a corresponding cessation of earthly activity. The people rest just as the gods rest; their houses and businesses are locked up. The "gates" of line 4 can also mean "city-gates," and I prefer this interpretation of the word because we are to see the entire city at rest. This is supported, on the one hand, by what we know about the Babylonian city—a hustling, bustling place by day, shut up and guarded by night, very much like the medieval city—and, on the other hand, by what we know of the relationship between the land and its gods. Land and city depend upon gods for guidance and protection and so represent a kind of "model" community that the gods rule through a prince and his priests and city rulers. When the gods turn from the affairs of governing to rest, the land and its cities also rest. But we are getting ahead of the poem.

Lines 5 through 9 return us to the image of the first line, but this time details are given. The divinities (both male and female) of the land— Adad, god of the storm; Ea, god of water; Shamash, the sun god; and Ishtar, the "Temptress"—have entered the inner room of heaven, having finished their tasks of judging and deciding celestial and terrestrial affairs. So we are to understand that the heavenly court is adjourned, for night (line 10) has come. The *Variant* shows that the same divine names were not always used in this type of prayer, for it substitutes Sin, the moon god, for Ea. Yet all these gods are principal gods in the Babylonian pantheon, and where there are variations in the use of the names, local religious custom has probably dictated the change.

The setting of lines 11 through 13 returns us once more to earth. The reference here to the total stillness of the palace and (its) sanctuary confirms our interpretation of lines 1 through 5, for these buildings represent the administrative centers of earthly power—political and religious—delegated to men by the gods, and the coming of night finds prince and priest, like gods above, at rest. Silence, gloom—this is the mood communicated by the poem so far. Specific instances of earthly rest are used in lines 12 and 13. In line 12, someone outside the city, in the vast wasteland that stretches between the points of human habitation, stops his caravan and calls upon his god for protection. The original says only "one who goes upon the road," but we should not translate this line as "traveler" because of the connotation of the English word: "traveler for any reason, pleasure or business." Traveling in the ancient Near East was undertaken mainly by business men, in caravans, or by soldiers. "Caravaner" is more to the point of the context.

Line 13 presents a contrasting image, a city man, now resting. The phrase in this line reads simply, "the one connected with the law (courts)." It could be anyone—judge, plaintiff, defendant, clerk. "Litigant" is probably closest, since a man involved in a pending case would be more than usually agitated; but even he, according to our line, is now completely at rest. A possible interpretation of these two lines would be that the caravaner of line 12 will, upon his arrival the next day in the city, be hailed into court by the person referred to in line 13, for this frequently happened as a circumstance of ancient Near Eastern business practices; but this interpretation is not necessary to the meaning of the poem.

Lines 14 and 15 return once more to heavenly activity. The sun god has retired into his chamber. This is not the unnecessary repetition it might appear to be, especially considering line 10, where night has been already said to have come on. The attributes of the sun god here deserve our attention. He is the father of truth, as well as the judge of it. (The *Variant* has "Judge of Truth, Father of the Orphan," an allusion to the time-honored obligation of Near Eastern gods and princes to protect the widow and the orphan.) In the reference to the sun god the main images of the poem blend. The sun qua physical object sets, the sun qua sun god retires with the other gods, and the sun qua author and judge of truth abandons his function in the face of night. This is the logical and poetic climax of the first fifteen lines.

With lines 16–19 of the poem, the prayer proper begins. Since the gods are adjourned, since night has come, since protection and guidance are needed by night as well as day, one prays to the star and constellation gods, here to be understood as representatives of the gods mentioned in line 6. Gibil, in line 16, is the god of fire; Irra, in the same line, is the god of the underworld. The meaning of Elamite bow is unclear. In line 18 the constellations have been identified as Pleiades and Orion, but the dragon, the mythical serpent of Babylonians, has not been identified with a star or constellation known to us. Line 19 contains the most enigmatic references, so we shall accept the traditional readings of "Chariot" and "Bison."

The direct address to the "Gods of grandest night" begins in line 20. The *Variant* positions this line earlier than it appears in our version, placing it before the catalog of constellations. For structural reasons this positioning seems preferable, and so we will adopt it in our translation.

It remains to consider the last four lines, 21–24. A worshiper prays. But he very often accompanies his prayer with the sacrifice of a sheep.

Our text does not make this clear, but the *Variant* at line 23 reads: "through this lamb which I offer up." This is the necessary meaning of the lines in our version for it explains the rest of the poem and especially the difficulty of line 24. A word is proper at this point about divination among the Babylonians. Omens were usually read from sheep livers. A worshiper petitions a god. An exorcist kills a sheep and examines its liver; and from the condition of the liver the exorcist interprets the will of the god. This is precisely the circumstance of our prayer. Our worshiper implores the Gods of Night, they who have taken over the function of judging and guiding until the day breaks once more, to make known their will regarding him by sending a favorable omen into the liver of his sacrificial lamb. Thus line 24—"truth confirm (for me)"—is explained and its references to lines 14 and 15 understood.

To briefly recapitulate the sense of the poem, night has come, and the gods' activities in governing the cosmos have ceased. The city itself is dark and still. And the worshiper-sacrificer now calls upon the Gods of Night for protection and guidance until the new dawn breaks.

It will be helpful at this point to present a first-draft version of the poem using the interpretations already discussed. I have not so far said anything about rhythm or meter, and I fear little can be said, for scholarship on the nature of Babylonian poetry is woefully inadequate. There appear, however, to be two main principles at work; first, a more or less consistent use of a four-beat line, each half of the line getting two beats; and second, an equally characteristic use of parallelism—paired or contrasted ideas and images, for example, lines 5, 6 and 7; 12 and 13; 14; 22 and 23. We should try to capture as much of the Semitic tone as possible in our translation.

Certain matters of structure and meaning need discussion here before we write the first draft. The *Variant* contains the thought "the locks are locked, the bolts are set" in a single line (line 2), while our version divides the thought between lines 1 and 2. The *Variant* version is preferable for clearness of the parallel between "locks" and "bolts"; no injury to sense results from adopting it. The *Variant* also preserves in a single line the pair "they judge not, they decide not," while our version splits them (lines 8 and 9). In line 12 of our version we should possibly replace "the caravaner implores Nergal" with the *Variant* version, "the caravaner calls out to *his God*," on the theory that the appearance of the name Nergal (god of the underworld) may reflect a local religious usage, while "his God" captures the general sense of prayer to any god. We have already decided to shift line 20 of our version to a position just before the catalog of constellations, for it fits more naturally there than farther down in the poem. And, finally, we should substitute the *Variant's* line 23 for that of our version, since it gives us the important image of the sacrificial lamb.

First Draft Version

1   The Great Ones sleep.
    Locked are the locks, the bolts are set,
    The crowds are still, the people, still,
    The city-gates are shut.
5   The Gods of the land, Goddesses of the land,
    Adad and Ea, Shamash and Ishtar,
    Have gone into the room (?) of Heaven.
    They do not judge, do not decide.
    Veiled is the Night.
10 Palace and shrine are very still.
    The caravaner calls out to his God;
    The litigant lies overcome with sleep;
    The Judge of Truth, the Father of Truth,
    Shamash has gone into his room (?).
15 O Gods of Grandest Night,
    Flaming Gibil, Valiant Irra,
    Elamite Bow,
    Pleiades, Orion, Dragon,
    Chariot, Bison
20 Stand by me, and
    through this ceremony I make,
    through this lamb I offer up,
    Grant favor unto me.

This will do for a start, but it is far from being a poem. We must decide what bothers us about it, for there are difficulties that must be resolved. We should also try to decide now what we are willing or not willing to do in the name of translation, by weighing the consequences of proposed alterations. On the one hand we do not want to be unduly bound by the demands of literalness for the reasons given at the beginning of this analysis. On the other hand we must not "mishandle" the original to suit any fancy that may strike us. We may put the question this way: What *must* be kept inviolate if the sense and mood of the original are to come through in translation? After we decide this, we are free to make alterations where they are needed to convey our perception of the original.

The main problem of this translation is whether it can accept the Babylonian structure as it stands, for certainly the awkwardness of the Semitic thought progression as it appears in English is noticeable. We are dealing with dichotomous construction in which the image scenes shift all too rapidly from heaven to earth and back again, although there is a progressive order in their presentation. A Babylonian's thought could range easily, intuitively, between gods and men, connecting and identifying divine affairs and human affairs. The transitions are unspoken, unwritten. They are *felt* primarily. Alas, *we* cannot feel them instinctively at all, but our translation must nevertheless accomplish these transitions as naturally as possible. We should not depend upon our usual English conjunctions: *but, while, so that, because,* and the like. These smack too much of logical prose transitions, and we should avoid the temptation to "fix up" the awkward shifts by using them. We can handle the problem another way and still remain faithful to the tone of the original, and that is by arranging the translation on the page so that we may perceive *visually* where the transitions come and thus intuit the sequence of thought without further ado, so that a reasonable use of position and punctuation will obviate the alternative of adding unwanted words.

This decided, we can now turn to the problems of word choice and rhythmic consistency. Several words need special treatment. In line 1 of our poem the synonym used for "gods" is, roughly, "Great Ones." But "Great" will not do in translation. It is a weak term for us at best, capable of describing cabbages as well as kings. We need something special, grandiose, powerful, to capture the idea of how the Babylonian *thought* of his gods. "Immortal Ones" might serve here to incorporate the total conception.

In line 7, the nature of the place to which the gods retire within the Babylonian "Heaven" is far from clear. A "room" or "quarter" seems indicated. Since the term is unclear, we should not settle upon anything precise, and so possibly "deep" of heaven should be used.

"Caravaner" of line 11 and "litigant" of line 12 have already been discussed.

In line 15 we should capture the physical nature of Shamash, the sun god, by changing the verb "entered" to "sunk." Again, as with the other gods, the nature of the sun's resting place suggests, very vaguely, an "inner chamber," so that "vault" may serve us better.

Considering now the prayer proper—lines 16–24—circumstances

would justify the use of reverential expletives carefully placed to preserve the personal, imploring tone.

Finally, in the matter of the lamb (line 23), no special effort should be
made to communicate information about divination *within the compass of
the translated poem itself.* The cultural "distance" between ourselves and
the Babylonians is too great to have a poem do the work of a historical
monograph.

Looking back, I think everything has been said that ought to have
been said, prior to the final translation about special problems and their
treatment, although more might profitably have been discussed on translation in general. In the final version we should try to catch the rhythm
or swing of the original, but that may easily elude us. The poem as a
whole has been *fairly* manageable. I cannot think but that it lets us off
very easily indeed.

Babylonian Prayer to the Gods of Night
> Now the Immortals sleep . . .

Locked are the locks, the bolts thrown home,
The crowds are still . . . , the people, still;
Shut, the city-gates—

> Now Gods of the land, now Goddesses—
> Adad and Ea, Shamash and Ishtar—
> Have gone into the Deep of heaven;
> They judge no more,
> > decide no more . . .

> Veiled is Night,
> > And palace, quiet;
> > > sanctuary, quiet . . . ;

Now caravaner calls out to his God;
> Now litigant lies overcome with sleep;

> > The Judge of Truth, Father of Truth,
> > Shamash has sunk into his vault.

So
> then
> > you Gods of Grandest Night,
> > > O flaming Gibil, valiant Irra,
> > > > Elamite Bow—

O Pleiades, Orion, Dragon God—
O Chariot, O Bison,
Stand by me now!
And through this ceremony I make,
And through this lamb I offer up,
Grant favor unto me!

Background

Physical Background

Landforms, Climate, and Hydrology
of the Near East

Think of the Near East as a single piece in the gigantic jigsaw puzzle of the earth's surface, the piece that joins the immense region of western Asia to the edges of Europe and northeastern Africa, respectively. These edges do not connect to Europe or to Africa in a firm or continuous way. The land mass at the European edge is interrupted by the Bosporus Strait, a narrow and treacherous waterway that connects the Black Sea on the north to the Sea of Marmara and the Mediterranean Sea on the south. The connection to Africa is a narrow coastal land bridge, which links Palestine to the northern Sinai Peninsula.

Altogether the Near East is a sort of "island," whose boundaries are great bodies of water, imposing mountain ranges, and deserts: on the west, looking from south to north, the Red Sea, including the Nile and its contiguous desert wastes, the eastern Mediterranean, the Aegean Sea, and the Bosporus; on the north the Pontic Mountains, which front the Black Sea; to the east the Zagros Mountains range, which divides present-day Iraq from Iran; and to the south the Persian/Arabian Gulf, the Arabian Sea, and the Gulf of Aden.

Our imagined island is composed of two geologically contrasted regions. The northernmost region, comprising what is today Turkey and including the border zone between present-day Iraq and Iran as well as the ranges of Lebanon and lower Palestine, is densely mountainous. The southernmost areas are underpinned by very ancient and stable rock structures. Differences in climate covering the entire territory of the

Near East account for surface differences between a verdant north and a desert south. Rain rarely falls in the Near East below the six-inches-per-year isohyet line except in the Mediterranean coastal areas, where winter and spring rains can produce raging floods. Where rain is absent, rivers and their tributaries and seasonal watercourses nourish crops; high water tables allow well-digging in the desert. Even morning dew can cause the desert surfaces to bloom as well as provide water for animals and their masters. All other conditions being considered, it is the presence or absence of water, in whatever available amounts and frequencies of occurrence, that determined the styles of life of ancient Near Eastern peoples.

Egypt

Beginning with Egypt, we note that the Nile, its eternal benefactor, flows a thirty-five-hundred-mile course on its way to the Mediterranean from its sources in the highland regions of east central Africa. Emerging from a vast watershed, two principal branches, the White Nile and the Blue Nile, unite at Khartoum to form the greater river itself. Between Khartoum and Aswan lies a zone in which six cataracts form impediments to travel. From Aswan northward, the Nile has cut a bed through a narrow, cliff-edged valley, whose width is about six miles until it broadens into the Delta below Cairo. At Cairo the Delta region begins, and the Nile flows to the sea in two main channels, the Rosetta Branch on the east and the Damietta Branch on the west, while innumerable little streams, larger lakes, and standing swamps cover the almost nine hundred square miles of Delta land and make it a formidable barrier to communication.

In the Nile Valley human life is oriented principally to the north and south, for the river is the main avenue of every habitable community. All villages, towns, and cities are thus inevitably connected by a common artery, whose rate of flow is easy and inviting to sailing craft. From the Nile Valley a small number of important routes lead to the outside. On the west caravan tracks connect to the northern oases of Natrun and the Fayyum, while at the latitude of Thebes they reach to the more southerly one of Kharga. To the east of the valley stand the eastern highlands, which are cut by a number of extremely deep wadis that serve to connect the Nile and the Red Sea. The one chiefly used in antiquity was the Wadi Hammamat, which lies slightly to the north of Thebes. Toward the south, river traffic can come without difficulty as far as the island of Elephantine, which lies at Aswan above the First Cataract, but further progress is possible along caravan routes leading into the Sudan, or the river may continue to be followed with greater inconvenience than earlier. At the extreme northern approach to Egypt, the Delta with its adjacent easterly Sinai Peninsula gives access to the coastal regions and the islands of the Mediterranean.

Ancient Egypt was thus united by virtue of having its population restricted to a narrow stretch of cultivable land, some one thousand miles long, all of it bordering on the Nile; and it benefited also from a strong defensive position created for it by virtually impassible deserts on the west and east and difficult approaches on the north and south. Well-controlled caravan routes allowed an extension of its commerce in all periods to the desert outposts of the Sahara and the Sudan, while the Red Sea route, made accessible from the Nile Valley, allowed profitable contact with trading stations in Punt (Somaliland). From the Delta, Egyptian ships made early contact with the Levantine Coast, an export region for Syrian and Lebanese woods destined for the great pharaonic structures in all periods. By coastal route across the neck of the Sinai Peninsula, whose interior complexes of rugged highlands and deeply eroded valleys gave added border protection to their valley homes, Egyptians could reach the Plain of Sharon in lower Palestine and eventually cross the upper Judaean Hills into Canaan and Syria. Thus, the topography of Egypt allowed its towns and cities more than adequate protection from outside disturbances in the early periods, thereby providing a physical basis for a gradual growth of national unity and for an early convenient contact with trading areas beyond its immediate borders.

Palestine (Canaan-Phonicia)

To travel northward from Egypt is to encounter the great exposed western coastland of the Near East. This is the threshold of entry to the entire area from the Mediterranean. A long, narrow strip of land, it is backed on its interior side by a continuous highland and mountain ridge, which forms the Judaean Hills in southern Palestine and the Lebanon and Amanus mountain ranges in the north. An additional barrier—the Great Rift Valley—further acts to set it off from the desert and steppe land of Syria. Through this valley the Jordan River winds on a southerly course to the Dead Sea. A bit farther north, at the edge of western Syria, the Orontes River flows westward to the Mediterranean Sea at Lattaqia.

Historically the entire region is better known to us as Canaan, although in ancient times it bore other names as well. After 1000 the southern region became the homeland of ancient Israel. The approach from the south is through the Negev and the Wilderness of Judaea, which together form a northeasterly extension of the Sinai Peninsula. This territory is generally inhospitable, although sites dating from about 2000 may be found scattered within its limits. These are generally small sites, primitively walled and occupying low elevations. They are usually situated near small, permanent streams or in the vicinity of oases. The one absolute criterion for permanent open settlement is the ability to channel the rampaging waters of winter rainfall into cisterns or other containment vessels. Those who brought the art to its highest level were the Nabataeans, during the centuries immediately preceding and following the Christian era. They were able to establish impressive settlements, in the Negev of present-day Israel, and make a farmland in the desert. Their settlements were installed on the desert trade routes, thereby linking their territory in Transjordan with the seacoast. By and large, however, the lifestyle of the Negev and contiguous territory has always remained a mixed pattern of small agricultural settlements and seminomadic herding activity.

The coastal plain, which connects the Judaean Hills with the Mediterranean coast below modern Haifa, is geographically more an extension of the Nile Delta than a connection to the hills of the interior. It was able to serve the Egyptians as a direct roadway into central Palestine. Several of its cities, such as Gaza and Ashkelon, are familiar names in Egyptian historical records of the second millennium. At about 1000 the Philistines appropriated this stretch of coastline as their own and formed a pentapolis, or five-city league, which included Ashkelon, Ashdod, Ekron, Gaza, and Gath. During the formative centuries of ancient Israel as a tribal community (1200–1000), the Philistines were a dominant military force in lower and central Palestine and remained so until the firm establishment of the Hebrew monarchy under David (ca. 1000–960). But even after the demise of the Philistines the coastal plain never served as an important settlement area for the Hebrews, possibly because of its distance from the political and religious capital at Jerusalem or again because of the many marshes and swamps that were to be encountered there. This particular stretch of Palestine's coastline is not as well-suited for harbors as were the more northerly Phoenician ports beginning at Dor and extending to the Gulf of Iskenderun. Solomon of Israel had access to these seaports after making political alliances with his Phoenician neighbors.

The cities of the southern hill country, especially Judaea, were off the main coastal route, which meant, from a practical standpoint, that the odd raid from Egypt into the north could usually pass them by. Even when the Assyrians from Mesopotamia were regularly invading lower Palestine in the eighth and early seventh centuries these cities were relatively unmolested unless they were openly rebellious. Their situation usually guaranteed that they would not be the first to experience the impact of new movements or aggressive policies from powers of the distant hinterland. But since the central highlands are unbroken and generally open to passage throughout their entire length, the southern hill communities could easily receive the influence of cultural trends developing elsewhere in Palestine or, on the other hand, the impact of regional warfare. At times southern Palestine was a transit corridor for foreign armies, at times a vassal province. But its position generally allowed it to display some degree of independence. The land was always exposed, and more often than not in ancient times it was actively or indirectly controlled by major powers located in Egypt or Mesopotamia. In periods when no strong power was on the scene its tribes enjoyed an ephemeral freedom of action.

Central and southern Palestinian terrain favored the establishment of the single fortified city, which directly controlled a moderately large surrounding area. The history of the region is the history of conflict or cooperation between individual cities. These cities were advantageously situated on heights or at the entrances to transverse valleys and resembled impregnable fortresses. Dominated as they were by efficient armies, they contributed to incessant warfare for most of their history. Even in periods of their vassalage to the Near Eastern empires of the first millennium, these cities strove to follow independent political courses and were hotbeds of continuous intrigue, if not open revolt.

Many of the same observations just made about central and southern Palestine may also be applied to the upper, or Lebanese, highlands, where the single city-state territory was the primary political form. However, the coastal strip of Lebanon deserves special attention, for this was the home of the famous Phoenician port cities of Tyre, Sidon, and Byblos, the outstanding maritime emporia of the ancient Mediterranean. Phoenician history is the history of competing seaports, not that of a national entity. Again geography supplies much of the reason. From the Lebanon mountain range approximately twelve wadis cut through to the sea. They divide the entire coastland into a series of small, compartmentalized units of land, each with a sheltering harbor, and thus tend to emphasize the autonomy of the single city over the concept of a united whole.

The Phoenician coast was the shipping coast par excellence of the ancient Near East. A number of fine ship havens were developed there into proper harbors through the construction of breakwaters and quays. The Phoenician city rulers were thus able to establish themselves at the eastern end of the great Mediterranean Sea roads that led outward toward the Straits of Gibraltar and into the Atlantic. The coastal regions containing traces of ancient Phoenician harbors were usually crescent shaped; the peninsular points were used as fire-signal stations for communication up and down the shoreline. When we think of the Phoenician cities we must consider them as terminals for commerce that originated as far east as Iran and as far south as Yemen. But they were not simply terminals. For as mother cities they sent out the colonists who founded Utica and Carthage on the North African coast of the western Mediterranean.

Asia Minor (West, Central, East)

At the upper regional border of Canaan, which is defined by the mountain walls of the Taurus and the Anti-Taurus, the features of the Near East change, for here geography begins to define the northern highland tier with its interior plateau that thrusts westward to the edge of Europe. The massive quadrangle of Asia Minor forms a physical unit distinct from Mesopotamia and Syria, and this distinctiveness has served to separate its human history from that of the lower lands. A true peninsula on a grand scale, it is the home of several autochthonous cultural styles that were never fully effaced by the march of civilizations over its terrain.

The civic world of this area is largely confined to the broad tableland that stretches from the rugged and broken coastal areas of the west to the eastern limits of the central Anatolian Plateau. The bordering mountains and seacoasts all contain pockets of urban life, but these are only sporadically engaged with the history of the interior.

There is scarcely any coastal plain along the entire southern edge of Asia Minor except for that of Cilicia and the Plain of Antalya. This is due to the sheer drop of the western Taurus to the edge of the sea over most of its territory, a drop that effectively closes this coast to significant penetration from the Mediterranean or the Aegean. The Cilician Plain, the terminus of important natural routes that lead south from the Anatolian Plateau through the great gorge called the "Cilician Gates," provided a meeting point for traffic from the interior and from Antalya. A narrow passage follows the coast and deflects toward Lebanon. The coastal pockets of southern Asia Minor are cul-de-sacs for cultural influences from the Mediterranean owing to the extreme difficulty of penetration inland through the towering mountain wall.

Where the western Taurus range reaches the sea of the European coast of Asia Minor it ceases to present as imposing a barrier as it does on the south, for its foothills there present entry routes to the upland steppes. A number of parallel ridges separate deep inlets all along the western coast, and between these, the rivers descended from the high-lands and have fashioned broad and fertile plains. In this region a con-tinuous zone of open land invites dense settlement. Since the coastal front is intersected by rugged ridges, there is no geological unity. The broken landscape tends to encourage formation of separate city-state ter-ritories. These have little enough contact with developments in the plateau behind them to the east because of the additional barrier pre-sented by the high plateau edge. The directional orientation of cities on the European coast is therefore westward, just as is that of the Phoeni-cian cities. Historically the city-states of western Asia Minor were always far more closely tied to contemporary developments in Greece and the Aegean than to those of their own hinterlands.

Along the Black Sea coast the Pontic Mountains reach a height of eight thousand feet and descend directly to the edge of the northern sea over much of the area. This precludes the existence of more than a few harbors over its entire length. Such sites as were founded along this coast were effectively used as "grain ports" by the Greeks of the first millen-nium. Earlier use of the coast is poorly documented. The mountain ranges that form the barrier behind these sites hug the shoreline. They consist of high ridges that enclose deep valleys. Natural routes through these mountains into the southerly interior are few, a circumstance that always effectively separated coastal inhabitations from their neighbors on the plateau.

In eastern Asia Minor the ranges of the Pontic Mountains meet those of the Taurus and the Anti-Taurus, which come up from the southwest. Their merger produces a rugged tangle of high peaks, narrow upland valleys, and large river basins and watersheds. The dominant point of this combined system is Mount Ararat, which caps the so-called Armenian Knot. There are few passes through the Taurus and the Anti-Taurus, such that communications were with Mesopotamia directly south and for the most part effectively limited.

The wild area here described has always resisted domination, even of the strongest neighboring powers. The placement of cities in this region was determined by the strongest strategic considerations. They are perched atop cliffs, at the entryways of passes, and near the convergence of the few routes that connect the mountain valleys and appear as fortress citadels, which dominated the mud brick villages beneath and around them. Although settlements have been known in eastern Asia Minor since the third millennium, the highest level and complexity of urbanism appeared only between 900 and 700, when the kingdom of Urartu was a major political opponent of the Assyrians to the south. For most of its history the area was subject to incursions from outside, and many an Asiatic migratory movement spilled over into its rugged valleys before gathering new momentum for further incursions southward and westward.

The heartland of Asia Minor, the central plateau of Anatolia, lies cradled between mountain walls that ring it on all sides. Here it is possible for a considerably-sized territorial state to develop and maintain itself as a center of power. The most outstanding example of such a state in antiquity was the Hittite Kingdom and Empire of the second millennium, which was a major participant in the Near East between 1500 and 1200. The basin of the Halys River, which flows through the Anatolian plateau, is not only a natural locus of organization but a passageway for routes that traverse Asia Minor from east to west and north to south. Here rainfall is abundant for agriculture; little or no irrigation is needed; and the grazing is plentiful for livestock, especially horses. The surrounding mountains are rich in silver, copper, and gold as reflected in the so-called Royal Graves at Alaca Hüyük. In all, the plateau was ideally suited for the establishment of a strong urban center, and indeed the archaeological record of village and town communities in the area goes back to the Seventh Millennium. Positioned between a westward-looking Aegean coast and the massive ranges of the eastern mountains, the Anatolian plateau was at once capable of receiving influences from both directions as well as absorbing and turning these into its own distinctive cultural styles.

Mesopotamia

If the Nile is the lifeline of a geologically narrow Egyptian homeland, the combined regimes of the Tigris and the Euphrates rivers are the arteries of a broad and complex geological structure. Both rivers rise within the tangled mountain zone of eastern Asia Minor, their head-waters sharing the Elazig Basin west of Lake Van. On their courses to the Persian Gulf each functions to water separate regions of Mesopotamia. The Tigris is a swift-flowing stream in its upper reaches and flows in a direct route down the western lowland flanks of the Zagros. The Euphrates winds westward from its sources in a large meandering half circle through upper Syria before it turns toward the southeast to cut through the Syrian and Iraqi plains. At the latitude of present-day Bagh-dad the Tigris and the Euphrates almost meet before they separate again to form a pear-shaped alluvial plain. From modern Qurna south they flow together through the Shatt al Arab to the Persian Gulf.

Because the Euphrates is considerably longer than the Tigris, and at its furthermost western bend lies but one hundred miles east of the Mediterranean coast, it, rather than the Tigris, has been the more impor-tant roadway in ancient Near Eastern history. Easily navigable from the Persian Gulf as far as present-day Raqqa, it was in ancient times a natural link between the cultures of the southern lowlands and those that stood at the gateways to Asia Minor and Lebanon. For its part, the Tigris linked Sumeria, and later Babylonia, with Assyria and the mountainous inhabitants of northern Iraq. The presence of these rivers ensured that the historical destiny of lower Iraq would be closely interwoven with that of the upland regions.

Both the Tigris and Euphrates rivers are amply supplied with tribu-taries, which form the heart of regional irrigation as well as communica-tion systems. The chief of these emptying into the Tigris are the Great and the Little Zab, the Adhem, the Diyala, and the Karun rivers. The Euphrates is joined by the Khabur and the Balikh, the former near mod-ern Meyadin, the latter near Raqqa. These streams supply the otherwise barren Syrian plain, where their headwaters branch out and make fertile the lands lying beneath the Anti-Taurus mountain range of Asia Minor. Across these headwaters passed several of the most frequently traveled caravan routes in ancient times.

The entire area that we call Mesopotamia ("the Land between the Rivers") was thus naturally well-watered by the great rivers and their dependent tributaries. Both large and small systems of irrigation canals tapping the rivers could serve to support urban life everywhere. Yet if such ample water resources could foster a system of sedentary life, they could also threaten it. Spring flooding was invariably destructive to many a settlement. Unlike the Nile, which gently and predictably inun-dates Egypt each year and whose waters can rather easily be harnessed and cached in field basins, the Tigris and the Euphrates frequently rampage over the countryside during the spring floods. No cliffs or high embankments keep their waters from spreading at will. In Mesopotamia few adversaries could be as powerful and troublesome as nature itself.

At the lower end of the valley formed by the Tigris-Euphrates system was situated the homeland of the Sumerians, the first prolific urban culture in the ancient Near East. The area was well-suited for early permanent settlement owing to the character of the broad plain, where many a channel and lake could be directed to supply small irrigation systems. Such systems allowed a number of individual cities to prosper long before there was a centralized state, and for centuries these independent cities combated each other for supremacy.

The land and water routes to the north of Sumeria are open and afford direct access to the highlands. Along these routes grew up dense clusters of inhabitation. The Diyala River Valley, in the vicinity of modern Baghdad, was an early important village and township area site, while further to the north the communities of the territory that would later become classical Assyria are among the earliest known in the Near East.

The open plains of northern Mesopotamia carry communication routes westward along the Sinjar Hills into the territories of the upper Khabur and Balikh rivers. Farther west the routes cross the Euphrates or follow the corridor leading to the Mediterranean coast of Aleppo. The people who lived along this extended passageway of the Anti-Taurus ranges were more immediately open to conflict with their nomadic neighbors than were the populations of the lower valley, and consequently the history of settlement in the early periods in this region was continuously troubled. Situated as they did at the threshold of Asia Minor, directly under the passes leading from the districts of contemporary Mardin, Urfa, and Marash, the peoples of this region were constantly invaded by armies from the north and south. When conditions conspired to set in motion the migrations of desert peoples, from whatever direction, the inhabitants of the upper Syrian plains were usually the first to bear the impact of war.

The land adjacent to Lebanon is separated from the lowlands and port cities of Phoenicia by the ranges of the Lebanon and the Anti-Lebanon mountains, which border on the western Syrian plain and the desert. A network of streams, dependent upon the Orontes River, waters the territory of upper Syria while adjacent lands receive enough rainfall to develop as an orchard and grain-growing district. But farther south, along the Jordanian highlands, opportunities for extensive settlement life are more severely limited. With the exception of some agriculture along the tributaries of the Jordan River, the land is chiefly suitable for herding. The long depression of the Jordan River Valley can support urban life in its upper districts. From here to the Gulf of Aqaba it is contiguous to the Negev of southern Palestine but limited as a difficult communications route.

Iran

Far to the east the northern geologic tier of the Near East runs out into the high mountains, steppe lands, and interior deserts of Iran. The combined Pontic and Taurus ranges of Turkey push toward the Caspian Sea, where they join the Caucasus and, farther eastward, the Elburz. Separating Mesopotamia from Iran is the Zagros Mountains chain, a rugged southerly extension of the Armenian Knot. The valley tributaries of the Tigris River form corridors eastward into the Zagros. These were important lines of communication between the nascent Mesopotamian and the western Iranian cultures.

From the northern plains of Iraq the Great Zab and the Little Zab rivers open passageways toward Lake Urmia and the fertile regions around Tabriz. Farther south the Adhem and the Diyala rivers become entryways to Luristan, the central province of the Iranian Zagros. Below Baghdad, the Karun River Valley leads toward Khuzistan. Thus while the Zagros Mountains forbid easy movement of population between Iran and Mesopotamia, they do allow selective points of contact. We know that the early Sumerian cities of lower Iraq and the Elamite cities just across the mountains were closely tied together in warfare, trade, and politics. Archaeologists recognize that southwest Iran was experimenting with the novelty of agriculture and village life at roughly the same time as the neighboring Mesopotamian highlands, between 5000 and 3000.

The urban nucleus of Iran was located in the southwest, as witnessed by the great Elamite city of Susa, whose career spanned over three thousand years. Much of earliest Iranian history in the north is unknown to us, although historical records from Mesopotamia, combined with archaeological surveys and excavations, depict this region as a mixed settlement and nomadic zone in the early second millennium. Toward 1000, people we know as Medes appear in the northern sectors and later organize a kingdom, with its capital at Ecbatana (present-day Hamadan).

When the Persians became masters of Iran in about 550, they built two great capitals in the south—Pasargadae, in the time of Cyrus the Great, and Persepolis, under Darius and Xerxes. The extant ruins of Persepolis, not far from present-day Shiraz, allow the mind to visualize the immensity and magnificence of a Persian royal seat of the mid-first millennium.

Arabia

Finally, below the lands of the Fertile Crescent we have been surveying lies the immense peninsula of Arabia. Its north is volcanic steppe land. Gigantic stretches of desert form its central regions. Along its seacoast high and dusty mountains afford few places for harbors. In the popular imagination this uninviting land is thought to be largely uninhabited, yet just the reverse is true. The desert is a veritable civilization unto itself. It teems with hundreds of tribes, villages, and towns, which have grown up around oases or wellheads. The life of the desert is often violent, occasionally anarchic, yet from earliest times there were discernible tribal and sedentary districts, with defended borders. When we speak of the world of the ancient Near East we cannot fail to examine and appreciate how even the inhabitants of the most desolate places in the area developed a rhythm of life in which sedentary settlement played a functional role.

Although Arabia is universally acknowledged to be the cradle of Semitic speaking peoples, the nomadic tribes that impinged upon the settlements of ancient Palestine, Syria, and Mesopotamia for centuries and millennia belong to the history of these areas and will be noted as relevant within the text of this book.[1]

FURTHER READING

Fisher, W. B. *The Middle East: A Physical, Social, and Regional Geography.* 6th ed. London: Methuen, 1971.

Kees, Herman. *Ancient Egypt: A Cultural Topography.* Trans. Ian F. D. Morrow. Ed. T. G. H. James. Chicago: University of Chicago Press, 1961. Phoenix ed., 1977. Paperback.

Historical Background

The Setting of Prehistoric Cultural
Development in Mesopotamia and Egypt

The prehistory of the ancient Near East is highlighted by two great transformations in human behavior. The first is the emergence of people from life within caves, or at the lips of caves, to new settlements in permanently open sites. The second is the knowledge gained by early men and women of how to grow the grains, vegetables, and fruits they previously had to collect from fields and forests and how to raise animals for food instead of hunting them in the wild. The observations and experiments necessary to produce these transformations are epic in nature and took millennia to accomplish. We cannot pause here to narrate the story in any expansively detailed way since our concern in this section is to provide a brief introduction to the rise of urban civilization in two focal points of ancient Near Eastern life—Mesopotamia and Egypt.

The Sequence to Urban Civilization in Iraq

End of the Cave Stage in Iraq

Type Sites

Barda Balka in the Kurdish Hill Country: A gravel layer contained the bones of elephant and rhinoceros in addition to coarse flint and limestone tools. (Date ca. 100,000.)

Zarzi and Palegawra in the near vicinity of Barda Balka (about forty miles away): Artifacts are all of flint, blade tools, and microliths. The animals hunted by the Palegawra people were of the modern type—sheep, goat, pig, gazelle, deer—but were undoubtedly wild. (Date ca. ?10,000–9,000.)

Karim Shahir, a temporary encampment in the Kurdish Hill country: excavators found a layer with erratic stones, perhaps indicating some kind of structure, but no architectural plan was available. Small objects include flint blades and microliths, some ground stone work, chipped axes, polished bits, mortars, and milling-stone fragments. Beads and bracelets also appear. The proportion of bones of domesticated animals was well over 50 percent. Karim Shahir was not yet a proper village. The area of site is about two acres.

M'Lefaat (twenty miles east of Mosul): An inhabitation layer about five feet in depth was uncovered, revealing several architectural levels. The site is mainly interesting for evidence it provides of architectural permanence. There was initially no evidence of plant food or domestication of animals. From the technical point of view heavier items (e.g., mortars) than those at Karim Shahir were manufactured. No fine beads or similar objects were initially discovered.

Transition to Earliest Available Village

Jarmo Phrase

Jarmo follows Karim Shahir and M'Lefaat in the sequence, seemingly after a short lapse of time. Jarmo is a mound over three acres and about twenty-five feet deep. There are traces of about a dozen successive levels, revealing continual renovation and change. Walls are of packed mud, sometimes placed upon stone foundations. The first two-thirds of its duration is without portable pottery but does contain floor basins throughout. The Jarmo people made unbaked clay figurines of animals and the so-called mother-goddesses. The flint industry is represented by blades and microliths. Obsidian also appears; it probably was traded in from Turkey. There is excellent production of ground stone materials: stone vessels, bracelets, pendants, and beads. Larger stone vessels include mortars, pestles, milling stones, stone axes, and hoes, as well as many flint sickle blades. The manufacture of bone spoons appears to have been a popular activity.

Two species of wheat have been discovered in addition to barley and peas. The wheat (emmer wheat and spelt wheat) and two-rowed barley represent early stages of breeding from the wild state. Of the animal bones found, 95 percent are of sheep, goat, pig, and ox varieties; only 5 percent appear to have been wild forms. An extremely high percentage of yearlings suggests a selection that would not necessarily be true if the animals had been hunted.

Jarmo certainly represents established village life. (Note that Jericho in Palestine also had a very long "pre-pottery" period even though the architecture for the "pre-pottery" was well developed and highly complex in form and technique; date ca. 7500.)

The Hassuna Phase

Following Jarmo, again after a short lapse of time, appear the materials known after the site of Tell Hassuna (near Mosul), where they were first discovered in any quantity. Hassuna materials are available from the type site, from the base of the great mound at Nineveh, from Matarrah (south of Kirkuk), and as surface occurrences on a number of mounds in northern Iraq.

The Hassuna phase is characterized by well-built mud-walled houses; several styles of pottery; a decadent flint industry; and a variety of simple tools in clay, ground stone, and bone. It was clearly a time in which the basic village economy had become well established. The major creative outlet seems to have been in pottery decoration, by incision or painting or both. In the latter half of the phase a particularly handsome pottery style occurs—the Samarran Ware. Other Hassuna materials include shells from the Persian Gulf and obsidian from Turkey. Hassuna-type pottery is found as far west as Syro-Cilicia.

Altogether, the Hassuna villages are not large, but they seem to have been fairly numerous in northern Iraq. The phase seems to represent a time of basic peasant-farmer activity, some craft specialization, and broadening trade relationships. From the Hassuna phase onward, the archaeological sequence in Iraq is essentially complete, though at no stage is it adequately represented. (Date ca. 7000–6000.)

From Halaf to the Beginnings of History in Iraq

The Halaf Phase

This phase is represented by materials at a number of sites in upper (Syrian) Mesopotamia, near the Turkish border, especially from Arpachiyah, near Mosul.

The phase is characterized by a peculiar round stone-foundation house type with a rectilinear antechamber leading off one side. Rectilinear rooms also seem to be available. An extremely handsome painted pottery style also characterizes the phase. According to archaeologists, the pottery represents the best of all the handmade wares, both from the technical and the artistic points of view. It is characteristically black and orange-red on buff or cream; designs are geometric as well as bird, animal, and human representations. Perhaps the earliest example of a chariot appears on a Halaf painted vase. Also characteristic are certain styles of beads and amulets and painted pottery figurines of the "mother-goddess."

Considerable technical advance appears in Halaf crafts. Halaf culture pottery has been found as far north as Lake Van in eastern Turkey and as a minor feature in Syro-Cilicia (Mersin, Ugarit). There is some evidence that it was contemporaneous with the latter phase of the Hassuna. (Date ca. 6000–5500.)

The Ubaid Phase

The earliest well-attested materials that have been found in southern Mesopotamia are Ubaidian. The type site itself, Tell-al-Ubaid, is found near Ur, which also yields Ubaidian materials, as do other sites south of Baghdad. Ubaidian materials also appear in northern Iraq, and there transition between Halaf and Ubaid cultures seems to occur.

In the north, at Tepe Gawra, and in the south, at Abu Shahrein (ancient Eridu), Ubaidian remains indicate towns of some size and the appearance of buildings that are standardly interpreted as temples.

The appearance of metal tools, with the implication of craft specialization, seems to be assured in northern Iraq. We are not so certain about southern Iraq, where, instead of metal axes and sickles, one finds very hard-baked clay tools of the same types. These would have been perfectly adequate to cope with reeds, soft woods, and grain.

Ubaid pottery is predominantly painted, a fine pale greenish ware with free geometrical designs in black or dark brown. There are suggestions of connections with Iranian pottery developments.

In architecture, uniformly molded mud brick appears for the first time. Mud-plastered walls are sometimes decorated with mosaics made of thin cones of clay, whose ends were left plain or were painted in red or black; the use of cones of this type provides effective waterproofing.

Regarding the temples, at Tepe Gawra (north) appears the oldest religious structure in Iraq. Toward the end of the Ubaid phase a very impressive acropolis is attested. Three monumental temple buildings surround a courtyard. The central shrine's exterior was painted white, and the interior rooms and shrine were painted purple.

In connection with Ubaid, sites with related materials appear along the Iranian Flanks of the hilly crescent, as well as over the grasslands to the north and west. The Iranian highland culture reaches eastward across the Plateau of Iran into Baluchistan, which itself is the bridge to India. Evidence of prehistoric sites suggests that Baluchistani cultures may have been in contact with the Indus Valley cultures, chiefly represented by Mohenjo-Daro, about 140 miles northeast of present-day Karachi.

Some facts suggest early contacts between Mesopotamia and India. For example, in the Ubaid period Mesopotamians are making beads out of lapis lazuli, an azure-blue stone that comes from central Asia, and out of amazonite, a green stone that is found only in central India and Trans-baikalia.

Also, in early tombs of Ur a little figure of a squatting monkey, precisely similar to figures from Mohanjo-Daro, was found. From about 2500 at Tell Asmar, other Indian animals on a seal of undoubted Indian workmanship have been identified. These animals are the Indian elephant, the rhinoceros, and the fish-eating crocodile.

A caution is in order here. One must be careful about assuming that because Ubaid pottery style appears widely diffused this implies movements or migrations *of people*. The Iranian materials may simply be regional variants of generalized Ubaidian cultural patterns.

In general, the Ubaid phase introduces important new elements into the Mesopotamia sequence and signals a general enlargement of population and population centers, as well as widespread cultural contacts. (Date ca. 5500–4000.) Our attention now shifts for the first time predominantly to developments in southern Mesopotamia.

Warka Phase (formerly Uruk)

Typical materials for this phase come from a few levels at ancient Uruk and Abu Shahrein (ancient Eridu). The pottery differs from Ubaidian, being red- or grey-slipped, and includes some new shapes (e.g., a beveled-rim bowl). A pottery resembling Warka and the last-noted bowl appears along the hilly flank zone from southwestern Iran to northwestern Syria. In northern Iraq, these materials are included in the remains of the so-called Gawran phase. All in all, the Warkan phase was a rather short one and was probably under way by circa 3500.

Protoliterate Phase (Formerly the Late Phases of Uruk and the Jemdet Nasr)

This phase gives evidence for a preponderance of what Braidwood and others call civilization and what I call *urban* civilization (as opposed to the ever-present and developing seminomadic civilization). *It is in the Protoliterate that southern Mesopotamia comes to the fore, exhibiting a cultural intensity that for the first time surpasses that of surrounding areas.*

The sites of Protoliterate towns are relatively large in area. Many of them seem to have been newly founded in this period, not simply built over the remains of earlier ones.

In architecture the best known example of a large and monumental temple-and-terrace complex at Eridu has a plan that suggests a connection to the Ubaid phase. But the chief distinction between the two phases is (a) the new appearance of a distinct and definitive temple platform and (b) the increased monumentality in scale, detail, and decoration.

In the Protoliterate, clay tablets appear bearing pictographic signs, the prototype of later cuneiform writing. By the end of the Protoliterate there is evidence that the rebus principle is being utilized. In addition, there is a highly developed architecture, a rise in the use of cylinder seals, and a richness of variety in the seal motifs. Sculpture in the round as an art form appears for the first time. (The Protoliterate is under way ca. 3500; writing appears ca. 3100.)

Sequence to Urban Civilization in Egypt

The materials from Egypt are less meaningful for a study of the early food-producing stages because most of the evidence comes from graves, which contain specialized objects of funerary interest, and because there is practically no stratification in Egyptian sites. Early chronological determination of materials was provided by typology (sequence dating), though carbon 14 dates have been standardly used in recent years.

The prehistoric findings may be defined regionally as follows:

The Northern (Lower Egypt) Assemblages: Fayyum A; Merimde; El Omari; Maadi

The Southern (Upper Egypt) Assemblages: Tasian/Badarian; Amratian; Gerzean

By the time of the food-producing economy in Egypt, the country appears as an isolated corner of the Near East. Its local cultures flourished without any outside stimulation. Even within the country contacts between north and south do not seem to have been especially active. In general, the affinities of these early Egyptian cultures may be found to lie with other African assemblages, such as those from the Sudan and the Kharga Oasis.

The Southern (Upper Egypt) Assemblages

Tasian Phase

On the spurs of the desert near Badari (275 miles south of Cairo), the Tasian people cultivated emmer and barley in the fifth millennium. Stone slabs for grinding flour have been found. However, the economy seems primarily to have been nonsedentary; that is, hunting and more commonly fishing were practiced. Axes, made by grinding or flaking, were used to cut trees in the then very marshy Nile Valley.

Tasian peoples made rough pottery to contain food and drink; vessels are grey to black in color and are unevenly fired. Shapes are simple, though exceptions are to be noted (e.g., beaker-shaped vessels of black ware with rounded base and flaring, trumpetlike rim; decorations are of incised lines filled with white paste for emphasis).

Some faint traces of linen have been found, in addition to alabaster eye palettes, Red Sea shell decorations, beads, and worked ivory.

Tasians were buried in a contracted posture, wrapped in skins, and enclosed in straw coffins in large pits. (Date ca. 4500–4000.)

Badarian Phase

Badarian culture is an elaboration of Tasian, found in Middle and Upper Egypt. Apparently the same agricultural and hunting conditions obtained as in Tasian.

Badarins, like Tasians, were encamped on desert spurs, not in the Nile Valley itself. Shelters were of matting, representing windscreens. Mud-lined storage bins appear to have been used for grain. Barley and emmer appear, but sickle flints are rare. Cattle and sheep are kept and appear sometimes to have been given ceremonial burial. Hunting and fishing are still very important, and among the artifacts found are boomerangs, hollow-based flint arrows, and fish hooks.

New economic factors are associated with Badarian finds. Malachite, used for painting eyes, appears to have been imported (from Sinai or Nubia). Shells from the Red Sea suggest continued contact with the coast. Of great importance, metallic copper becomes known, though it was poorly fused. Pottery models of ships were also found. Ceramic skill is very fine, especially in the funerary vessels, which are models of perfection.

Badarians were still clothed in skins, but they also knew how to make coarse cloth out of vegetable fibers. Items of everyday use include ivory combs and pins as well as bracelets. Ornaments of copper tube, shells, and ostrich eggshells are known.

In some graves were found figurines of ivory or clay and amulets represented by carvings of hippopotamus and antelope. Badarians were buried flexed or crouched, wrapped in skins or encased in hampers of sticks in trench graves, which were sometimes lined with matting and grouped to form small cemeteries. Corpses generally faced west, but rules for orientation of body apparently were not strict. (Date ca. 4500–4000.)

Amratian Phase

This phase is named from its type site at Amra, about 350 miles south of Cairo. It represents a continuation of the old hunting and fishing techniques, but with an implied increase in commerce and communication.

There is still considerable hunting and fishing alongside farming. The evidence of stone-disk mace hands suggests some military activity. Items of everyday use (combs, cosmetics, etc.), are a continuation of earlier materials. The pottery is red, with white-crossed lines and decorations. Also ivory vases are used for ointments, and stone jars of black basalt appear. The pottery decorations show boats with oars and many desert scenes as well as figures of animals—elephants and hippopotamuses. (Date ca. 4000–3600.)

Gerzean Phase

The Gerzean phase appears over Middle as well as Upper Egypt and reveals wholly new features in the Egyptian sequence.

Copper is cast for the first time. In architecture, mud bricks appear. Lapis lazuli appears from Asia. In decoration, ships having cabins are represented, and these have rows of oars and emblem standards. Similarly, on pottery, there appear representations of people as well as symbols of deities. The south was probably already divided up into nomes during the Gerzean, each having a chief god as well as lesser ones.

The previous phase (Amratian) was mainly a Chalcolithic (copper-stone) culture, a wholly Egyptian and localized culture. By contrast, the Gerzean seems to have a broader extent. The new features seem to have connections to the Delta or to Asia. In the latter part of this period religion and the state may have reached their most advanced prehistoric forms.

The first clear example from Egypt of foreign connections occurs in the Gerzean—the presence of ledged, or wavy-handled, jars, originating in Palestine. Also, there appears a class of pottery vessels whose spouts are completely un-Egyptian in origin; they seem to have affinities with Protoliterate vessels in Mesopotamia. Other connections of Gerzean with Mesopotamia include the following:

Cylinder seals of the Jemdet Nasr style (Protoliterate), two of which were found in well-documented late Gerzean graves.

Examples of jars with four triangular lugs, a type known throughout the Protoliterate.

Figures of Mesopotamian high-hulled ships on the walls of the Wadi Hammamat. Mesopotamian mythological motifs, the Gilgamesh hero, in one instance dressed in Mesopotamian clothing. Also, the appearance of serpent-necked panthers and entwined snakes on late Gerzean vase decorations and carvings. Mesopotamian myth motifs appear carved on knife handles of artifacts from Jebel-el-Arak and Jebel Tarif. (Date ca. 3600–3100.)

The Northern (Lower Egypt) Assemblages

Fayyum Phase

Fayyumic settlements are to be found slightly south of Cairo, along the edge of an extensive lake that then filled the Fayyumic depression to a height of circa 180 feet above this present level.

Here there is evidence of the cultivation of emmer and barley and some flax. The cereals were harvested with serrated flint sickles set into wooden shafts. Cereals were stored in silos dug into the earth and lined with straw matting. Flour was ground on stone "saddle querns" as at Badari in Upper Egypt. Swine, sheep or goats, and cattle were kept. Hunting and fishing were primary economic activities.

Pottery techniques are about the same as at Tasa/Badari, and the forms are somewhat similar. Basketry techniques at Fayyum were excellent. There is some suggestion of weaving, as well as use of skins for clothing. Shell materials from the Red Sea and the Mediterranean Sea suggest potential for foreign contract.

No graves were found, hence burial practices are unknown. (Date ca. 4500–4000.)

Merimde Phase

Located on the western edge of the Delta, Merimde has revealed a culture closely allied to that of the Fayyumic settlements. The first settlers built flimsy shelters in an area circa six hundred by four hundred meters. Only hearths and rubbish heaps remain. A second phase shows more substantial shelters, oval or horseshoe shaped and outlined by posts, which probably supported reed matting. In the third phase some structures appear fully developed on a similar plan but are now walled with humps of mud. The huts are arranged along "streets," and each seems to have its own yard.

Barley and emmer were cultivated as at Fayyum and harvested with sickles. Grain was also stored in silo pits; in the second phase, in mud-coated baskets; in the third phase, in large pottery jars. The catalog of artifacts is very similar to that of Fayyum and indicates a strong dependence upon hunting and fishing.

The dead were buried among the dwellings, flexed, and generally facing east. No vessels have been found among graves.

(Date ca. ?4500–3600. Note that some scholars date the end of Merimde ca. 4000, while others bring it down to ca. 3600.)

El-Omari Phase

This is a closely allied culture to Merimde, discovered at El-Omari near Helwan. As at Merimde the dead are buried among the dwellings, but the orientation is different; they face west. Corpses are wrapped in skins or woven mats. One burial contained a wooden baton carved at both ends and said to resemble the so-called ames scepter of historical times, the insignia of kingship over Lower Egypt. (Date is roughly contemporary with Merimde.)

Maadi Phase

Maadi, located just south of Cairo, represents the last phase of northern (Lower Egypt) development.

Its pottery, stone vessels, and flints are linked to the Gerzean of Upper Egypt. The Maadi culture appears to be a development from the Merimde phase by way of El-Omari.

The foreign relations of Maadi are indicated by the wavy-handled Palestinian jars found in Middle and Upper Egypt during the Gerzean, but a real problem exists about the chronological priority. (Date ca. 3600–3100.)

Civic Background

Cities and Gods in the Ancient Near East—
Mesopotamia, Egypt, and Israel

Mesopotamia

The ancient mounds that dot the surface of the Near East conceal inhabitation layers testifying to several thousand years of occupation at the most outstanding sites to perhaps only several hundred to a thousand at others. Their locations were not arbitrarily chosen. The availability of water was the paramount consideration, as was, in the earliest periods, the natural protection afforded by sheltered valleys and defensible heights. Between about 9000 and 5000 protovillage and town sites clustered in the highlands or hilly flank regions of Northern Iraq, where rainfall provided adequate to abundant crops for harvest. In the earliest phases one encounters combinations of cave and open-site habitations as well as semipermanent hunting stations, followed in the later phases by incipient agricultural peasant villages. Typical of the period in general is the seasonal migration of clan and tribal units, which also occupied settlements supporting agriculture on a semipermanent basis. By the fifth millennium the prototypical agricultural village of the highlands has become an efficient unit, and some have become small towns, that is, regional centers upon whom a network of smaller enclaves of the same essential type depended for protection and which were in turn supportive of the logistical requirements of the centers. In the fourth millennium the Mesopotamian lowlands enter a village and town phase, in which settlements now appear on riverbanks, on canals, in wadis, and on marshy sites. The style of life parallels that of the north—small herding and agricultural pursuits to which has been added intensive fishing activity.

The historical era in Mesopotamia is ushered in with the appearance of the Sumerian city-states of the lowland by the end of the fourth millennium. This is the era of the large walled city with monumental architecture (ziggurats, temples, palaces, warehouses) and extensive residential areas both within and outside the walls. Typical of the period are such cities as Ur (Tell Muqaiyar), Uruk (Warka), Eridu (Abu Shahrein), Lagash, Larsa (Senkereh), Umma (Djokha), Nippur (Niffar), Kutha (Tel Ibrahim), Isin (Bahriyat), and Adab (Bismaya).[1]

The typical Sumerian city (*uru*) was composed of three parts: the inner city, or city proper, which contained within its walls the temples, palaces, official residences, and citizen's houses; the *kar,* which was the business or port district par excellence and which was situated on the banks of a canal or river spur so as to conduct and control intercity trade; and the *uru-bar-ra,* or "suburbs," whose aspect suggested more a rural than an urban setting since farmhouses, fields, gardens, stables, and corrals all could be seen there. The entire complex was guarded by outposts at some distance away.

Within the uru, probably the closest we can come to the notion of discernibly different sections or districts is through the role of the city-gate as organizational focal point for various activities. There were, of course, numerous gates to the city. Each opened on to a particular precinct. Such precincts might include inhabitants of particular tribes or ethnic or language-speaking groups or practitioners of single trades, such as metalworking or cloth weaving, very similar in appearance and function to what can be seen in contemporary Near Eastern cities, although in Sumerian times the overwhelming amount of hand trade seems to have been practiced within the temple enclosures. The city-gate was the place where legal matters might be adjudicated, where sales and contracting for services might be performed, or where ad hoc markets might appear and disappear in a relatively short period of time. The city-gate also served as a kind of public loitering or gathering place, where conversation and gossiping might take place. Leading from the city-gates were roads heading in the particular direction of one or another town.

In a real sense life did not radiate outward from the center of a Sumerian city but appears to have funneled inward from the outside, from the steppe or desert. This is because the nucleus of the city constituted a kind of dead end as far as freedom of movement went. This was the holy area, housing the largest, tallest, and most important building of the city. On a high terrace stood the main religious shrine, a massive stated tower called a ziggurat. Nearby stood the temple of the city's tutelary god. Also within the inner area of the city stood the many ancillary temple courts, chapels, storehouses, and granaries, with living quarters for the temple personnel. In some cities the religious enclosure was walled in, hence separated from the palace and city residences. In others palace and temple shared the inner enclosure and together were walled off from the citizens' settlement, which was further enclosed by a second wall. The subtleties of these variations cannot be treated in this short résumé. Suffice it to say that the inner temple—or temple/palace—complex was essentially isolated from the rest of the city.

Originally the Sumerian city appears to have had open land within its confines and some semblance of easy passage within its midst, but increasing population gradually eliminated all but the absolutely necessary passageway areas, a circumstance that resulted in narrow streets and crowded residential areas. What personal or family space there was resulted from the courtyard style of house, which served as the private, open-air domain of a household.

Numerous textual references inform us of Sumerian (and later Assyrian and Babylonian) city and town features, landscapes of temple towers, walls, and palaces. Pleasant gardens are mentioned (usually in reference to the holdings of the king or city governor), as are town houses and lands planted with trees. The setting of temple sanctuaries against the sky also attracted the attention of the ancient scribe. The famous *Gilgamesh Epic* of Old Babylonian times tells us that the ancient city of Uruk (biblical Erech) had, in addition to the lands of the temple estate of the goddess Ishtar, an area the size of the uru itself for orchards and a similar area for clay pits.

The passage of time in Mesopotamia found a new dominant population group—the Semites—who, following the demise of the Sumerian state at about 2000, formed the two chief political communities of Mesopotamia until the later first millennium. These were Babylonia, whose capital was Babylon in the area north of the Mesopotamian alluvium, and Assyria, which was originally governed from Assur (Qal'at Sherqat) on the upper Tigris. We cannot here recapitulate the ebbs and flows of fortune experienced by these states. Rather, it should be stressed that the second and first millennia were ages first of the national state, with an ever-growing involvement in international affairs by the leading participants, and then, after 1000, of imperialism, in which Assyria (900–612), Babylonia (ca. 625–539), and Persia (539–330) were respectively masters of the Near East.

During these two thousand years all regions of the area were linked through war as through trade. Many old cities were cruelly destroyed. Many new cities were founded. In the period we can recognize the growth of the national or imperial capital city: in Assyria, the Kalhu (Nimrud) of Assurnasirpal (883–859); the Nineveh (Kouyunjik) created by Sennacherib (704–681); the Dur-Sharrukin (Khorsabad) of Sargon II (721–705); in Babylonia, the Babylon of Nebuchadrezzar II (604–562) and metropolitan Borsippa (Birs Nimrud), also accomplished by Nebuchadrezzar; in Iran, the rise of Ecbatana (Hamadan) under the Medes and the foundation of Persepolis in the time of Darius and Xerxes (521–465).

For this entire period we may also mark the initial appearance of some or the dramatic growth of other *district capitals,* in which governors of Mesopotamian kings ruled; of market and caravan cities, as well as port cities; of border outpost cities; and of fortresses and garrison cities. There was also the type of city whose specific nature was that of a holy place par excellence, for example, Nippur from earliest Sumerian times. Perhaps the greatest spur to urbanization in the ancient Near East was provided by the Neo-Assyrian practice of forced urbanization of rebellious tribes. Similarly the Assyrian policy of transfer and exchange of rebellious populations in the first millennium tended to make cosmopolitan regions and settlements out of formerly unmixed population areas.

The Western mind makes a sharp distinction between *urban* and *rural,* but this dichotomy is considerably vaguer in Mesopotamian usage. For the city owned lands both outside and inside its walls; and within the city the temple, palace, and free citizenry also had their possessions. The countryside, while generally contrasted to the city, as we shall see, is but an extension of the area understood to be controlled, or potentially capable of being controlled, by the city. The city dweller, who actually lived within the walls of the largest urban complexes, and his peasant counterpart, who lived perhaps less securely in the small towns and villages round about, were not only mutually dependent (the former for food, the latter for protection and sharing certain advantages of city life) but may well have had many cultural and social notions in common. *Together they may be contrasted to a third type of population—the pastoralist or seminomad, who was often the object of scorn for his lack of "civilization."* The situation here described, the urban/agricultural on the one side and the seminomadic or pastoral on the other, is the basic division of human subsistence styles in the ancient Near East. It may be seen where, in Gertrude Bell's memorable phrase, "the desert and the sown" appear side by side. It applies almost without modification to the Palestinian and the West Syrian areas and is recognizable to a somewhat lesser extent in Egypt.

Archaeological studies of early Mesopotamian urban/village complexes stress that the earliest Sumerian communities existed within an identifiable ecological system, based on canal irrigation, in which the larger and more important centers served as focal points for the smaller towns and villages in a specifically exploited agricultural region or subregion; the entire functioning network suggests a clearly interacting organism. For the first millennium we continually read of the Assyrian conquest of the principal city or town of a valley or other defined district, along with the towns, villages, and hamlets of its surroundings. This type of reference confirms the archaeological picture of much earlier times and urges us to see the Mesopotamian idea of the urban as a subtle mixture of what we would call the *urban* with the *rural*. However, individual cities—walled cities—are identifiable in their own right and were celebrated as such in literature.

Our texts in all periods distinguish between uru (Akkadian *alu*), on the one hand, and its antonyms, which denote agricultural or pastoral regions: *a-dam* ("pasture"); *a-ra-a/e-ri-a* ("that which is fructified with water"); *e-duru* ("the moistened ground"); and *a-gar* ("the irrigation district"). As regards uru, or "city," only rarely is it used to distinguish one type of urban settlement from another. Both city and village are described by the term.

We must conclude this all too brief and general survey of function and form in Mesopotamian urbanism by alluding to a subtle balance of institutional forces within the historic cities of the region. The chief of these were the temple, the palace, and the free citizenry. A recent study of Sumerian Lagash showed that about one-fifth of the entire territorial holdings belonged to the temple; of the rest the majority acreage was possessed by the ruling princes and their families, high officials of both temple and palace, and various administrative dependents of these. Such individuals often possessed huge estates of hundreds of acres. What was left of the land beyond that owned by temple or nobility was possessed by the free population organized into patriarchal family units, which comprised perhaps half of the entire population of Lagash, the rest being clients in some relationship of dependency to the large estate owners or slaves outright. Toward the end of the second millennium the palace institution had become vastly more powerful than it had been at the beginning; it was the dominant institution, and its rulers and their associates had bought up most of the land previously held by the free population. The temple maintained a secondary, though still very influential, role. Each of these institutions—palace and temple—formed one order of political and socioeconomic institutional reality within the city complex. Each gained income from agricultural holdings, from products produced in their workshops, and from tribute, as well as from gifts of the pious. Each stored up income and redistributed surplus to dependent personnel.

The other great component in the Mesopotamian city was the community of persons of equal status, whose traditional organization was an assembly directed by elders and whose decisions were arrived at by consensus. Altogether, palace-temple and citizen community functioned symbiotically within the city. The palace was the seat of kingship, the office that mediated between gods and men. The temple provided a permanent dwelling place where the deity might live within the city. The citizenry looked to their assembly and their own traditional, if often waning, legal status to provide a focal point for their intimate concerns. For a literal chasm existed between king and subject, as between god and worshipper. An interesting explanation of the existence of the three components or civic "forces" described previously has been offered. Various scholars have seen an early movement of prosperous individuals toward either the palace or the temple nucleus for reasons of influence and prestige. Such persons constituted the membership of these institutions, which were self-subsistent and primarily concerned with intracity economics. The ordinary city dweller, primarily a manor-household producer, found his economic outlet in intercity trade, which was run from the business district, or kar—thus the unusual existence of three economic and sociopolitical components within one and the same urban complex. To the end of classical Mesopotamian history one can note not only the specific functions of palace and temple as power centers but also the continuing existence of civic assemblies, however much their influence was reduced in relation to the former in the late period.

Egypt

The development of culture in Egypt is essentially different from that of Mesopotamia, although in large, broad terms there are similarities. Egypt emerged from prehistory as a unified state by about 2800. The cultural situation of an era of city-states existing previous to the coalescence of national and imperial entities in Mesopotamia is not visibly paralleled in the Nile Valley, though most historians appear to agree that some sort of provincial, or nomic, division of the land may have existed. There never was a single city center that served as the heart of the land. Rather, Egypt was an agricultural nation replete with small agricultural villages that were spread out along the many miles of her extent. The more important ones were already small cult centers before the great ages of Egyptian historical development. One or another of these could become a capital city if a dynasty made its home there or for other reasons chose to honor it—witness Memphis in the early phase of the Old Kingdom or Thebes from about 2000 onward. Particular places may be seen as focal points for the religious and intellectual life of the country, for example, Abydos, Heliopolis, Hermopolis, and others. By and large, archaeology does not support the idea of any large and continuing size for such places as Memphis, Thebes, or Heliopolis.

The typical capital "city" appears in Egypt as a highly specialized religious and political enclave, which was often of immense proportions. It was dominated by the temple complex of the local god, to which might then be added auxiliary complexes of other gods who functioned centrally in the nation's pantheon. Although there now exists no trace of the populated areas of Memphis, two rectangular enclosures oriented north and south have been found. The former contained the palaces, the latter the temples. At Thebes a processional avenue bordered by sphinxes, about three kilometers long, connects the temple of Amun at Luxor with that of Amun at Karnak; together with adjacent courts and building complexes dedicated to other gods (Ptah, Montu, Osiris, Mut, Khonsu), the Theban agglomeration of massive religious architecture served de facto as the heart of the capital. The remainder of the town has not survived.

Archaeology in Egypt reveals a variety of village and town types, encompassing the period from prehistory to the Greco-Roman era. Unlike Iraq, where we can observe a rather full sequence of development from the tiny protoagricultural village to the walled city of historical times, in Egypt we must be content with a far less complete record. In its final prehistoric phases we encounter at first the barest habitation enclaves—encampments without architecture, protected by wind screens. These existed on the hilly spurs of the Nile cliffs, which border the river. Between 5000 and 3500, roughly the period of the Neolithic in Egypt, we encounter embryonic towns both at Merimde-Fayyum in the southwest Delta region and within the Tasian-Badarian cultural zone of Upper Egypt. By about 3200 numerous sites are at hand in Upper Egypt (at Hierakonpolis, Naqada, and Abydos) and in the Delta south of present-day Cairo, at Ma'adi and El Amra. Two predynastic slate palettes offer pictorial representations of fortified towns of this period. Additionally, two hieroglyphic signs allow the inference that early towns were small groups of structures, perhaps situated at a crossroads and surrounded by walls, and that the district, or nome, was a rectangular area, intersected into squares, whose sides represented irrigation dikes or canals.

For historic Egypt, in addition to the smaller or larger agricultural village and the administrative and religious capital, we may cite certain settlements that had specialized characteristics, such as those of the Delta (e.g., Sais, Busiris, Bubastis and Tanis) that were port or harbor towns, especially Tanis of the thirteenth century, through which trade with Phoenicia was funneled. Border fortress towns guarded the approaches to the Delta and, in the south, the approaches to Upper Egypt. Perhaps the most interesting and unusual type of "city" was the pyramid complex, a veritable "city of the dead," which in addition to the pyramid and surrounding streets of tombs contained preplanned settlements for the workmen on the mortuary buildings and orthogonally laid out quarters for funerary priests.

Short of reviewing the entire panoply of town and village forms in Egypt, we may arrive at some views of the nature of urbanism in the Nile Valley. The basis of this was the agricultural estate, the manor. The population was strung out along the entire narrow length of cultivable land in the valley. In a sense the Nile is the Main Street of every Egyptian settlement. The religious orientation of the ancient Egyptians affirmed that the pharaoh was a living god dwelling in their midst. The site of his palace became the actual center of the country, and as we have seen this center could shift from period to period. The monumental buildings erected while he was alive—whether to accommodate his administrative activities or to celebrate the worship of the national gods or alternatively to provide him, in a massive funerary complex, with home after death—all became the nuclear structures around which specific concentrations of population (administrators, clergy, workmen) settled. *As in Mesopotamia, the dominant idea of the urban enclave is a combination of such concentrations and the agricultural setting in which they appeared; there was no real dichotomy between the "urban" and the "rural."* The farmer and the townsman maintained a naturally close relationship. As also in Mesopotamia the "other" was the "sand-dweller," he who was not a civilized person, the one who perennially threatened Egypt with chaos from his home in Sinai or Libya.

Finally, in Egypt from the beginning of dynastic rule, there was a harmony of the parts, an integrated system of rule in which the pharaoh's residence guided the fortunes of the entire land. Only in the predynastic period and in periods of national breakdown does the Egyptian "city" appear as a completely autonomous entity. We do not encounter a tradition of strong personal and civic rights that exist independently of the powerful state and religious organizations, although this is not to say that norms of law and conduct were not pervasive in the land.

West Semitic/Hebrew

Within the Syro-Palestinian culture sphere there was a dichotomy of attitudes toward the city brought about by the historical imposition of Hebrew culture and religion, which were originally pastoralist, upon the autochthonous Canaanite city-state culture. The development of proto-urban and urban forms can be traced from as far back as the tenth millennium. With the exception of an occasional monumentally developed site, such as Jericho, the entire area was dotted with agricultural villages and towns, the larger ones dominated by the palace-temple systems that have already been discussed for Mesopotamian cities. These were the seats of usually autonomous dynasties. After about 2000 we discern a veritable system of small city-states distributed on heights, at entrances to valleys and wadis, and at communications crossroads. These cities are massively walled and may dominate an entire region. Yet we cannot speak of any large national state in Palestine until after 1000, when the Israelites established themselves in the land.

The Canaanite city-state system survived numerous threats—constant attacks by pastoralist tribes, conquest by Imperial Egypt in the fifteenth through fourteenth centuries, and vicious intercity warfare—until it was finally subjugated by Israel under David (about 1040–1000) and incorporated under Hebrew rule. The cities of this system were every bit as imposing as their Mesopotamian counterparts except in the matter of size. None, for example, attained the population concentration of a Babylon in its heyday. Some of them could depend upon irrigation agriculture; others developed elaborate storage facilities for grain and large cisterns for collecting rainwater in the absence of permanent streams in their environment. In all, the typical Canaanite city had at its power center that same complex of palace and temple administration that we observed in Mesopotamia; the population within it was a combination of fully free and half-free individuals who were routinely taxed, subjected to the corvée, and generally directed by an autocratic monarchy, although some evidence for citizen assemblies does exist.

The success of the Hebrews against the Canaanite city-states was very slow in coming and was achieved at great loss. The Hebrews had originally a strong loathing of urban life; the experience of slavery in Egypt (for some) and in various Canaanite cities (for others of the group) was strongly impressed upon the tribal consciousness of the constituent members. The crisis for Israel came with the practical need for a permanent leader, who could organize the often individualistic member tribes into an effective fighting force. Where Saul failed David succeeded. David's achievement was the reduction of the last Canaanite strongholds in the land, the capture of Jerusalem, and the establishment of the nucleus of a palace-temple complex in a capital city now selected to rule a sedentarized Hebrew-Canaanite mixed population. In 1 Sm 8 we get a capsule view, probably dating to premonarchic times, of what the institution of kingship would mean to the tribes: the image of a king's autocratic actions there given is a reflection of what city-based Canaanite kingship actually was. After David's victories the old tribal covenant with Yahweh was altered so that the deity now became the guarantor of David's dynasty and also the patron of his newly established temple in Jerusalem (although biblical thought strongly affirms that Yahweh was not limited to the temple but ruled everywhere in the universe).

In general, the chief distinction in appearance between city, town, and village was that the city was walled. As elsewhere in the Fertile Crescent the walled city was the economic and military center for a group of smaller settlements, which are often called its "daughters" (b^{e}nôth), a term that can mean, in special contexts, "town." Some further distinction between city and village may be seen in the legal sphere, where the redemption of houses after sale is subject, in each type of settlement, to different laws.

Throughout the Bible occur references to various types of settlements: we encounter the "store-city," the "chariot-city," and the city for horsemen. There are royal cities, as contrasted with country towns. Some cities were also built especially as fortress or garrison cities.

Although Israel was not itself a maritime power, it acted in concert with Phoenician fleets in the pre-Exilic period; the ports of Sidon and

Tyre figured strongly in its economy, as did Gaza and later Joppa. In the third and second millennia, well before the establishment of the Israelites in Palestine, Byblos on the Lebanese coast had been the major port in the Levant and had vigorously traded its cedarwood to Egypt. From the point of view of overland trade, the caravan cities, such as Sela (later Petra), Teman, Tadmor (later Palmyra), and Damascus, also figured strongly in the prosperity of early monarchic Israel.

Finally should be mentioned a special feature of the Israelite urban system—the "City of Refuge." Six cities of the Levites were selected to provide sanctuary for those who had killed accidentally. The right of asylum in biblical law was restricted to accidental homicide alone, and the provision of safety for the perpetrator was vital under Israelite religious conceptions, "lest innocent blood [i.e., because of consequent blood vengeance upon the guiltless] be shed in your land . . . so the guilt of bloodshed be upon you" (Dt 19:10).

Images of the City in Ancient Near Eastern Literature

Mesopotamia

We return once more to the ancient mounds of the Near East. We begin the second part of our discussion by noting that the remains of ruined cities in the pre-Hellenistic period all share a common feature, albeit with variations in execution. They are physically dominated by a high spot within their precincts, and we have pointed out that within this focal area, which was usually walled in, stands a temple complex and a palace. These represent the habitations, respectively, of the tutelary god of the city (and other gods) and the king. The latter, in Mesopotamia, is only the human representative of the gods, though in Assyria he is also the chief priest. Our particular concern here is not with the palace and the king but with the temple and the god. Whatever the size or shape of the ruin, however important the site may have been in its own time, whatever its specialized function, *the city contained a temple area that represented the literal house or houses of particular deities, places in which the gods were actually conceived to live.* The temple in an ancient Near Eastern city not only represented an important civic institution; it was, to my view, the civic institution par excellence. It was, as seen in the literature, the first institution of the city to be created and the one that directly linked heaven with the affairs of men.

In actual idea the cities of the ancient Near East are understood to belong to a god. They are therefore counters in the great swings of destiny determined by the gods. History is of urbanites, destined to live out their lives as tenants in residences created by the gods. It is an affair of cities, and the affairs of cities are held to be exclusively determined by the will of the gods.

Nowhere is this more clearly seen than in the creation and organization myths of ancient Near Eastern societies (a special case is Israel, to be discussed subsequently). Since these societies were traditionally oriented, looked back, that is, to mythic foundations for the ultimate source of the authority that governed them, the stories about the founding of cult places and cities assume an especially central position in the religious and historical consciousness of their members. Even for Israel, which did not acquire cities until long after it had come into being as a religious community of covenanted tribes and for whom creation myths were of secondary importance, the sanctity of Jerusalem as *the* cult center—that is, the true city of God—was an undisputed fact.

Most analysts of ancient Near Eastern myth have occupied themselves with the *content* of the literary works that show the gods in action in one or another kind of plot. *Setting,* as a key component of such works, has been almost entirely neglected. But if we now turn to Sumerian myths of creation and organization, we encounter not only repeated statements about the creation of cities but also the circumstance that the plots involving the gods frequently take place in an urban setting, in cities *before* the creation of man had taken place. We may allude to a group of nine myths that S. N. Kramer has studied over the years, five of which have such characteristics.

Enlil, the air god and tutelary deity of Nippur, figures in a number of these. This god separated heaven from earth and united with earth to set the stage for the organization of the universe, the creation of man, and the establishment of civilization. In the myth *Enlil and Ninlil: The Begetting of the Moon God, Nanna,* a long introduction celebrates Nippur as "the bond of heaven and earth." As yet no human lives within it. The plot concerns the begetting of Nanna and three underworld deities; the action is set within the city, at its gate, or in immediately surrounding areas—Nippur which has a pure river, a quay where the boats stand, a well of good water, and a pure canal. Nippur again figures as the spiritual center of Sumeria in the myth *The Journey of Nanna to Nippur.* Nanna, now the tutelary deity of Ur, comes to the shrine of Enlil in Nippur bearing gifts in order to obtain Enlil's blessing, even as the tutelary deities of the other important Sumerian cities were expected to do. Here again Nippur is celebrated in the introduction and is described as fully built before any human inhabited it. On his way to Nippur Nanna is described as visiting five cities, in each of which he is courteously greeted.

A particularly interesting myth, *The Creation of the Pickaxe,* which contains passages of special importance for the Sumerian conception of creation of the universe, tells how Enlil brought the pickaxe into existence and gave it exalted power. He bestowed it upon the Anunnaki (subordinate gods, usually described en masse), who in turn gave it to the Sumerian people to hold. This is the pickaxe, which with the basket

> . . . builds cities
> The steadfast house the pickaxe builds,
>   the steadfast house the pickaxe establishes,
> The steadfast house it causes to prosper . . .

With a slightly different orientation the myth of *Enki and Ninhursag* celebrates the land Dilmun, a veritable paradise except that it lacks sweet water. When the latter is supplied through the order of Enki, the water god, and the action of Utu, the sun god, Dilmun is described thus:

> Her (Ninhursag's) city drinks the water of abundance,
> Dilmun drinks the water of abundance . . .
> Her city, behold, it is become the house of the banks and quays of the
>   land.

We see that the celebration of cities within which the gods lived and were conceived to function is no less an important part of the essential Sumerian (and later Mesopotamian) conception than the activities of the gods themselves. A further excellent example of this, particularly pertinent because it makes an identification of the god's house with his city itself, comes from the myth *Enki and Eridu: The Journey of the Water God to Nippur.* Here it is the ancient city of Eridu that is described. After the creation of the earth and of agricultural abundance, the water god Enki

> Built his house of silver and lapis lazuli;
> Its silver and lapis lazuli, like sparkling light
> The father fashioned fittingly in the abyss.

After creating his temple Enki brings Eridu into being and fills it with gardens and animal life. All that is now required is Enlil's blessing for the new temple and city. To get this, Enki journeys to Nippur, where, at a divine feast, Enlil says,

My son has built a house, the king Enki;
Eridu, like a mountain, he has raised up from the earth,
In a good place he built it

Eridu, the pure house having been built,
O Enki, praise!

No real distinction is made between the temple of Eridu and the city itself, which is also a sacred creation of Enki.

Beyond the particular myths that celebrate the gods and their shrines in particular cities, we can point to a pattern in Sumerian cosmogonic thought that stresses, first, that natural abundance was created, and then, and completely naturally and matter-of-factly, that cities came into being. The Sumerian gods fashion a universe in which the culmination of creative activity is the founding of cult centers and their attendant cities, so that the chief gods of the pantheon may be revered in their own special places. Concomitant with the idea of the gods creating their earthly residences is, in relation to the creation of man, that first, in the state of nature, men were like animals, did not know how to eat bread or clothe themselves. Through a gift of the gods men became agriculturalists and partakers of the civilized arts. Thus to the Sumerian poets it is the seminomadic, the tribal Amorites, who are described as "uncivilized"—they who do not know grain, who do not know houses, who do not know cities. Recall here that in the *Gilgamesh Epic* of the Old Babylonian period (1900–1600) Enkidu, who is created as a companion for Gilgamesh, at first runs wild with the animals but is enticed into "civilization" in Uruk, whence his adventures with Gilgamesh ensue. Usually, as a parallel to the notion of the gods building their own shrine cities, mankind is assigned the task, and men are further relegated to serving the gods as their mission in life.

To return to the notion of the civic setting of myths of creation and acquisition of civilization, the myth *Inanna and Enki: The Transfer of the Arts of Civilization from Eridu to Uruk* purports to show how Uruk claimed its place within the milieu of the ancient Sumerian cultural centers. Inanna, the Queen of Heaven and tutelary goddess of that city, brought the arts of civilization to it after numerous adventures. This and other myths, too numerous to discuss, emphasize the unique role of particular ancient cities (Nippur, Ur, Eridu, Uruk) as the setting for the origins, growth, and diffusion of the civilized arts. It is the gods in and from their resident cities and temples who ultimately decree and work out the form of Sumerian civilization.

So pervasive is civic consciousness and the city in Sumerian views of the universe and human destiny that their major forms of literature other than myths reveal this theme consistently. In what little epic materials we have from Sumeria, we can nonetheless see that the epic hero par excellence is the king of a city, whose actions take place against a backdrop of civic responsibility. For example, the tale *Gilgamesh and Agga* shows the king defending his city despite the reluctance of the elders in the assembly. Also in the tales in which Gilgamesh seeks to establish an immortal name, as in *Gilgamesh and the Land of the Living,* or undergoes adventures involving the *huluppu* (willow?) tree planted by his city's goddess in Uruk, the city is as natural and important to the background setting as any of the magical or divine realms within which the action takes place.

Of the many Sumerian genres that deserve probing relative to our theme, only two more will be mentioned. The first is the genre of historical writing; the second, that of the lamentation. While we have very little in the way of Sumerian historical records as such, we do have a "King List," composed in the later stages of Sumerian development (about 2200). From this we learn that five cities were alleged to have existed before the onset of the Deluge and that history begins when kingship is lowered from Heaven to the first city, Eridu. The scribe records the transfer of kingship then to Bad-Tibira, Karak, Sippar, and finally Shuruppak. The scribe assumes that Sumeria was always a unified nation (which it was not) and presents a view of the transfer of political power from one capital city to another at the behest of the gods, who purely and simply direct the process. Even the Deluge is not held to disrupt the process for too long for kingship is again lowered to a dominant city.

Finally, the Sumerians brought to a high point of artistic development the form in which the fate of a city becomes the subject of elegiac treatment. Probably the most famous lamentation that has come to us from pre-Classical antiquity, other than the biblical book of Lamentations, is the *Lamentation over the Destruction of Ur.* This work commemorates the destruction of Ur III by the Elamites and the Subarians at about 2000, although the poem may have been written at some time later than the actual event. In eleven songs or stanzas of uneven length the poet describes how the tutelary deities of various Sumerian cities, including Ur, have abandoned their cult centers, their cities, and how Anu and Enlil, the chief Sumerian deities, have ordered Ur to be destroyed and its people killed. Even Ningal, wife of Nanna (the protector of Ur), cannot prevail through her pleas. The narration of destruction pitifully informs the reader of the catastrophe that has befallen humans and gods alike. Nothing could be worse than a deity who abandons or is forced to abandon his city through a decree of the superior gods. We see affirmed most movingly that, just as the greatest wish of a deity is to claim a cult place in a city for himself, the greatest calamity is to see the city destroyed. It is as though all significant life has ceased.

Later Mesopotamian literature continues to display the high regard for the city that we encounter in the earliest materials. Only two major works need to be cited to make the point. The great Babylonian *Epic of Creation* gives us a vivid insight into the founding of the Temple of Marduk at Babylon and the promotion of that city to the most renowned place in the Mesopotamian political sun. In the *Gilgamesh Epic* of the Old Babylonian period, a work that persisted in popularity through the Neo-Assyrian period, the poet skillfully uses Gilgamesh's city, Uruk, as a literary setting, along with the various cosmic and mythical regions that function in the plot. Although the reader is taken along on the various adventures undertaken by Gilgamesh and his companion, Enkidu, he is never allowed to forget that he is observing the king of Uruk in action, and a number of key scenes in the work take place within the walls, even on the walls, of that city. Both the introduction to the poem and its postlude direct the reader's attention to the civic setting, and the entire poem invites the reader to see the plot and theme as involving both the terrestrial and the divine worlds in an integrated fashion.

The Mesopotamian city was conceived in spirit to be a divine rather than a human creation in the first instance. At creation the gods fixed the plans of things that were to be. Indeed, we have a reference in Sennacherib's inscriptions (704–681), describing the king's building activities in Nineveh, to "Nineveh, whose ground plan has been drawn since the beginning in the stars in the sky." Other sporadic references refer to the gods' activities as city founders. Recent detailed reference has also been made to the Mesopotamian notion of "the eternal city." At least four Mesopotamian cities bore this designation: Sippar, Babylon, Nippur, and Uruk. The supreme deity of the pantheon, Anu, bears the epithet "lord of the eternal city," a significant equation of the primordial universe with the image of the city.

Egypt

For the Egyptian as for the Mesopotamian, the "city," or, better, the monumental religious complex that passed for such, was primarily thought of in divine contexts. *The Theology of Memphis* gives an account of the creation through the actions of Ptah, patron of that city. After Ptah had completed his work he was satisfied with all that he had made:

> He had formed the gods, he had made cities, he had founded nomes, he had put the gods in their shrines, he had established their offerings, he had founded their shrines, he had made their bodies like that (with which) their hearts were satisfied.

More than this, Ptah had also created the *ka*-spirits within all created things, which is to say, the vital energy and the creative force that sustained them. Hence the cities, too, were animated by the divine creative will.

In addition to the *ka,* it is important to mention the *ba.* The *ba* that a god *possesses* is the manifestation of his power, or, according to a most fascinatingly complicated concept, a god can also *be* a *ba.* And not only a god, but also kings (who were theoretically gods) and ordinary men. Even inanimate objects possessed a *ba* or *bas;* they have been cited for such diverse entities as the Sphinx at Giza, pylons of the Temple of Isis at Philae, threshing floors, doors, and of special purport for towns. It has been pointed out that Egyptian texts frequently refer to groups of *bas* connected with religiously and politically famous ancient cities (e.g., Buto, Hierakonpolis, Heliopolis). Louis Zabkar, after a careful study of the use of the terminology, was left with the impression that the *bas* of Buto, Heliopolis, and so forth, "all indicate the same thing, that is, the divinized dead kings of the ancient cities." He further concludes that "In their various aspects of *kas, bas,* . . . the divinized kings reside in those famous religious centers but are at the same time present in all important events in the pharaoh's life as guarantors of the divine kingly office and as protectors of their successor, the living Horus, who at death joins their company and becomes one of the divinized members of the ancestral corporations of dead kings." Put another way, in Egypt there is an unin-

terrupted line of divine ancestors, beginning in mythic times with a
dynasty of gods ruling on earth and emerging as the divinized kings of
historic times, which has always been worshiped in their various cult
cities; this line of deities literally animates the cities. The current king is
just the living, terrestrial representative of all the kings or gods who have
ever ruled, and his residence is the site where his and, by implication, all
the ancestor gods' power is manifest at all times. Thus we can begin to
grasp, however dimly, how intimately the divine world and the human
world are understood to meet in the cities, the cult centers of Egypt.

Last but not least, we may refer to texts that especially extol the cities
of Thebes and of Ramses. Thebes is described as the place where the
primeval hillock emerged from Nun (the original watery chaos); hence
it is the site where creation took place. Thebes is also described as the
norm of every other city; that is, only under its domination were other
Egyptian cities allowed to be designated as cities. As one text reports,
"Every (other) city is under (her) shadow, to magnify themselves
through Thebes. She is the *norm.*"

In the thirteenth century, pharaohs of the Nineteenth Dynasty built
the city of Ramses as their residence city in the eastern Delta. A poetic
composition is lavish in praise of the new foundation, which was likened
to Thebes itself. A picture of the city as a veritable paradise is presented,
and the poet ends with an address to Ramses II (User-maat-Re), its resident pharaoh:

> (So) dwell content of heart and free, without stirring from it, O
> User-maat-Re . . . life, prosperity, health!—Montu in the Two-
> Lands, Ramses Meri-Amon—life, prosperity, health!—thou god!

Here again the viable referent of the city is the pharaoh-god, for whose
support and well-being the city exists in the first instance.

West Semitic/Hebrew

This final section proposes to concentrate exclusively on biblical materials, although some motifs of extant Ugaritic (Canaanite) myths might
profitably be discussed were there sufficient space. A dramatic plot that
relates how Baal acquired a "house" (or temple) at Ugarit and therefore
became Lord of the City is of a piece with Mesopotamian motifs,
although its setting is more vividly concerned with fertility than the
usual Mesopotamian examples. Accordingly we shall pass on to present
some key biblical ideas and images of the city.

In the two major creation stories of the Bible, Genesis 1–2:4 and Genesis 2:4–3, it is vital to note that Yahweh is *not* considered to be the creator of cities. The former (a late story within the tradition) reveals creation through phases or stages. After the natural world is brought into being man is created as the crowning achievement, but there is no stage of urban civilization as is encountered in Mesopotamia or Egypt. The latter story, of early vintage, simply stresses an agricultural paradise (Garden of Eden) as the original setting of man. The created universe is a Nature that exists *before* the onset of civilization. It is, in fact, the loss of Paradise that initiates human history, with all its travail. In a real sense civilization is sort of "punishment" that results from disobedience to the divine decree in the Garden of Eden.

In Genesis 4:17 it is Cain who is the first builder of a city. That Cain was first a farmer, an inferior to Abel, the sheep herder, suggests a double theme: first we are introduced to a typical pastoralist view of the world, that God loves the herder more than the tiller of the soil; second, following a phase of agriculture, a phase of urban life is introduced in human development. There are further numerous examples of antiurban bias in the myth fragments and quasihistorical tales in Genesis, for example, the Tower of Babel story, which shows God confounding the desire of men to achieve fame and unity by interrupting their building of a city (with a Mesopotamian ziggurat!) and scattering them over the face of the earth. Also the generally peaceful and pious life of the patriarchs is starkly contrasted to the corruption of such cities as Sodom and Gomorrah. Nor should we forget that according to the book of Exodus the bondage of the Hebrews in Egypt consisted of their being forced to build the store cities of Pithom and Raamses in the Delta.

In the Patriarchal period (pre-thirteenth century) encounters with God occur at sacred shrines or individual trees or rocks or even at the patriarch's tent. The Mosaic period (thirteenth century) reveals a god who speaks from a burning bush or leads the wandering tribes through the deserts in the form of a pillar of cloud. Always the image of Palestine as a "land of milk and honey," where Yahweh will dwell with the tribes, is vividly contrasted with the reality of the hostile Canaanite cities and their well-armed warriors, their kings, and their resident alien gods.

With the establishment of Jerusalem as the capital of an Israelitic state, the Hebrew attitude toward city life underwent a dramatic change, although the diehard antiurbanist could always be found. Some eight psalms specifically celebrate Jerusalem as the habitat of God, while many of the rest have Jerusalem and its temple as an implied setting. "Great is the Lord and greatly to be praised in the city of our God!" sings the psalmist of Jerusalem. "His holy mountain beautiful in elevation is the joy of all the earth" (Ps 48:1–2). In a time of danger Psalm 46 asserts that "God is in the midst of her [i.e., Jerusalem]" (l. 5). God's abode "has been established in Salem, his dwelling pace in Zion" (Ps 76:2). In Psalm 87 God is assumed to have created Jerusalem: "On the holy mount stands the city he founded; the Lord loves the gates of Zion more than all the dwelling places of Jacob" (ll. 1–2). Psalm 132 further elaborates this idea: "For the Lord has chosen Zion; he has desired it for his habitations: 'This is my resting place for ever; here I will dwell, for I have desired it'" (ll. 13–14). In two psalms a view of Jerusalem is given through the point of view of pilgrims to the city: "How lovely is thy dwelling place, O Lord of hosts!" sings the psalmist. "My soul longs, yea, faints for the courts of the Lord; my heart and flesh sing for joy to the living God" (Ps 84:1–2), and the lovely "For a day in thy courts is better than a thousand elsewhere. I would rather be a doorkeeper in the house of my God than dwell in the tents of wickedness" (l. 10). Again, in Psalm 122 the pilgrims celebrate "Jerusalem, built as a city which is bound firmly together, to which the tribes go up, the tribes of the Lord, as was decreed for Israel, to give thanks to the name of the Lord. There thrones for judgment were set, the thrones of the house of David" (ll. 3–5). One final reference worth quoting is from Psalm 2, where the Lord says, in derisive anger at kings who would attack Israel, "I have set my king on Zion, my holy hill" (l. 6).

Following the destruction of Jerusalem in 586 and the exile of much of its population to Babylonia, Israel was a community that experienced an obsessive longing for its lost home and capital city. "How lonely sits the city that was full of people!" writes the poet of Lamentations. "How like a widow has she become, she that was great among the nations! She that was a princess among the cities has become a vassal" (1:1). The biblical elegy echoes the Sumerian lament of fifteen hundred years earlier, with the critical difference that Yahweh is understood to be punishing Israel and Jerusalem for their moral derelictions. In two marvelous passages the prophet Ezekiel describes visions of the Lord leaving his temple and his city. While Ezekiel watched, "the glory of the Lord went up from the cherubim to the threshold of the house; and the house was filled with the cloud and the cloud was full of the brightness of the glory of the Lord. . . . Then the glory of the Lord went forth from the threshold of the house, and stood over the cherubim. . . . Then the cherubim lifted up their wings, with the wheels beside them; and the glory of the God of Israel was over them. And the glory of the Lord went from the midst of the city" (10:4, 10:18, 11:23). Further visions depict the rebuilding of the temple, and Ezekiel sees, from a very high mountain, "on which was a structure like a city opposite me" (40:2). What follows is an elaborate description of an idealized temple, in the earlier Solomonic style. The temple having been "seen" and carefully described, Ezekiel then describes the return of God to it and his holy city: "And behold, the glory of the God of Israel came from the east . . . and the vision I saw was like the vision which I had seen when he came to destroy the city" (43:2–3). The book of Ezekiel ends with a description of the new Jerusalem, whose name henceforth shall be "The Lord is there" (48:30–35).

The earthly Jerusalem was rebuilt but slowly after the exiles were allowed to return after 539 by benevolent Persian rulers, who now were masters of the Near East. By 445 it still lay in disrepair, and by 398 its community had still not fully been reorganized. Gradually, as the destructive tempo of history made of the small postexilic Jewish community a pawn between warring successors of Alexander, then a resisting vassal of Rome, the idea of the Jerusalem where God would rule forever was translated into the heavenly sphere, and it is appropriate to draw this vignette to a close by alluding to the vision of the "new Jerusalem" that we find in the Book of Revelation. An angel carries John, the "seer" of the book, "to a great, high mountain, and showed me the holy city Jerusalem coming down out of heaven from God, having the glory of God, its radiance like a most rare jewel. . . . And the city has no need of sun or moon to shine upon it, for the glory of God is its light, and its lamp is the Lamb. By its light shall the nations walk; and the kings of the earth shall bring their glory into it, and its gates shall never be shut by day—and there shall be no night there" (21:10–11, 23–25). Significantly there is no temple in the city, "for its temple is the Lord God the Almighty and the Lamb" (21:22). The image of the "new Jerusalem" entered Europe as a key doctrine of Christian thought for centuries; even today it is implicit in much millenarian thought.

FURTHER READING

Adams, Robert. *Land Behind Baghdad: A History of Settlement on Diyala Plains.* Chicago: University of Chicago Press, 1965.

Kraeling, C. H., and R. Adams. *City Invincible: A Symposium on Urbanization and Cultural Development in the Ancient Near East.* Chicago: University of Chicago Press, 1960.

∾ Especially for Students ∾

LANGUAGES AND LITERATURE

A Brief Note on Languages

The ancient Near East was never unified under a single political rule until the conquest of Alexander the Great (late fourth century) and subsequently the Romans. It existed as territorial blocks, each dominated by peoples of different origins, traditions, and modes of life. Quite apart from the geographical unity of the entire area, its inhabitants were especially defined by differences in the languages they spoke and in which they wrote. At least four major linguistic families can be identified. These are the Hamito-Semitic or Afro-Asiatic; the Semitic; the Indo-European; and the Iranian, a sub-branch of the Indo-European.

A family of languages is a group whose members are related as connected to an earlier language in matters of features such as grammar, vocabulary, and formative processes; prefixes, suffixes, and voiced and unvoiced consonants; and a number of other technical comparisons. Looking just at the Hamito-Semitic, ancient Egyptian is but one division of this category, which also includes many languages of present-day West Africa and Berber of North Africa. Ancient Egyptian was written in hieroglyphics from about 3000 and in cursive writing on papyrus from about 1900.

The Semitic family was by far the most widespread in Near Eastern antiquity. Scholars recognize three branches: East Semitic, Northwest Semitic, and Southwest Semitic.

East Semitic includes Akkadian, spoken by the ancient Babylonians and Assyrians. The northern dialect of Akkadian was employed by the Assyrians; the southern, by the Babylonians. The language in both areas was written in cuneiform, or wedge-shaped writing on clay tablets and

183

monuments. This writing system was invented by the Sumerians, the earliest historical inhabitants of Mesopotamia, and adopted by subsequent Semitic invaders. The cuneiform system of writing endured for more than two thousand years and was even adapted to express non-Semitic languages, such as Indo-European Hittite.

North Semitic is the Semitic spoken by Amorites, Canaanites, Phoenicians, Hebrews, Moabites, Edomites, Ammonites, and others in the Palestinian corridor. The term *Canaanite* proves difficult because it is imprecise. It has been used to describe many Palestinian dialects, excluding Aramaic. The outstanding members of the Northwest Semitic family, along with the already mentioned Aramaic, are Hebrew, Phoenician, and Ugaritic.

Southwest Semitic includes in its family ancient South Arabic, Ethiopic, and North Arabic.

The third great linguistic division of the ancient Near East is the Indo-European. Hittite was the dominant language of the Old Hittite kingdom and New Empire between 1750 and 1200. It was written in cuneiform as borrowed from Mesopotamia.

Finally, the Iranian, or Indo-Iranian, family is represented by Old Persian, sixth to fourth centuries BC, written in cuneiform.

Five additional languages employed in the ancient Near East, having left larger or smaller numbers of texts in the cuneiform script, have not been shown to belong to any known language family. These are Sumerian (lower Mesopotamia), Elamite (early southwest Iran, also an official language of the Persian Empire), Kassite (mid-second millennium in Mesopotamia), Hurrian (northern Mesopotamia and Asia Minor), and Urartaean (northern Mesopotamia and Asia Minor).

A General View of
Ancient Near Eastern Literature

Ancient Near Eastern literature comprises works from at least seven major cultures that thrived some three thousand years before the time of Christ in the lands bordering upon the eastern Mediterranean. For convenience they may be spoken of as belonging to three dominant cultural streams: (a) the *Mesopotamian-Anatolian,* which includes productions written in cuneiform (wedge-shaped) characters on clay tablets, as well as on stone stelae or prepared rock surfaces, by the Sumerians (lower Iraq, ca. 3000–2000), the Babylonians (lower Iraq, ca. 2000–539), the Assyrians (upper Iraq, ca. 2000–612), and the Hittites (central Turkey, ca. 1750–1200); (b) the *Syro-Palestinian,* which is characterized chiefly by Canaanite literature from Ras Shamra (ancient Ugarit) on the Syrian coast, written in a cuneiform alphabetic script on clay tablets and dating to about 1400, and by the Bible, the sacred book of the Hebrews, which contains materials that begin to appear in written form some five hundred years later in the Hebrew script on papyrus and other soft materials; and (c) the *Egyptian,* which contains works inscribed on stone (such as pyramid, temple, and tomb inscriptions) and on papyrus, the whole extant body covering a time period from about 2500 to 330. A small corpus of royal inscriptions emanating from Achaemenid kings (ca. 539–330), produced in cuneiform on stone stelae and on prepared rock faces, when added to the limited number of clay tablets emanating from Elamite culture (ca. 3000 et seq.), represents the chief written materials of the oldest classical Iranian culture.

Since the totality of the literatures just delineated comes from an area where the three continents of Europe, western Asia, and Africa meet, it is characterized by works in a number of both related and unrelated languages. The chief language subdivisions represented are Semitic, Indo-European, Indo-Iranian, and Hamito-Semitic. The classical representations of the eastern branch of the Semitic languages are Babylonian and Assyrian; of the western, Canaanite (Ugaritic), Hebrew, Phoenician,

Aramaic; and Hamito-Semitic by ancient Egyptian. The major unclassified languages include Sumerian, upon whose literary heritage of themes and forms much of Assyrian and Babylonian literature is founded; Hurrian (the biblical Horite), which contributed much to Hittite religion and literature; and Kassite and Elamite, each of which remains little known.

It should be appreciated then that ancient Near Eastern literature is the result of a process of continual transmission of themes and forms between cultures of vastly different origins and modes of life and of different degrees of sophistication all interacting for almost three millennia in a single geographical arena. What facilitated this transmission throughout the region were the two dominant writing systems—the cuneiform, developed by the Sumerians, which became the normative form of expressing the many different languages of peoples inhabiting the northern tier of regions in the Near East, and the hieroglyphic, which although limited for the most part to Egypt gave the impetus for the development of experiments in cursive writing within the Syro-Palestinian corridor. But what most allows us to speak of ancient Near Eastern literature as a category, in addition to the circumstance that it comes from a definable time period and a circumscribed area and that it is expressed in a few common writing systems (although in different languages), is the characteristic that it has been elaborated from some half dozen major genres and but a slightly larger number of lesser genres. For the former we have myth, epic, historical narrative, wisdom literature (i.e., theodicies, instructions, meditations, proverbs, and sayings), hymns and prayers, and incantations and omens. For the latter we may add fables, folktales and legends, lamentations, songs, dialogue debates, autobiography, satire, riddles, and the like. This nucleus was already established in the earliest times by the Sumerian and the Egyptian "core" civilizations and was continually favored in all subsequent phases of society in Mesopotamia and Egypt, as well as by new societies of the intermediate and the fringe areas. The traditionalist bent of production of ancient Near Eastern peoples, in particular of the ruling cadres that controlled the production of literature (see later discussion), fostered continual copying and recopying of ancient works (as much to train new scribes in the art of writing as to preserve the outstanding works), so that where fresh themes appear, they do so most often within recognizably older literary forms.

Accordingly one may experience a sense of an underlying pervasive spirit of common cosmic awareness on the part of ancient Near Eastern cultures that is reflected, despite regional variations, in the literature from all parts of the area. The one outstanding exception to this statement is the religious vision of the Hebrews and Christians as presented in the Bible, but even here, despite the appearance of new genres reflecting that vision (such as the books of prophecy in the Old Testament and the gospel, the epistle, and the apocalyptic of the New Testament), there is constant use of traditional genres developed by the older, nonbiblical societies.

It is important to issue a few cautions before passing on to a presentation of guides to understanding the literature here discussed. For the contemporary Western reader, *literature* means belles lettres, but in the ancient Near East, works such as myths, epics, and the various forms of short imaginative literature that we would include under the term are but a very small minority of the written materials produced by a representative society. Far more important were what we would call "scholarly" texts and religious texts of everyday use. The excavation of Assurbanipal's library (ca. 650) at Nineveh in the last century disclosed that in this great repository (the ancient Near Eastern equivalent to the noted Library of Alexandria) the majority of works comprised omen literature, magical formulae and instructions, lexical materials of all types, and lists of objects belonging to both the natural and the human spheres of activity. Even historical texts and legal codes were minimal in number by comparison with the others. In Egypt the situation was not much different, with highest priority in all periods being reserved for funerary texts, the myriad of textual materials relating to priestly training and activity, to charms, omens, amulets, and the like. The great medical and mathematical texts also represent practical compendia. It might be wise to remind ourselves that writing was not necessarily invented to preserve the great thoughts and feelings of mankind; the evidence too frequently suggests that this precious intellectual tool was most often applied to the purposes of political and religious administration.

Furthermore, the Western reader thinks of literature as being predominantly produced by private persons, with the assistance of independent publishing houses. By contrast, however much the single literary creator lies behind a work that has become known to us from the ancient Near East, the work is preserved and continually recopied in what the late A. L. Oppenheim of the University of Chicago has called "the stream of tradition." The original writer fades into obscurity, and the work enters the public realm to serve a social purpose. Too often we are completely ignorant of the essential background details of any particular piece of literature. We do know that the greater and lesser works served to both train scribes and to form a corpus of consultative materials for the king's benefit. Of course the great myths and epics may have entertained the public through being declaimed by accomplished readers; certainly they existed in oral form. We simply do not know very much about the creation of, and audience for, a good many of the nonscholarly and nonliturgical works we encounter. The only really "private" materials in the ancient Near East are the thousands of business documents and letters that have been excavated and the imaginative writings, perhaps some anonymous love poems, that have gained great popularity.

Finally, two additional points must influence our approach to the literature of the ancient Near East. Because this literature was *produced* long before the time of Aristotle and the invention of literary theory, it defies classification into neat and precisely defined genres, although *genre* as used previously is a generally useful term. The Hammurabi Law Code is today recognized less as a document giving an accurate reflection of the legal usage of its time than as a calculated laudation of Hammurabi, the king, as "law giver," something that its highly florid prologue and epilogue and its idealistic tone confirm. One of the urgent tasks for present and future scholars is to propose principles of literary theory and criticism that are valid in terms of the evidence available in the absence of any such aids produced internally by the societies in question. The second point worth emphasizing is that the line between religious—or, more properly, sacred—literature and secular literature is by no means clear. It is truly difficult to accept any such distinction for societies in which religious perspectives were as totally pervasive as they were in each of the societies of the ancient Near East. We forget that most societies in the history of the world have been what we should call "religious societies," and their literatures, unlike that of Greece (where individual mental and aesthetic activity was not influenced by the existence of a restrictive religious outlook), usually reflect the dominant sacred viewpoints of the tradition. Consequently one must be as careful to not read Western secular viewpoints into ancient Near Eastern literature as one normally would be to not interpret ancient actions and institutions by contemporary standards of motivation and accomplishment.

DECIPHERMENTS

The Decipherment of Cuneiform Writing

Not all voyages of discovery lead to lost civilizations, hidden continents, or material treasure. Some of the most exciting have been intellectual adventures. A classic example of the latter is the nineteenth-century decipherment of cuneiform (wedge- or nail-shaped) writing, which was used to express at least eight different languages and many dialects of these in the ancient Near East. Its use for three thousand years before the birth of Christ makes it, along with Egyptian hieroglyphs, the longest used writing system in recorded history. By conservative estimate there exist today some hundreds of thousands of clay tablets and other surfaces, such as brick and stone, that bear cuneiform writing. These were found in the ruins of long-lost cities such as Nineveh, Babylon, and Ur and at many older sites in countries known today as Iran, Iraq, Syria, and Turkey. These writings represent not only public (state and temple) archives but also innumerable records of the day-to-day life of ancient Near Eastern peoples.

Cuneiform writing was invented by the Sumerians, who in about 3100 were founding city-states in the areas adjacent to the head of the Persian Gulf. So functional was their invention that it spread to every region that had contact with Sumerian civilization and to every people who attained political domination in the Tigris-Euphrates (Mesopotamian) River Valley for centuries, even millennia, thereafter. Thus it became the single most significant "civilizing" agent for many previously illiterate populations.

The chief inheritors and beneficiaries of the system were the Assyrians and Babylonians (who, respectively, occupied northern and southern Iraq after the fall of the Sumerian civilization in about 2000), the Hittites of central Turkey, the Elamites of earliest Iran, and the Achaemenid Persians of the sixth century and later. During the Achaemenid period, the use of cuneiform, an essentially cumbersome method of recording alphabetic and syllabic sounds and ideograms, gave way to the more easily written cursive Aramaic and became obsolete altogether about the time Christ lived. Knowledge of the cuneiform system appears to have died out with the gradual demise of the Old Persian and Babylonian scribal schools after Alexander the Great conquered the Persian Empire.

The rediscovery of the script, its identification, and subsequent decipherment is a saga of international scholarship whose heroes nonetheless are identifiable. Each made a contribution, whether a discoverer or copier of inscriptions, a linguistic experimenter, or (in the later stages) a professional scholar. The triumph came in 1857 AD, when four leading researchers—Henry Rawlinson, Edward Hincks, Fox Talbot, and Jules Oppert—independently studied a longish text and were found by the Royal Asiatic Society of London to agree on essential points of translation.

Before we turn to the key principles of the solution that made modern research into the vanished civilizations of the ancient Near East possible, it is interesting to consider the slow, often frustrating, but always fascinating progress of the early course of the decipherment.

Ruins and inscriptions in Persia came into focus first. At Isfahan the brilliant reign of Shah Abbas I (1587–1629) attracted European attention, and various royal courts sent diplomatic and commercial travelers eastward. In keeping with the seventeenth-century Renaissance spirit of discovery, many of these voyagers took a deep and scholarly interest in the unfamiliar peoples and places, and especially in the evidences of great antiquity, that they found.

As early as 1472 the Venetian ambassador Giosafat Barbero had admired the ruins of Takht-i-Jamshid northeast of Shiraz (later identified as ancient Persepolis), the reliefs at Naqsh-i-Rustam close by, and the ruins of Murgham (Cyrus the Great's Pasargade) further to the northeast. Antonio de Gouvea, ambassador of Philip III of Spain and Portugal, first noticed the writing at Takht-i-Jamshid and in 1602 commented on its complete unfamiliarity. The next Spanish ambassador, Don Garcia Silva Figueroa, was the first to identify the ruins at Takht-i-Jamshid with Darius's palace at Persepolis, using the historian Diodorus of Sicily's description as the basis for his determination.

In 1621 the Italian traveler Pietro della Valle sent to a friend in Venice a letter containing an inaccurate copy of five characters from an inscription in Persepolis. Four years later in another letter he described characters inscribed on sun-dried bricks he had collected at Ur of the Chaldees in southern Iraq. But it remained for later researchers to correlate the Persian and Mesopotamian writings.

Other contributors to the discovery of and earliest speculation about cuneiform inscriptions are too numerous to list, but special notice is due Sir Thomas Herbert (1606–82), who as a young man had been in the service of the British ambassador to Persia; Samuel Flower, an agent of the British East India Company, who collected characters at random from several inscriptions (these were the first to be published in England in 1693 after his death); and Jean (later John) Chardin, a naturalized Briton of French birth, who provided the first copy of a complete inscription from Persepolis.

After 1711, the date of Chardin's major communication, several avenues for future work opened up. First, whatever else they might turn out to be, the inscriptions thus far found appeared to belong within the milieu of old kings of Persia, although nearly a century was to pass before the Danish scholar Friedrich Münter (in 1802) presented reasonable grounds for the conclusion that they originated with the kings of the dynasty of Achaemenes (ca. sixth century to 310). This, of course, led the scholars to the writings of numerous ancient Greek historians (among them Herodotus) who had written vivid descriptions of ancient Persia and its rulers.

Second, it became clear that the three columns usually found in Persian cuneiform inscriptions did not represent one continuous text but rather were three copies of the same text. Chardin's first communication of a complete Persepolitian text had been of one of these. By 1778 another Danish savant, Carsten Niebuhr, had perceived that the Persepolis inscriptions utilized three different systems of writings; he labeled these I, II, and III. The first system contained the fewest characters (Niebuhr 42), the second seemed a more complicated script, while the third was richest in characters. Fourteen years later Münter, building on Niebuhr's fundamental perceptions, reasoned from his general knowledge of antiquity that multilingual inscriptions were commonly issued by the scribes of ancient courts and that the Persepolis texts, rather than comprising one pronouncement in three parts, were probably the selfsame message presented in three languages or dialects used by the Old Persians.

Further, he suspected that the writing in Column I was alphabetic script and that the writing in Column II was syllabic script, and he proposed that Column III contained ideographic or word signs. These suspicions were supported by his observation that, wherever a word appeared in the first column, corresponding groups of signs always appeared in the second and third columns of the same inscriptions. Last, he identified the groups for "king" and "king of kings" but made practically no progress in determining the phonetic values of the characters.

Meanwhile, it was becoming clear that cuneiform signs similar to those of the third column (Niebuhr's III) were commonly observed on inscribed materials in southern Mesopotamia. In 1762 (forty years before Münter's publication in 1802) the Frenchman Jean Jacques Barthelemy had already noticed the connection between the cuneiform signs of both areas. By the dawn of the nineteenth century, the Mesopotamian and Persepolitan examples of cuneiform were being given parallel attention, and this broadened the scope of the work leading toward eventual decipherment of both varieties of characters.

The next half century would bring the crucial breakthroughs, culminating in the Royal Asiatic Society contest of 1857 that proved—in the independently reached solutions of Rawlinson, Hincks, Talbot, and Oppert—that a new linguistic science had been born.

The first step in the final phase of translation was taken by a young high school teacher in Göttingen, Germany—Georg Friedrich Grotefend—who in 1802 succeeded in producing a legible reading before the Learned Society of Göttingen. Not a trained linguist but a hobbyist in secret code decipherment, Grotefend applied his remarkable talents of observation and reasoning to the inscriptions at his disposal. Four years previously the German Orientalist Olav Tychsen had noted that in the Column I script a diagonal wedge appeared to serve as a word divider. But Grotefend reasoned that since ten signs might appear between consecutive diagonal wedges, it was inherently improbable that any ten syllable words existed. Grotefend also shared Münter's belief that Achaemenid Persian kings had produced the inscriptions. Logically, then, the language at issue was an old form of Persian, and Grotefend reasoned that if he were dealing with royal inscriptions, he could look for patterns expressing royal names and titles in later Persian inscriptions of the same type, notably Sassanian inscriptions. He applied this method to two of the Persepolitan texts before him. One may understand Grotefend's approach from the English translations, without the names of kings, for he himself at first was entirely ignorant of them. The letters *X, Y,* and *Z* are used to present the unknown names.

Inscription No. 1: [Y], the great king, king of kings, [X's] son, the Achaemenid

Inscription No. 2: [Z], the great king, king of kings, [Y's], the king's son, the Achaemenid

By close comparison of the cuneiform signs in the inscriptions, Grotefend was able to identify a feature that indicated the possessive case. He was now faced with this intriguing question: Was there an Achaemenid (great) king whose son was also a great king but whose father was not a king but a member of the Achaemenid dynasty or related to it?

From Herodotus's writings Grotefend made up a list of the Old Persian kings. He eliminated the first two, Cyrus and Cambyses, because their names began with the same sounds, while none of those in the inscription, designated Y in the translation, had to be Darius, the *father* of Xerxes (the Z in the second inscription) and the *son* of Hystaspes (the X in the first inscription).

Darius had seized the throne after the death of Cambyses, the second ruler. Darius's father, Hystaspes, had been in the collateral line of royal descent—that is, of royal ancestry but not in the direct line of succession—and so had never himself been a king. Thus Grotefend eventually was able to assign phonetic values to the signs that express the names of the Old Persian kings, although he had to abandon the Greek writings of their names in favor of the more correct Avestan forms. In all he proposed fifteen phonetic values, of which eleven proved to be correct.

Grotefend's original discovery merited only a short notice in a Göttingen scientific journal, and his work did not receive general circulation until 1815, possibly because he was not an academically trained philologist. In any event, however belatedly, his contribution turned out to be pivotal. In the second, third, and fourth decades of the nineteenth century, a combination of professionals and talented amateurs further advanced the prospects of decipherment. The professionals—Eugene Burnouf, a French student of the Avesta, and the German Christian Lassen, a professor of Sanskrit at the University of Bonn—contributed to the listing of Old Persian phonetic values. The greatest advance was accomplished by a British officer who entered Persian governmental service as a military adviser in 1835. Major (later Colonel) Henry Rawlinson, working independently of Grotefend and using two texts by Darius

and Xerses similar to those used by Grotefend, arrived at the same conclusions as Grotefend had.

Rawlinson's most brilliant and exciting accomplishment was the discovery of the longest and most substantial Old Persian trilingual: Darius's
huge inscription carved into the cliffside at Bisitun, located about mid-
way between Teheran and Hamadan. It consisted of more than one
thousand lines on the sheer face of the cliff about three hundred feet
above the road, clearly inaccessible except to good climbers. Undaunted,
Rawlinson climbed as high as he could, despite the anxiety of his Persian attendants, and began to copy the inscription. Thereafter, whenever
he had time, he returned to the Bisitun inscription and continued his
copying, but he could not reach the highest part.

He later enlisted the help of a "wild Kurdish boy," who scaled the
bare face of the rock "in a manner which to the looker-on appeared
quite miraculous," Rawlinson wrote. With ropes and a short ladder the
boy formed a swinging seat, like a painter's cradle, "and fixed upon this
seat, he took under my direction a paper cast on the Babylonian translation of the records of Darius."

Rawlinson's publication of the Old Persian column of the inscription
in 1846 and his subsequent studies of the relationship of Old Persian to
Avestan and Sanskrit, along with the contributions of Edward Hincks
and Jules Oppert, brought the decipherment of Old Persian to a successful conclusion.

With work well advanced on the Column I alphabetic cuneiform,
the focus shifted to the next most complex writing of the trilinguals,
Column II, since it could be reasonably assumed that, with one language
in the fold, the other two as copies could be solved with far less
difficulty.

This proved to be more or less the case with Column II, but only in
1853 and subsequently, after the publication of Column II of the Bisitun
inscription (which contained numerous proper names and word equivalents to the Old Persian text), could significant progress be made. The
language of the column was called Elamite, and we now know that it
was Persia's oldest written language, contemporaneous with Sumerian of
southern Mesopotamia. However, knowledge of the features of Elamite
has lagged behind; its study is now a rarity even within the generally rare
study of cuneiform languages.

The remaining third column of the Old Persian trilingual inscription,
which seemed to contain the greatest number and variety of signs,
proved to be almost as difficult to decipher as the Old Persian. The writ-

ing contained more than three hundred signs, no word dividers, and the incredibly difficult circumstance that, as would be discovered, a single word could be conveyed either by several phonetic signs or, conversely, by a single word sign. Such a system within a language was unknown to the pioneer decipherers.

Again, lack of space precludes listing all of the contributors to the decipherment of Column III, which, as it turned out, contained the language we now call Babylonian. Some of the names are already familiar, beginning with Grotefend and with Rawlinson, whose career efforts would earn him the title "Father of Assyriology" from his British compatriots. The Swedish scholar Isidor Löwenstein was the first to propose, in 1845, that the language of Column III was Semitic and therefore related to the later Hebrew and Arabic writings. Edwards Hincks, in 1850 and thereafter, asserted that the Column III signs were syllabic and not alphabetic and also that a single sign could be used either as a syllable or as an ideogram (that is, a sign for an entire word), even as a determinative (a sign used to mark a class of objects to which a following word belongs). The French excavator of Sargon's palace at Khorsabad, Paul Emile Botta, contributed the accurate observation that a single word, expressed by one sign used as an ideogram, could also be written by several signs used as syllables. Finally, Rawlinson discovered what has since been termed *phonetical polyphony*—the principle that a single sign could be read as one of several syllabic values according to its context.

Interestingly, the ancient Mesopotamians contributed to the decipherment of their own language. For the Assyrians and their culturally and linguistically related neighbors to the south, the Babylonians, full lexical lists were developed for the use of scribes as aids in reading each other's languages (actually dialects) and the radically different Sumerian language, which cuneiform writing was invented to express in the first place. These lists proved helpful to the modern decipherers.

When the Royal Asiatic Society of London in 1857 resorted to the device of asking four outstanding cuneiform researchers to work independently on a then recently discovered longer text, and when the results of Rawlinson, Hincks, Talbot, and Oppert agreed in essentials, a wish expressed by another royal society in 1666 had found its fulfillment. The British Royal Society had inquired, "whether, there being already good Descriptions in *Words* of the Excellent Pictures and Basse Relieves that are about *Persepolis* . . . some may not be found sufficiently skill'd in those parts, that might be engaged to make a Draught of the Place and the Stories there pictured and carved."

Two hundred years later a whole company of observant and inquiring scholars delivered to mankind the knowledge of three lost languages written in cuneiform—Indo-Iranian Old Persian, the Semitic Babylonian and Assyrian (together known as Akkadian), and Elamite—all of which helped to open the door to our ancient Near Eastern heritage.[1]

The Discovery of Hittite Civilization
and the Decipherment of Hittite

ong before the modern discovery and the correct identification of
the Hittite civilization, a people known as the Hittim in the Old
Testament and as the Hetheen in the Greek translation of the Bible
came to the attention of historians. These people appeared to belong to
the roster of ancient Near Eastern peoples. They appeared in Assyrian
records as Hatti and in Egyptian records as Ht'. From biblical accounts
they seemed to be one of the many tribes of Palestine with whom the
Israelites made contact.

As a result of the great European surge of interest in exploring the
Near East and its border areas in the nineteenth century, travelers began
to report discoveries of ruins and monuments that they encountered in
North Syria, southern and northern Cappadocia, Phrygia, and western
Asia Minor (Turkey). In the years immediately following 1833, two
important sites later identified as Hittite—Alaca Huyuk and Bogazkoy
(the Hittite capital, Hattusas), both in central Anatolia—were discovered. What could be learned about these new sites and the unfamiliar
inscriptions there discovered?

Biblical accounts showed the Hittim to have had numerous and varied relationships with the Israelites. In Genesis 23:3–20, Ephron (a Hit-
tim/Hittite) sells the field and the Cave of Machpelah to Abraham as a
burial site and tomb for his wife, Sarah, and himself (see also Gn 35:9,
49:29–32). It is also of great interest that Israelites could customarily
marry Hittite women (Gn 26:34–35; 1 Kgs 1). Beyond this, the Hittites
are cited as a major settled group within the Palestinian milieu in Exodus 3:8–9, again in Exodus 33:2 and 34:11, and throughout the books of
Joshua, Judges, Numbers and 1 Kings. (See also biblical references to
Hittite individuals as confederates of Hebrew heroes: 1 Sm 26:6; 2 Sm
11:3, 23:39; and 1 Kgs, where "all the kings of the Hittites, and the Kings
of Syria," are mentioned.)

Through careful analysis of chronological and historical information from the archives of contemporary peoples, it was established that the biblical accounts referred to a second period of Hittite existence and activity—the first a national and imperial period when Hittites were based in Anatolia (central Turkey), and the second a period when population remnants after the main collapse of Hittite imperial power at about 1200 migrated to, and established themselves in, North Syria and Palestine. The Israelites encountered and interacted with these postimperial Hittites.

Gradually, scholars working on Mesopotamian historical archives and Egyptologists concentrating on Egyptian New Empire campaigns in Palestine and Syria began to assemble important pieces of the puzzle. These pieces included sculptures, which celebrated the campaign of Rameses II against the Hittite king Muwatallis (ca. 1299), and a copy of the peace treaty between the Egyptian pharaoh and the Hittite king Hattusilis III (ca. 1284). In addition to these pictorial and inscriptional materials, there was also a fund of tablets, written in cuneiform, known as the Amarna Letters. These were found in the palace built by Akhnaton (Amenhotep IV, ca. 1370–53) at El Amarna in central Egypt. Akhnaton and his father, Amenhotep III, controlled a system of Palestinian and Syrian city-state vassals, who were constantly plotting against each other, although all were nominally under the authority of Egypt. The pleas in these letters are for the Egyptian ruler to send troops to stabilize the territory. Little was done on the Egyptian side, which made the situation very advantageous to Hittite and Hurrian powers of the north, who either watched the situation carefully or actively meddled in the affairs of the Egyptian vassals. Of almost four hundred tablets from Amarna, about three hundred are from the vassals, but about half of the rest comprise letters essentially between Egypt and heads of state in the areas of Mesopotamia, Mitanni (southeastern Anatolia), and the Hittites. Within this group, two of the letters are in the Hittite language.

An additional documentary source of knowledge about the Hittites came from Assyrian annals composed from about 1100 through 700, when Assyrian kings made references to Hatti and Hittites during their military campaigns.

Finally, excavations at Bogazkoy beginning in 1906 and continuing to the present day have uncovered Hittite records written in the cuneiform script that the Hittites borrowed from Mesopotamia to express their own language. These have given insight into this people's identity and the major role they played in ancient Near Eastern history. The process of decipherment began in 1913, when the Deutsche Orient

Gesellschaft commissioned a group of scholars to begin work on a sampling of Hittite tablets. One of these scholars, Bedrich Hrozny, a Czechoslovakian professor from universities in Prague and Vienna, struck gold through an alert, though fortuitous guess.

There were several vocabularies among the Bogazkoy tablets that gave the ancient scribes equivalents in Semitic Akkadian cuneiform signs to Hittite words and terms. Single signs known as logograms in the Sumerian and Akkadian languages allowed an understanding of the meaning of a word without necessarily indicating how the word was to be pronounced. Hrozny discovered in his sample a Mesopotamian logogram within an apparent Hittite phrase. The logogram read *ninda,* which means "bread." The phrase he perceived read: "Nu Ninda-an e-iz-za-at-te-ni wa-tar-ma e-ku-ut-te-ni."

In ancient oriental literary and pragmatic style, there is a feature of composition known by scholars as "the parallelism of the members." Hrozny believed that he was looking at such an expression in the line he studied, as described by the following: the term translated as "bread" appeared to be balanced by what looked suspiciously to Hrozny like the Indo-European/English word *water,* especially because the syllable *ma,* meaning "and" or "but" in Akkadian, suggested a parallel construction. He also recognized that the two verbs that followed the nouns for "bread" and "water" had the Indo-European roots for the terms *to eat* and *to drink.* Hrozny then proposed that Hittite belonged to the Indo-European family of languages, with the translation of his specimen sentence as "you eat bread; water, however, you drink."

Continuing international research has established Hittite on a sound linguistic basis. With no bilingual text to aid him, Hronzy was nonetheless able to solve the initial mystery of an unknown language.

Conclusion

Who Will Know about Us When We're Gone?

While the heads of the most powerful nations in the world regularly met to discuss how to keep civilization from destroying itself with nuclear weapons, this writer, as a historian, often engaged his university classes in ancient Near Eastern history with summit conferences of his own. A favorite subject: barring an overwhelming natural or manmade disaster in the future, what did my students think our civilization would be remembered for thousands of years from now? I believed the question to be timely. If life is to be preserved in the future, what of our achievements should we be looking to pass on?

The answers were many and varied. Heading the list were our medical and engineering successes. Not far behind came an eagerness to have future people know about our constitutional system, our political ideals, and our concern for social equality. Then music, art, and literature; sports and other recreations; even the shape of our cars, fashions, films, and TV programs—all to be preserved and somehow available for future societies to admire.

"And what are we doing to make sure that our distant descendants will know about us what we *want* them to know?" I would ask. This question usually elicited disbelief. How could our successors *not* know about us? One student summed up the innate confidence of all by speaking about all the institutions—libraries, museums, specialized archives, and institutes—we have devoted to preserving our achievements, including film depositories, CDs, electronic data banks, and millions of other sources such as newspapers, magazines, diaries, letters, and personal items. Then came a list of all material remains—buildings, bridges, and vehicles, plus scads of machines of all types. How, again, could any future people fail to know about or appreciate us?

My counter to this question always begins with the fact that there are basically two types of sources—the written and the unwritten. For written sources, I include photographs as well as paper and surfaces of all kinds, including inscriptions on stone, wood, metals, and the like. Nonwritten sources include all material objects, from pottery to monumental buildings. The historian and his colleagues are chiefly concerned with the former; archaeologists are concerned with the latter. Together these scholars attempt to "decipher" particular cultures and individual societies, as much as is possible to do so. The key phrase here is "as much as is possible." The investigator of the past has no choice but to take what is left of a civilization's written and material remains and work from there.

Time is a cruel mistress, and whether we like it or not, she is bent on destroying everything that mankind has produced. Poets know this, as do professional investigators of the past, but the ordinary person ignores this fact and thinks his or her achievements are immortal. As one historian put it, "We are as immortal as the materials we write on."

It is ironic that the peoples of Mesopotamia of five thousand years ago, who invented writing and inscribed on clay tablets, have a better chance of being known in the future than do Americans of the last two centuries, precisely because of the *durability* of their records. Baked clay is rocklike. Paper and film, by contrast, are extremely perishable (ask any librarian), yet virtually all of our daily records are recorded on these delicate materials. No matter how much we experiment to produce acid-free paper, longer-lasting film, and better air-conditioning systems for our precious documents, all are eventually doomed to failure. The paper production of our society is truly phenomenal. What the historians know is that our records are on a road to certain destruction.

But let's suppose that we're lucky and that some of our writing does survive. What then? It depends on what happens to have gotten through: maybe some historical documents, although not necessarily the ones you might have *wanted* to get through, or some literature maybe, things like that. But maybe also a lot of other things survived, like mortgage writs, box scores of baseball games, the rules of order of a local service lodge. Maybe nothing on medicine or how our courts work or what people think about death and taxes in our society. You simply can't know unless you find a way to determine precisely *what* is important to leave for the future and then actually *find a way* to assure that those things survive. To stress once again, *we* know how the things we've produced work, but can we assume that down the centuries or millennia ahead the occupants of the earth will automatically know what we know? They may, in fact, have only the slightest understanding of our language or even none at all.

As for our material remains, also consider how regularly we build, tear down, or alter all types of houses, civic structures, and office buildings. When a building comes down it is usually razed right to the ground. Nobody today builds on top of the remains of a previous structure, unlike the ancients. It's cheaper to haul the earlier foundations away, and with them goes the opportunity for archaeologists to study the stratigraphy of a building site.

To drive home what I've been saying, let's examine a most ordinary object, one we use every day—the Jefferson nickel. Someone may find a coin like this a few thousand years ahead. It might be badly corroded, but some future scientist could discover its metallic content and learn some things from that. But for illustration, let's say the coin is intact and both faces can be made out. What impression might the coin make on an investigator who might have little else to go on?

First of all, on one side, there is a picture of a man wearing his hair in a particular style. *We* know him to be Thomas Jefferson. But what on the coin helps our investigator of the future to know that? Around Jefferson's head are words and a date. Several questions come to mind: Assuming something of English is known, even as a most ancient language, what might the words *In God We Trust* signify to a stranger? Is the picture of Jefferson perhaps to be interpreted as a deity, silly as that seems to us? What about the word *Liberty*? What does that mean? And what of the four numbers? Will our investigator know that they are numerals and that they represent a date? Are they perhaps the sacred number of the deity of the coin?

Now turn the coin over to reveal more words and an impression of a building. Is the building the deity's house, his temple? How about *E Pluribus Unum* at the top? *We* know the phrase to be Latin, but will our investigator? Necessary corroborating language not being available, how long will it take for future scholars to learn that, although links exist between English and Latin, they are really separate languages? And why is this phrase on the coin anyway?

Immediately below the building is another word, *Monticello,* which *we* know to be the name of Jefferson's home. But how about that investigator?

Finally, we have the words *Five Cents* and *United States of America* on the bottom. The same questions can be asked as before: What do they mean and how can the solution be found?

It's a frustrating business, but that's what historians and archaeologists have to do all the time. You hope for the best.

The solution to our dilemma may be at hand. We have apparently indestructible plastic materials, such as our milk bottles, which now advertise everything from cooking recipes to alerts about missing children. We also know how to manufacture artificial stone, on which selected information taken from our national archives and literature can be imprinted. If national commissions could be formed to decide what to tell future peoples about ourselves and where this information is to be found, we may still not be forgotten. Nor should we forget to incise English on the manufactured stone in order to leave descriptions of how to read our language and, just as important, how our cars, trucks, trains, and planes were intended to run, along with the thousands of other inventions we use in our lives.

A Summary of Culture Growth in Mesopotamia and Egypt

Mesopotamia

I. Establishment of Mesopotamian culture. Prehistoric, proto-historic phases. (5000 to 3100)

    A. Original agricultural villages in hilly flank areas of northern Iraq with implied concomitant pastoralism of contemporary groups. (5000 to 3900)

    B. Continuation of this type of life at base, with new rise of large urban centers in southern Iraq. Appearance of Sumerian culture and the beginning of written records. (3900 to 3100)

        1. Rise of canal-irrigation pattern of agriculture with small craft specialization

        2. Emergence of "authoritarian" pattern in religion

        3. "Authoritarian" pattern perpetuated through standard religious practices and through scribal system of education

II. Protodynastic era in Mesopotamia. (2600 to 2000)

    A. City-state pattern of rule, with occasional larger territorial unities. City assembly form of government loses ground to permanent monarchies

    B. Extension of trade to international scope, facilitated by the rise of the professional merchant

    C. Increased productivity of the economic establishment owing to continued attention and control under Third Dynasty of Ur. (ca. 2100 to 2000)

III. Establishment of Semitic power. (1900 to 1600)
   A. Entry of the Semitic Amorite populations with almost complete submergence of Sumerian identity; widespread adaptation of Sumerian culture by new Semitic population elements
   B. Period where seminomadism had its greatest effect upon the cultural situation along the arc of the Fertile Crescent
IV. Period from 1600 to 323.
   A. 1600 to 1100: Long period of stable and quiescent reign under Kassite invaders; few noticeable changes in Mesopotamian cultural patterns
   B. Period of "balance of power" among Near Eastern kingdoms (Egypt, Hittites, Hurrians, Assyrians, Kassite-Babylonians)
   C. 900 to 612: Rise of full-scale, area-wide imperialism under the Assyrians
   D. 600 to 323: Continuation of Assyrian Empire, first under Neo-Babylonians and Medes, until Aegean reaction against Persia under Alexander the Great

Egypt

I. Prehistoric period through the Old Kingdom. (4500 to 2200)
   A. Original agricultural village nomes; practically no pastorialism; at first settlements located on the spurs of the Nile, then in the Nile Valley
   B. Organization into a "nation" with a few large urban centers. (ca. 3000 to 2200)
      1. Emergence of typical Egyptian "authoritarian" establishment, god-king at the apex
      2. Again, as with Mesopotamia, perpetuation of "authoritarianism" through a controlled scribal system of education
      3. Diffusion of Egyptian culture via trade and small military probes, south and north
      4. Rise of administrative complexity in pharonic administration with increased demands by government officials for rewards within the established values of the "authoritarian" pattern
      5. Breakdown of Old Kingdom. (2200 to 2000)
II. Middle Kingdom. (2000 to 1780)
   A. Reestablishment of order, restrengthening of control by central political establishment
   B. Reopening of sources of external wealth through renewed economic and military thrusts, both into Palestine and south to Nubia

C. Perpetuation of authoritarian establishment, with internal, perhaps relatively minor shifts in the religious outlook and values

D. Broadening base of participation in the official religion through the inclusion of middle classes (rise of Osirian beliefs and practices as fairly normative)

E. Rise of imperial consciousness; end of Middle Kingdom a result of inability to resist the inroads of seminomadic groups with a superior military technology (Hyksos)

III. Establishment of New Empire to Alexander the Great. (1550 to 323)

A. 1550 to 1200

1. Tightening and centralization in politics, complete transformation of the military establishment, adaptation of the Hyksos technology by the army

2. Thrust to maintain Palestine as a strongly dependent area; greatest contact with Semitic and Hittite cultures Egypt has had so far; greatest adaptive abilities of Egyptian religion

3. Internal tears in the "authoritarian" establishment; loss of empire in Palestine and Syria and check upon Egyptian imperialism

B. 1200: Inroads of sea peoples and consequent disruption of economic and military solidity; Egypt enters weak postimperial period

C. 900 to 323: Decline of Egypt and successive conquests by Assyria, Persia, and Macedonia

Methodological Fallacies in the Study of Ancient Near Eastern Religion

1. That there is something called Ancient Near Eastern Religion (ANER), a single area-wide religion of a homogenous type. Each society had its own religion, however similar it appeared in content and types of observance to another. It may occasionally be useful to speak of ANER as we might of "Western culture," but caution is required.

2. That ANER is to be viewed through the lenses of the biblical Old and New Testament.

3. That ANER is simply an earlier form of modern religion in function.

4. That an ANER is primarily conceptual in nature. By contrast, it was primarily behavioristic.

5. That modern religious terminology has necessarily any objective correlatives in ancient religions.

6. That religion is a separate but equal component of society.

7. That parallels between religious features of ancient Near Eastern societies are easily made.

8. That an ANER may be studied without reference to the developmental history of the society involved.

9. That the personnel of an ANER are purely "religious" in function.

10. That an ANER may easily be categorized by type.

11. That an ANER is primarily concerned with the individual. Most were as much or more concerned with the fate of the community.

12. That all translations of ANER texts will agree on the meanings of the ancient texts.

13. That an ANER is static in form and represents a fixed form. The reality is that the religion studied may exhibit contradictory features even in a fixed chronological period. Furthermore, the sources may be provincial rather than mainstream even though there are huge numbers of them.

14. That the "official" documents of the ANER represent the religion as actually practiced.

Chronology

This chronology is offered for the convenience of the general reader. Students in ancient Near Eastern history classes will already have access to textbooks and specialized studies that offer fuller chronologies and take up controversial chronological issues. See, most recently, *HANE*, 14 and 281–96.

Mesopotamia	*Egypt*	*Anatolia*	*Palestine*
Prehistoric 5000–3600		Prehistoric	
	Prehistoric 4500–3100		
Protoliterate 3600–3100			
Early Dynastic 3100–2400	*Old Kingdom* (Dynasties I–VI) 3100–2200		
Akkad 2350–2200			
	1st Intermediate Period 2200–2000	Small Hattic City-States ???–1750	
Ur III 2100–2000			
	Middle Kingdom (Dynasty XII) 2000–1800		
Old Babylonian 1800–1600	2nd Intermediate Period (Dynasties XIII–XIV) 1800–1600	Old Assyrian Trading Colonies 1900–1750	

		Old Hittite Kingdom 1750–1550	
Kassite 1600–1200	*New Empire Period* (Dynasties XVIII–XX) 1600–1100	Hittite New Empire 1500–1200	Conquest of Palestine by Israelites ?1250–
Middle Babylonian 1200–750	*Decline* (Dynasties XXI–XXVI) 1100–500 Persian (Dynasties XXVII–XXX) 500–332		Period of the Judges ?1200–1020 Saul ?1020–1000 David ?1000–961 Solomon ?961–922 Division of Israel into Judah (south) 922–587 and Israel (north) 922–721
Neo-Assyrian 750–612 Neo-Babylonian 612–538 Persian 538–323	Persian (Dynasties XXVII–XXX) 500–332		

Glossary

Akkadian   The term that identifies all dialects of the East Semitic Babylonian and Assyrian languages.

Amorites   West Semitic tribes appearing all around the area of the Fertile Crescent from about 2000 and earlier in Mesopotamia.

Anatolia   The great central plateau of modern-day Turkey.

Aramaeans   West Semitic tribal units who ultimately settled in Syria and parts of Lebanon and whose form of alphabetic writing in the first millennium influenced Persian, Hebrew, and Arabic.

Assyrians   Kingdom established in northern Mesopotamia about 2000 that became a great imperialistic power in the first millennium until its demise in 612, when its capital, Nineveh, fell to an alliance of the Medes and Babylonians.

Babylonians   Inhabitants of lower Mesopotamia, whose historical career rivaled that of Assyria to the north until Cyrus the Great of Persia captured Babylon in 538.

Canaan   The land of Palestine.

Cappadocia   Synonym for the Upper Territories of Anatolia.

Caria   A small country in the southwest corner of Western Anatolia.

Cilicia   The coastal plain of southern Anatolia.

Cimmerians   An eastern horde of raiders who swept across Anatolia in the late eighth, seventh, and sixth centuries and sacked Sardis (ca. 652).

Edom   A tribal state in southeastern Palestine that interacted with the ancient Israelites in the late second and early first millennia.

Elam   An area of the Zagros Mountain range bordering southern Mesopotamia. Its inhabitants interacted in war and peace with Mesopotamian dynasties for more than twenty-five hundred years. Their capital, Susa, was destroyed circa 640 by Ashurbanipal of Assyria.

Gutians   Hill peoples from the eastern borders of Babylonia who ruled that country for about a century (ca. 2200–2100).

Hattites   Name of the Late Prehistoric peoples of central Anatolia, as distinguished from the historical Hittites.

Hittites   Indo-European-speaking immigrants into central Anatolia in the early second millennium. They formed first the Old Kingdom, circa 1750, and then an extended empire, circa 1450–1200, and were a major competitor to the Egyptians in Syria and Palestine.

Hurrians   Early- to mid-second-millennium immigrants to eastern Anatolia from beyond the Elburz Mountains bordering on Iran. Their language, not well known, appears in cuneiform documents. Their small kingdoms were consolidated into a state known as Mitanni.

Hyksos   Rulers of foreign countries who invaded Egypt from Palestine and areas north, a mixed horde of Semites and non-Semite raiders who occupied Egypt in the mid-eighteenth century.

Kassites   Mountaineers from the eastern Zagros Mountain range who invaded Babylonia and occupied the country from 1600 to about 1200. We know very little about them.

Lycia   A small kingdom in the southwest corner of Anatolia in the time of the Persian Empire.

Lydia   A major kingdom in west central Anatolia on the coast of the Aegean Sea in the Persian period.

Media	A small kingdom in northwestern Iran in the ninth and eighth centuries that became an empire under Cyaxeres and joined with Babylon to destroy Nineveh (ca. 612) and the Assyrian Empire.
Mitanni	A mid-second-millennium state occupying eastern and southeastern territories of Anatolia and counting its major population as Hurrian.
Moabites	A tribal state in south central Palestine that interacted with the ancient Israelites in the late second and early first millennia BC.
Persians	A people who inhabited southern Iran, overthrew Medean suzerainty in 550, and established an empire under Cyrus (II) the Great in 550 that extended from the Mediterranean to India.
Philistia	A small tract of coastal land in southwest Palestine on which Aegean warriors established a coalition of five cities—Gaza, Ashkelon, Ashdod, Ekron, and Gath.
Phoenicia	Name given to northern coastal areas of Palestine.
Phrygia	First-millennium state in northwest Anatolia bordering on ancient Lydia.
Samaria	Ninth-century capital of northern Israel and later the name of the territory itself.
Sumeria	Earliest village/city territory, located at the head of the Persian Gulf, where their non-Semitic language was first expressed in cuneiform writing on clay tablets; the earliest nucleus of Mesopotamian historical development.
Urartu	First-millennium kingdom in the territory of Lake Van of eastern Anatolia and military rival of the Late Assyrian Empire.

Notes

In the Tablet Houses of Mesopotamia

1. Mogens Weitemeyer, "Archive and Library Technique in Ancient Mesopotamia," *Libri: International Library Review* 6 (1956): 220–21.
2. Ibid., 225–32.
3. See further Ernst Posner, *Archives in the Ancient World* (Cambridge, MA: Harvard University Press, 1972), 12–70.

New Year's Day in Babylon

1. See the translation of the "New Year's Day Ritual" in *ANET* (1969), 331–34.
2. See the translation of the "Creation Epic" in *ANET* (1969), 60–72 and 501–3.

Decoding the Hammurabi Law Code

A complete translation of the Hammurabi Law Code appears in *ANET* (1969), 163–80.

1. See further J. J. Finkelstein, "Ammisaduga and the Babylonian 'Law Codes,'" *Journal of Cuneiform Studies* 15 (1961): 91–104.

On the Lighter Side of Mesopotamia

The technical information upon which this vignette is based is found in I. J. Gelb's article "Homo Ludens ["playful or recreational man"] in Mesopotamia," *Studia Orientalia* 46 (1975): 43–76. A Festschrift dedicated to the Assyriologist A. Salonen.

Wild Animals and Game Parks

1. See *ANET* (1969), 433, col. B.

2. See J. K. Anderson, *Hunting in the Ancient World* (Berkeley: University of California Press, 1985), especially chap. 1; and R. D. Barnett, *Sculptures from the North Palace of Ashurbanipal at Nineveh, 668–627 B.C.* (London: British Museum Publications, 1976). On the role of ivory in ancient Near Eastern art (here Syria), see Irene J. Winter, "Ivory Carving," in *Elba to Damascus (Art and Archaeology of Ancient Syria)*, ed. Harvey Weiss, 339–46 (Washington, DC: Smithsonian Institution Traveling Exhibition Service, 1985). See further "Zoology," in *Anchor Bible Dictionary,* ed. D. N. Freedman, 6:1109–67 (New York: Doubleday, 1972).

Theme and Variations on Herodotus's Statement

Herodotus, *The Histories,* trans. Aubrey de Selincourt, rev. John Merincola (1996; repr., London: Penguin Classics, 2003), 97, paragraph 5.

1. The indispensable work in English for information about the topographical influences on Egyptian culture is Herman Kees, *Ancient Egypt: A Cultural Topography,* trans. Ian F. D. Morrow, ed. T. G. H. James (Chicago and London: University of Chicago Press, 1961; Phoenix ed., 1977 [paperback]).

2. Ibid., 28–29.

3. On tombs and burial customs of the Egyptians, see Carol Andrews, *Egyptian Mummies* (Cambridge, MA: Harvard University Press, 1984); and James E. Harris and Edward F. Wente, eds., *X-Ray Atlas of the Royal Mummies* (Chicago: University of Chicago Press, 1980).

4. An admirably competent short introduction to ancient Egyptian religious ideas, a good choice to begin with, is J. Cerny, *Ancient Egyptian Religion* (London: Hutchinson's University Library, 1952).

The Seagoing Phoenicians

1. On Egyptian, Phoenician, and Syro-Levant ships and sea routes, see Shelly Wachsmann, *Seagoing Ships and Seamanship in the Bronze Age Levant* (College Station: Texas A&M University Press and London: Chatham Publishing, 1998), 310–14, 327–28.

2. The text of the original story of Wen-Amon appears in *ANET* (1969), 25–29.

From Tribal Coalition to Statehood in Ancient Israel

The translation of the Bible used in this account is the *Oxford Annotated Bible with the Apocrypha, Revised Standard Version* (New York: Oxford University

Press, 1965). The historical account of the rise of Israel to statehood is contained in the books of Joshua, Judges, 1 and 2 Samuel through 1 Kings 12. The reference to Merneptah's victory stela, which mentions Israel, appears in *ANET* (1969), 376–78. The single line containing the name appears seven printed lines from the end of the otherwise unnumbered text and should be read with footnote 18 of p. 378. The interpretation of Israel's rise to statehood here presented follows the proposals of W. F. Albright and George Mendenhall, though the reader should be aware that the issue is very complex and has been the subject of longstanding and often heated debate among historians and theologians.

Ancient Persia and a Tale of Two Cities

1. Robert B. Strassler, ed., *The Landmark Thucydides* (New York: Simon and Schuster [Touchstone], 1996), 111–14; and see the *Oxford Annotated Bible,* the books of Ezra and Nehemiah for the return of Jews to their homeland.

On Nomads and Nomadism

1. See M. B. Rowton's articles "Enclosed Nomadism," *Journal of the Economic and Social History of the Orient* 17, pt. 1 (1974): 1, 2–30, and "Dimorphic Structure and Topology," *Oriens Antiquus* 15 (1976): 17–31. See also Jorge Silva Castillo, ed., *Nomads and Sedentary Peoples,* Thirtieth International Congress of Human Sciences in Asia and North Africa (Mexico City: El Colegio de Mexico, 1981), especially the essays by M. B. Rowton, "Economic and Political Factors in Ancient Nomadism," 25–36; D. O. Edzrd, "Mesopotamia Nomads in the Third Millennium, B.C.," 37–45; and J. N. Postgate, "Nomads and Sedentaries in the Middle Assyrian Sources," 47–56.

An Old Assyrian Trading Enterprise in Asia Minor

1. See my *Assyrian Colonies in Cappadocia* (The Hague and Paris: Mouton, 1970), especially 45–46, 224–25.

Some Observations on Ancient Near Eastern Treaties

1. On ancient Near Eastern treaties in general see Dennis J. McCarthy, SJ, *Treaty and Covenant: A Study in Form in the Ancient Oriental Documents and in the Old Testament* (Analecta Biblica 21) (Rome: Pontifical Biblical Institute, 1963), especially its excellent bibliography, xiii–xxiv, and also 80–81, 89.

2. See my *Assyrian Colonies in Cappadocia* (The Hague and Paris: Mouton, 1970), 73–158.

3. See O. R. Gurney, *The Hittites* (London: Penguin Books, 1990).

4. See Ilya Gershevich, *The Avestan Hymn to Mithra* (Cambridge: Cambridge University Press, 1967), the Avestan Hymn, section 1.2, p. 75, with commentary, 152–57.

5. See R. C. Zaehner, *The Dawn and Twilight of Zoroastrianism* (New York: Putnam, 1961), 108–9.

6. On multiple biblical covenants, consult the subject index of John Bright's *A History of Israel* (Philadelphia: Westminster Press, 1959).

On the Greatness of Gilgamesh

A literal translation of the epic appears in *ANET* (1969), 72–79 and 503–7. For readers interested in the textual tradition of the *Gilgamesh Epic,* see Jeffrey H. Tigay, "Summary: The Evolution of the Gilgamesh Epic," in *Gilgamesh: A Reader,* ed. John Maier, 40–49 (Wauconda, IL: Bolchazy-Carducci Publishers, 1997).

Reflections on Ancient Near Eastern Myth

1. Alex Preminger, ed., *Princeton Encyclopedia of Poetry and Poetics* (Princeton: Princeton University Press, 1965), 538, col. B, under the section "Myth."

2. W. G. Lambert's article "Myth and Ritual as Conceived by the Babylonians," in the *Journal of Semitic Studies* 13, no. 1 (spring 1968): 104–12, basically challenges the connection between myth and ritual in Mesopotamia.

Wisdom Literature

1. Samuel Noah Kramer, "Sumerian Literature: A General Survey," in *The Bible and the Ancient Near East (Essays in Honor of William Foxwell Albright)* ed. by G. Ernest Wright, Garden City, 249–66 [258] (New York: Doubleday, 1961).

Physical Background

I have supplied this detailed chapter on the geological and geographic features of the Near East because I believe that to understand its ancient history requires an appreciation of how the natural environment offers both opportunities for and restrictions upon political and social developments. I have also divided the subject matter into divisions of regional significance.

1. For this brief survey of the Near East as a geological and geographic entity I am greatly indebted to the technical information contained in W. B. Fisher, *The Middle East: A Physical, Social and Regional Geography,* 6th ed. (London: Methuen, 1971), and Charles L. Redman, *The Rise of Civilization* (San

Francisco: W. H. Freeman, 1978); to frequent discussions during my years of teaching with friends and colleagues in the University of Michigan's Departments of Geography and Geology; and to my own field notes taken during the course of numerous explorations in most countries of the area.

Historical Background

I have included this general account of the prehistoric backgrounds of culture in Egypt and Mesopotamia simply as a foundation study and not as current "state of the art" results. Readers with special interests in the archaeology of the Near East, should consult the *Oxford Encyclopedia of Archaeology in the Near East,* ed. by E. M. Meyers for individual cultures and sites.

Civic Background

This vignette is an adaptation and condensation of my article "Ancient Near Eastern Cities: Form, Function, and Idea," which appeared in *Janus: Essays in Ancient and Modern Studies,* ed. L. L. Orlin, Part 1: "The City in History: Idea and Reality." This volume was published following an interdisciplinary conference entitled "The City in History" sponsored by the Center for Coordination of Ancient and Modern Studies of the University of Michigan in 1975. All references to the Sumerian myths quoted in this section are to the translations of Samuel N. Kramer in his *Sumerian Mythology,* rev. ed. (New York: Harper and Row, 1961). Additional essays on ancient Near Eastern cities and city life appear in Ira M. Lapidus, ed., *Middle Eastern Cities* (Berkeley and Los Angeles: University of California Press, 1969); A. Badawy, *Architecture in Ancient Egypt and the Near East* (Cambridge, MA: MIT Press, 1966); and W. W. Hallo, "Antediluvian Cities," *Journal of Cuneiform Studies* 23 (1970): 57–67. This last article, with its bibliographical notes, is an especially valuable contribution for both professional and nonprofessional readers.

1. A basic book with city plans and illustrations of ancient Near Eastern cities is Paul Lampl, *Cities and Planning in the Ancient Near East* (New York: George Braziller, 1968 [paperback]).

The Decipherment of Cuneiform Writing

1. See Svend Aage Pallis, *The Antiquity of Iraq: A Handbook of Assyriology* (Copenhagen: Ejnar Munksgaard, 1956), 94–159.

Bibliography

Akurgal, Ekrem. *The Hattian and Hittite Civilizations*. Ankara: Republic of Turkey Ministry of Culture, 2001. Profusely illustrated.

Andrews, Carol. *Egyptian Mummies*. Cambridge, MA: Harvard University Press, 1984. Paperback. Additional reading list on p. 70.

Badawy, A. *Architecture in Ancient Egypt and the Near East*. Cambridge, MA: MIT Press, 1966.

Barnett, R. D. *Sculptures from the North Palace of Ashurbanipal at Nineveh 608–627 B.C.* London: British Museums Publications for the Trustees of the British Museum, 1976.

Beckman, Gary. *Hittite Diplomatic Texts*. 2nd ed. Atlanta: Scholars Press, 1999.

Bienkowski, Piotr, and Alan Millard, eds. *Dictionary of the Ancient Near East*. Philadelphia: University of Pennsylvania Press, 2000.

Borowski, O. *Every Living Thing: Daily Use of Animals in Ancient Israel*. Thousand Oaks, CA: AltaMira Press, 1997.

Bright, John. *A History of Ancient Israel*. Philadelphia: Westminster Press, 1959. Pt. 5, secs. 9 and 10, pp. 321–86.

Brower, Rueben A. *On Translation*. Harvard Studies in Comparative Literature 23. Cambridge, MA: Harvard University Press, 1959.

Cambridge Ancient History. Ed. J. Boardman et al. 3rd ed. 4 vols. Cambridge: Cambridge University Press, 1982.

Castillo, Jorge Silva, ed. *Nomads and Sedentary Peoples*. Thirtieth International Congress of Human Sciences in Asia and North Africa. Mexico City: El Colegio de Mexico, 1981.

Champion, Sara. *Dictionary of Terms and Techniques in Archaeology*. New York: Everest House, 1980. Paperback.

Contenau, Georges. *Everyday Life in Babylonia and Assyria* (in French). Paris: Hachette, 1950. English translation, New York: Norton, 1966.

Curtis, John. *Ancient Persia.* Cambridge, MA: Harvard University Press, 1990. Paperback. Additional reading list on p. 71.

Dalley, S. M. *Myths from Mesopotamia.* Oxford: Oxford University Press, 1989.

De Camp, L. Sprague. *The Ancient Engineers.* New York: Barnes and Noble, 1993.

Driver, G. R., and John C. Miles. *The Babylonian Laws.* 2 vols. Oxford: Clarendon Press, 1952–55.

Erman, Adolph. *The Ancient Egyptians.* Trans. Alyward M. Blackman. New York: Harper and Row (Harper Torchbooks), 1966. Paperback.

Firmage, E. "Zoology." In *Anchor Bible Dictionary,* ed. D. N. Freedman, 6:1109–67. New York: Doubleday, 1992.

Fisher, W. B. *The Middle East: A Physical, Social and Regional Geography.* 6th ed. London: Methuen, 1971.

Foster, Benjamin R. *Before the Muses: An Anthology of Akkadian Literature.* Bethesda, MD: CDL Press, 1993.

Frankfort, Henry, H. A. Frankfort, John A. Wilson, and Thornkild Jacobsen, eds. *The Intellectual Adventure of Ancient Man.* Chicago: University of Chicago Press, 1946.

Freedman, D. N. *Anchor Bible Dictionary.* New York: Doubleday, 1992.

Gershevich, Ilya. *The Avestan Hymn to Mithra.* Cambridge: Cambridge University Press, 1967.

Ghirschman, R. *Iran from the Earliest Times to the Islamic Conquest.* Harmondsworth, England: Penguin Books, 1954.

Gibson, J. C. L. *Canaanite Myths and Legends.* 2nd ed. Edinburgh: T and T Clark, 1978.

Grunfeld, Frederic V., ed. *Games of the World.* New York: Ballentine Books, 1977. Paperback. Cf. "The Royal Game of Ur," 57–58.

Gurney, O. R. *The Hittites.* London: Penguin Books, 1990. Paperback.

Hallo, William W., and William K. Simpson. *The Ancient Near East: A History.* 2nd ed. Fort Worth: Harcourt Brace College Publishers, 1998.

Harden, Donald. *The Phoenicians.* London: Thames and Hudson, 1962.

Hart, George. *A Dictionary of Egyptian Gods and Goddesses.* London and New York: Routledge, 1986.

Hodges, Henry. *Technology in the Ancient World.* New York: Barnes and Noble, 1970.

Hoffner, H. A. *Hittite Myths.* Atlanta: Scholars Press, 1990.

Jacobsen, Thorkild. *The Harps That Once . . . Sumerian Poetry in Translation.* New Haven, CT: Yale University Press, 1987.

James, E. O. *Myth and Ritual in the Ancient Near East.* London: Thames and Hudson, 1958.

James, T. G. H., and W. V. Davies. *Egyptian Sculpture.* Cambridge, MA: Harvard University Press, 1983. Paperback. Additional reading list on p. 69.

Joint Association of Classical Teachers' Greek Course. *The World of Athens: An*

Introduction to Classical Athenian Culture. Cambridge: Cambridge University Press, 1984. Paperback.

Kees, Herman. *Ancient Egypt: A Cultural Topography.* Trans. Ian F. D. Morrow. Ed. T. G. H. James. Chicago: University of Chicago Press, 1961. Phoenix ed., 1977. Paperback.

Kirk, G. S. *Myth: Its Meaning and Function in Ancient and Other Cultures.* Berkeley: University of California Press, 1970.

Kramer, Samuel N. *Sumerian Mythology.* Rev. ed. New York: Harper and Row, 1961.

Kuhrt, Amelie. *The Ancient Near East c. 3000–330 BC.* 2 vols. London and New York: Routledge, 1995.

Kuhrt, Amelie. "Usurpation, Conquest and Ceremonial: From Babylon to Persia." In *Rituals of Royalty,* ed. D. Caundaine and S. Price, 20–25. New York: Cambridge University Press, 1987.

Lampl, Paul. *Cities and Planning in the Ancient Near East.* New York: George Braziller, 1968.

Lapidus, Ira M., ed. *Middle Eastern Cities.* Berkeley and Los Angeles: University of California Press, 1969.

Lichtheim, Miriam. *Ancient Egyptian Literature.* 2 vols. Berkeley and Los Angeles: University of California Press, 1975. Paperback.

Lloyd, Seton. *Mounds of the Near East.* Edinburgh: Edinburgh University Press, 1963.

Maier, John, ed. *Gilgamesh: A Reader.* Wauconda, IL: Bolchazy-Carducci Publishers, 1997.

McCarthy, Dennis, SJ. *Treaty and Covenant: A Study in Form in the Old Testament.* Analeca Biblia 21. Rome: Pontifical Biblical Institute, 1963.

Mercatante, Anthony S. *Who's Who in Egyptian Mythology.* 2nd ed. Ed. and rev. Robert Steven Bianchi. New York: Barnes and Noble, 1998.

Meyers, E. M., ed., *Oxford Encyclopedia of Archaeology in the Near East.* New York: Oxford University Press, 1997.

Mieroop, Marc Van De. *The Ancient Mesopotamia City.* Oxford: Clarendon Press, 1997.

Mieroop, Marc Van De. *A History of the Ancient Near East, ca. 3000–323 B.C.* Oxford: Blackwell, 2004.

Moran, William L. *The Amarna Letters.* Baltimore and London: Johns Hopkins University Press, 1992.

Moscatti, Sabatino. *The Face of the Ancient Orient.* New York: Doubleday Anchor, 1962.

Moscatti, Sabatino. *The Phoenicians.* New York: New York University Press, 1988.

Murnane, William J. *The Penguin Guide to Ancient Egypt.* Harmondsworth, England: Penguin Books, 1983. Paperback. Additional reading list on pp. 357–58.

Nissen, Hans J. *The Early History of the Near East, 9000–2000 BC.* Chicago and London: University of Chicago Press, 1988.

Nissen, H. J., P. Damerow, and R. K. Englund. *Archaic Bookkeeping: Writing and Techniques of Economic Administration in the Ancient Near East.* Chicago: University of Chicago Press, 1993.

Oppenheim, A. L. *Ancient Mesopotamia: Portrait of a Dead Civilization.* 2nd ed. Chicago: University of Chicago Press, 1977.

Orlin, Louis L. *Assyrian Colonies in Cappadocia.* The Hague and Paris: Mouton, 1970.

Orlin, Louis L., ed. *Janus: Essays in Ancient and Modern Studies.* Ann Arbor: University of Michigan, Center for Coordination of Ancient and Modern Studies, 1975.

Orlin, Louis L., ed. *Michigan Oriental Studies in Honor of George G. Cameron, Department of Near Eastern Studies.* Ann Arbor: University of Michigan, 1976.

Özgüç, Tahsin. *Kültepe-Kaniš/Neša Saraylari ve Mabetleri* (The Palaces and Temples of Kültepe-Kaniš/Neša). Ankara: Türk Tarih Kurumu Basimevi, 1999.

Pallis, Svend Aage. *The Antiquity of Iraq: A Handbook of Assyriology.* Copenhagen: Ejvar Munksgaard, 1956. Chaps. 2 and 3 provide a very comprehensive description of early explorations and the decipherment of cuneiform writing.

Posner, Ernst. *Archives in the Ancient World.* Cambridge, MA: Harvard University Press, 1972.

Preminger, Alex, ed. *Princeton Encyclopedia of Poetry and Poetics.* Princeton: Princeton University Press, 1965.

Reade, Julian. *Assyrian Sculpture.* Cambridge, MA: Harvard University Press, 1983. Paperback. Additional reading list on p. 71.

Reade, Julian. *Mesopotamia.* Cambridge, MA: Harvard University Press, 1991. Paperback. Additional reading list on p. 70.

Religions of the Ancient Near East: Sumero-Akkadian Religious Texts and Ugaritic Epics. Ed. Isaac Mendelsohn. New York: Liberal Arts Press, 1955. Paperback.

Roaf, Michael. *Cultural Atlas of Mesopotamia and the Ancient Near East.* Oxford: Equinox, 1990.

Roth, M. T. *Law Collections from Mesopotamia and Asia Minor.* Atlanta: Scholars Press, 1997.

Sasson, Jack M., ed. *Civilizations of the Ancient Near East.* 4 vols. New York: Charles Scribner's Sons, 1995.

Schwartz, G. M. "Pastoral Nomadism in Ancient Western Asia." *CANE,* 249–58.

Soden, Wolfram von. *The Ancient Orient: An Introduction to the Study of the Ancient Near East.* Trans. Donald G. Schley. Grand Rapids, MI: Wm. B. Eerdmans Publishing, 1994.

Stassler, Robert B., ed. *The Landmark Thucydides.* New York: Touchstone (Simon & Schuster), 1996.

Stead, Miriam. *Egyptian Life.* Cambridge, MA: Harvard University Press, 1986. Paperback. Additional reading list on p. 71.

Trigger, B. G., et al. *Ancient Egypt: A Social History.* Cambridge: Cambridge University Press, 1983.

Trustees of the British Museum. *Reading the Past.* New York: Barnes and Noble Books, 1998. Contains excellent authoritative essays on ancient scripts; those relevant to the present book include C. B. F. Walker, "Cuneiform," 15–73; W. V. Davies, "Egyptian Hieroglyphs," 75–135; and John F. Healy, "The Early Alphabet," 197–257.

Van Buren, E. D. *The Fauna of Ancient Mesopotamia as Represented in Art.* Rome: Pontificium institutum biblicum, 1953.

Veenhof, K. R., ed. *Cuneiform Archives and Libraries.* Leiden: Nederlands Historisch-Archaeologisch Instituut te Instanbul, 1986.

Wachsmann, Shelley. *Seagoing Ships and Seamanship in the Bronze Age Levant.* College Station, TX: Texas A&M University Press, 1998 and London: Chatham Publishing, 1998.

Wilheim, Gernot. *The Hurrians.* Warminster: Aris and Phillips, 1989.

Wilkinson, Richard H. *Reading Egyptian Art: A Hieroglyphic Guide to Ancient Egyptian Painting and Sculpture.* London: Thames and Hudson, 1992.

Wright, G. Ernest, ed. *The Bible and the Ancient Near East: Essay in Honor of William Foxwell Albright.* Garden City, NY: Doubleday, 1961. Appendix 1.

Index

Some of the assembled materials in the part of the book entitled Especially for Students have not been indexed.